SEX DISCRIMINATION:

The EDD, EEOC, & Superior Court Legal Forms

("*The ABM Papers*")

Paralegal Publishing Group™

Case Study:

[Plaintiff] v. CUIAB

(2017)

Los Angeles Superior Court – Central District

Copyright. © 2020-2022. Paralegal Publishing Group.

All rights reserved. No part of this publication may be reproduced or transmitted in any form or by any means, electronic or mechanical, including photocopy, recording or any other information storage and retrieval system without prior permission in writing from and of the publisher, except in the case of brief quotations embodied in secondary or post-secondary educational papers and for certain other noncommercial uses permitted by copyright law. For permission request please contact the publisher at the email address with "Attention: Permission Request", at the address below.

This publication does not substitute the advice of a licensed attorney. Please consult an attorney at law for legal advice.

Printed by Paralegal Books Publishing.

First Edition. 2020-2021. Second Edition. 2022.

DISTRIBUTOR CONTACT:

PARALEGALPUBLISHINGGROUP@GMAIL.COM

Sex Discrimination

Contents

INTRODUCTION 4

JUDGEMENT FOR PREMPTORY WRIT FOR ADMINISTRATIVE MANDAMUS IN FAVOR OF EMPLOYEE (California Court – Los Angeles Superior Court) 5

VERIFIED PETITION FOR WRIT OF ADMINISTRATIVE MANDATE UNDER CALIFORNIA LAW (Paralegal Format) 8

THE ADMINISTRATIVE RECORD CERTIFIED BY THE EDD INCLUDING ALL PAPERS FILED DURING THE 1ST APPEAL 24

    CERTIFICATE OF THE ADMINISTRATIVE RECORD 25

    NOTICE OF DETERMINATION & APPEAL FORM 27

    EDD APPEAL FORM 29

First Appeal Legal Argument to the EDD & CIUAB: The State of California Mandates Anti-Harassment in the Workplace But the Board and EDD Ignore the Law 31

    DECLARATION FOR PROOF OF SEXUAL HARRASSMENT IN THE WORKPLACE 46

    ABM INTERNAL COMPANY POLICY REGARDING EQUAL EMPLOYMENT 49

    EEOC CORRESPONDENCE REGARDING FILING CHARGE(S) ffddss 51

NOTICE OF HEARING BEFORE ADMINISTRATIVE LAW JUDGE 73

EDD & CUIAB'S ADMINISTRATIVE LAW JUDGE MICHAEL KURZ'S DISCRIMINATORY LEGAL DECISION NEGATING THE CIVIL AND LEGAL RIGHTS OF THE DISCRIMINATED EMPLOYEE AT ABM INDUSTRIES 76

DECISION BY THE ADMINISTRATIVE LAW JUDGE MICHAEL KURZ (DISCRIMINATORY) 179

NOTICE OF DEFAMATION OF CHARACTER AND DEMAND FOR RETRACTION TO THE EDD 184

CONSTITUENT SERVICES AUTHORIZATION FORM (SENATOR RICARDO LARA) 193

CUIAB DECISION BY CALIFORNIA UNEMPLOYMENT INSURANCE APPEALS BOARD MEMBERS ELLEN CORBETT AND MICHAEL ALLEN (UNLAWFUL) 210

NOTICE OF RELATED CASES 214

CUIAB COVER LETTER AND BLANK DISCRIMINATION FORM IN RESPONSE TO LEGISLATIVE COMPLAINTS 217

INTRODUCTION

Please note when suing for unemployment benefits there are strict rules in the process. Before filing a lawsuit called a "Writ of Mandate", you must first have been denied by the EDD such as in the "Notice of Determination". Second, you must have filed a timely appeal to the Administrative Law Judge and been denied by written decision such as in this case. During this appeal process it is necessary to lodge and subpoena all of the documents and evidence necessary for the prove up of your case.

Thirdly, you must have filed a timely appeal to the "California Unemployment Insurance Appeals Board" and have been denied by the "Final" written decision.

Then you must have timely filed what is called "A Verified Petition for Writ of Mandate" such as in this case study. Please read, study, and learn the rules required for filing, serving, and lodging all of the legal documents necessary for success of you case.

There are many legal rules, procedures, and short time limits to submit and file all of this paperwork. This legal case offers a good source for research and analysis in an academic setting, public library, and general legal research.

We do not offer nor solicit legal advice and encourage any aggrieved party to seek the advice of several qualified attorneys at law in their jurisdiction.

The "Administrative Record", which is a collection of documents filed and lodged with the EDD during the first appeal process. The EDD certifies any paperwork and 'evidence' a claimant or employer submits to the EDD for review after the first appeal process to the ALJ. The Record must be certified by the Department and there is a procedure that must be performed within a certain time limit in order to be considered timely requested.

Many of the rules, procedures, and time limits can be found on the government's websites such as the EDD and CUIAB websites. In this information age, there exists a lot of resources for legal research and contacts for lawyers and general legal information. In this publication you find advanced legal research such as case citations, statutes, and public policy which specifically pertains to the State of California.

This publication does not substitute for the advice of a qualified attorney nor solicits any legal advice, please consult a local attorney for legal advice.

SEX DISCRIMINATION

JUDGEMENT FOR PREMPTORY WRIT FOR ADMINISTRATIVE MANDAMUS IN FAVOR OF EMPLOYEE
(California Court – Los Angeles Superior Court)

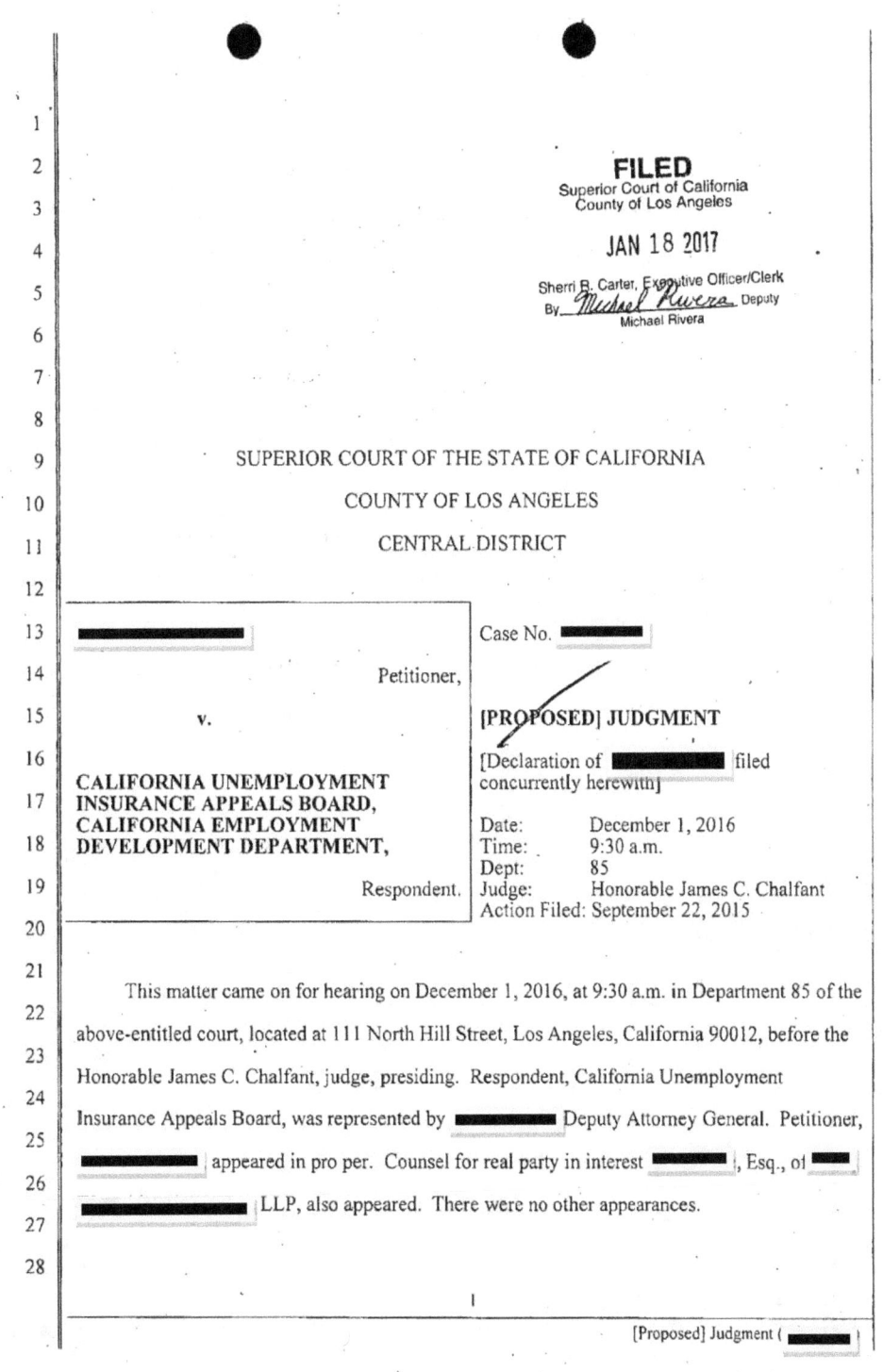

This Court issued its tentative ruling on December 1, 2016. This Court, having reviewed the pleadings on file and the record of the administrative proceedings, and having heard oral argument makes the following ruling.

IT IS ORDERED, ADJUDGED, AND DECREED that:

1. The Court's Tentative Ruling, ~~attached herein as Exhibit A and~~ incorporated by reference herein, shall constitute the Final Order of the Court. Judgment is hereby entered in favor of petitioner ▮▮▮▮▮ and against respondent California Unemployment Insurance Appeals Board. A Peremptory Writ of Administrative Mandamus shall issue commanding respondent to:

    a. Set aside respondent's decision in the Matter of ▮▮▮▮▮, Hearing No. ▮▮▮▮▮ and

    b. Issue a new and different decision consistent with the Final Order of the Court.

2. The Peremptory Writ of Administrative Mandamus shall be in the form submitted herewith, approved as to form by counsel for the parties.

3. Respondent shall make a return to this Court within 60 days following entry of judgment, stating what respondent has done to comply with the writ.

///
///
///
///
///
///
///
///
///
///
///
///

[Proposed] Judgment

Sex Discrimination

IT IS SO ORDERED.

Dated: 1/18/17

_____
HONORABLE JAMES C. CHALFANT
JUDGE OF THE SUPERIOR COURT

APPROVED AS TO FORM

For Petitioner:

Dated: 1-18-2017

By: [redacted]
Petitioner

For Respondent:

Dated: 01/18/2017

KATHLEEN A. KENEALY
Acting Attorney General of California
JENNIFER M. KIM
Supervising Deputy Attorney General

By: [redacted]
MALINDA LEE
Deputy Attorney General
Attorneys for Respondent
California Unemployment Insurance
Appeals Board

[Proposed] Judgment

VERIFIED PETITION FOR WRIT OF ADMINISTRATIVE MANDATE UNDER CALIFORNIA LAW (Paralegal Format)

Petitioner in pro per

SUPERIOR COURT OF THE STATE OF CALIFORNIA

COUNTY OF LOS ANGELES - CENTRAL DISTRICT

STANLEY MOSK COURTHOUSE

PETITIONER, v. Unemployment Insurance Appeals Board, RESPONDENT, ABM Onsite Services West, Inc., Real Party in Interest.	Case No.: **VERIFIED PETITION FOR WRIT OF MANDATE** **MEMORANDUM OF POINTS AND AUTHORITIES**

THE PARTIES

1. The Petitioner is ▒▒▒▒▒ also known as ▒▒▒▒▒, the Claimant (herein "Petitioner"). The Respondent is, and at all times herein incorporated by reference as the "Employment Development Department" (herein "Department") and the "California Unemployment Insurance Appeals Board" (herein "Board").

2. The Board is an inferior lower tribunal in where the Petitioner has exhausted all of his administrative remedies, appealing first to the "Administrative Law

SEX DISCRIMINATION

Judge" (herein referred to as "ALJ Kurz") with a final decision issued by the Board. The "Real Party in Interest", is ABM Onsite Services West, Inc., (herein "Employer"), and at all times herein mentioned is a Corporation with sufficient, significant, and/or substantial presence and is subject to the existing laws and jurisdiction of the State of California, which its principal place of business, corporate, and/or regional office location is in Los Angeles County, California.

I.
RESPONDENT FAILED TO PERFORM LEGAL DUTY AND PETITIONER EXHAUSTED ALL ADMINISTRATIVE REMEDIES

3. The Respondent had a legal duty and obligation to perform the Act sought to be compelled by this Writ. The Petitioner in this case had a clear and beneficial right to performance of that Act; the Petitioner has had no plain, speedy, or adequate remedy which normally exist in the ordinary course of law.

4. The Petitioner has undisputed facts and lawful declarations that have been unjustly suppressed, excluded, and omitted by the Respondent in this case.

5. The Respondent's decisions were not supported by the true facts and uncontested evidence of this case. The Petitioner can and shall prove up how the Respondent used their discretionary administrative powers to censor the undisputed facts and disregard the factual weight of the unchallenged evidence.

II.
PETITIONER'S STATEMENT OF FACTS & EVIDENCE WERE IMPROPERLY EXCLUDED WITH BIAS & PREDJUDICE

6. Since October 5, 2014, The Petitioner complained to his Employer about the continuous sexual harassment at the worksite but *no immediate corrective Action was ever taken*, "Exhibit 4". The Petitioner complained to his Employer and to his Union leader about the harassment at the worksite and lack of correction thereof. The Petitioner asked his Employer several times if they were going to

do anything to stop the near daily harassment or at least investigate the problem but they ignored his requests. The Petitioner shifted the legal burden onto the Employer to take immediate corrective action in the workplace but they never did.

7. On October 30, 2014, the Petitioner was called by his Employer to attend a "meeting" with the "district manager" in regards to his Complaint in Exhibit 4. The Petitioner had asked the Employer about if he would need his union representation but the Employer responded, "I don't know" and "you'll just have to talk to the district manager when you get there".

8. On November 3, 2014, at 2:45PM, a meeting was held with the Employer and it was stated that it was "commendable" the Petitioner reported the sexual harassment but he had to be disciplined for "fraternization" and transferred to another work location.

9. The Employer had prepared a disciplinary advisory notice ("notice") for the Petitioner to sign. The notice was the first written warning ever issued by the Employer to the Petitioner. The notice stated a term for separation and termination of Petitioner's employment at anytime thereafter.

10. The Employer stated that the "Union would not disagree with them" and they had no other job for him if he did not sign it. The Petitioner wanted to preserve his employment relationship and was under duress to sign it. The Petitioner was deceived to believe the Employer and was to be demoted.

11. The Petitioner had went along with the transfer in order to preserve his employment and a first opportunity to remove himself from the hostile work environment. The Petitioner did not know that he was going to be demoted, threatened with a paycut, and no longer be allowed off duty meal periods.

12. On November 5, 2014, at approximately 9:00AM, the Employer held another meeting with the Petitioner at the new worksite. The Employer then informed the Petitioner that he is no longer a Shift Supervisor and has been demoted. The Employer further stated that the Petitioner was to receive a lower

Sex Discrimination

wage and he must remain on premises at all times for all future rest/meal periods.

13. There is sufficient and substantial evidence that the Employer had intentionally discriminated against the Petitioner due to his sex (male) and gender, in retaliation of complaining, in violation of California Government Code Section § 12940 (a),(h), (i), (j)(3), and (k); Title VII of the Civil Rights Act of 1964; and the California Constitution art I, § 8.

14. By the Employer's adverse employment actions, the Petitioner was intentionally deprived of his equal opportunities. Under California law the Employer cannot have demoted him from his supervisory position from Shift Supervisor nor unilaterally waive his meal periods. For this action set forth, under Unemployment Insurance Code §1256, the Petitioner was deemed to have voluntarily left for good cause through no fault of his own. Thereafter, Petitioner duly filed a claim as a "voluntary quit" through no fault of his own for unemployment compensation benefits online via the Department's website on November 5, 2015. "Exhibit 1".

15. The Respondent neglected and omitted the fact of a bona fide EEOC Complaint was lodged and has been pending investigation. Exhibit 4.

16. The Respondent was presented with direct evidence by the Petitioner of these facts but were omitted and excluded by them, "Exhibit 6".

III.
PETITIONER WAS DEPRIVED OF EQUAL OPPORTUNITIES AND RESPONDENT IGNORED THE UNDISPUTED EVIDENCE

17. No lawful reason was provided by the Employer for the sexual harassment or the lack of corrective action thereof. No legal reason was provided by the Employer for the discipline, demotion, threat of paycut, and intended separation as a series of adverse employment actions against him from October 5, 2014.

18. The Respondent was presented with direct evidence by the Petitioner of these facts in Exhibit "4, 5, & 6" but had omitted these facts.

-4-
PETITION FOR WRIT OF MANDATE

19. The Petitioner presented evidence that the Employer had deceived and discriminated against the Petitioner in the November 3, 2014 meeting.

20. The Employer never revealed their intent to demote him, demand on duty meal periods with no compensation, and cut his pay until after the "transfer".

21. The Respondent excluded these facts and intentionally falsified some information in their "Claim of Status Report".

22. On November 19, 2014, Petitioner did ask the Union, one last time, to file a grievance against the Employer. Pursuant to CBA Article 25, Section 25.1, which states that the Union can present a grievance within 14 days from the date of the CBA violation. The Union declined Petitioner's request and deferred him to the EEOC. "Exhibit 4".

23. The Petitioner still asked the Employer for reinstatement but they have refused to do so to date. Although the Petitioner signed the separation notice, "Exhibit 11", he was under duress and deceived into signing it.

24. The Petitioner has since rescinded his signature since December 1, 2014, herein attached in "Exhibit 11", in sub-Exhibit "A", see "Recession and Breach of Contract" email attachment dated 12/1/14 at 2:09PM to Employer. The Petitioner has presented this to the Respondent as direct evidence but they have neglected to include it into the record, thus showing substantial prejudice.

IV.
THE DEPARTMENT EXAMINER ACTED WITH BIAS, LIBEL, AND DISCRIMINATORY MOTIVE AGAINST THE PETITIONER

25. The "Unemployment Insurance Eligibility Interview", delayed and untimely, took place on December 10, 2014, herein attached as "Exhibit 2".

26. An "Examiner" of the Department claimed that *Employer did not have to do anything to stop "anyone" from harassing the Petitioner* at work.

27. The Examiner disbelieved, denied, and excluded this information into their "Claim of Status Report". The Petitioner request the record and this report.

SEX DISCRIMINATION

28. The Examiner treated Petitioner with bias when he further informed the Department that the Employer was consistently violating labor laws, in Exhibit 6.

29. The Employer was consistently cheating him on his paychecks within the company and violating OSHA regulations at the worksite regarding chemical spill(s) in violation of health and safety regulations. The Respondent treated the Petitioner with bias and then begin to falsify and alter his statements against him in their "Claim of Status Report".

30. The Examiner acted with bias by falsely presuming that she believed that the Employer did a lawful "investigation" into the sexual harassment at the workplace.

31. The Examiner had no evidence to presume this as "fact" and libels the Petitioner in the "Claim of Status Report". The Petitioner specifically informed the Examiner of no lawful Employer "investigation" but it was omitted and falsified.

32. The Examiner proceeded to construct words, sentences, and phrases against the Petitioner in the "Claim of Status Report" that were simply not true. The Examiner had intended to defame the Petitioner in order to unlawfully exclude him from the benefits of this insurance claim. The Department also disregarded Petitioner's right to privacy pursuant to the sensitive nature of this legal matter. The Petitioner has reserved all rights afforded to him by the  California Constitution§ art 1, § section 1, privacy.

33. The Respondent denied and falsified their findings regarding his demotion because of his sex, gender, and in retaliation for protesting discrimination in the workplace. The Respondent ignored the undisputed fact that he was transferred to a location not in compliance with the CBA Article 4 & 25; and California law.

34. The claim was ultimately denied by the Examiner of the Department on grounds that the Petitioner did not "explore all reasonable solutions" before 'voluntarily leaving' and claims to have considered their decision based on all the "available information". Exhibit 3.

35. On December 17, 2014, the Petitioner wrote the Department a two-page letter, herein attached as "Exhibit 5", reminding them of the undisputed and uncontested facts regarding the constructive termination and the demeaning treatment of Petitioner in the eligibility interview by the Department Examiner.

36. Then on or around December 30, 2014, the Department received the Petitioner's 13 page written appeal to the Department and it was denied deliberately with an intent to harm and cause economic injury. "Exhibit 6".

V.
THE DEPARTMENT ALLOWED BIAS & LIBEL AGAINST PETITIONER'S UNDISPUTED FACTS & EVIDENCE

37. The Employer never submitted any information in writing to the Department disputing or setting forth any facts to the contrary against the Petitioner. The Department had made up its own facts and conclusions in sharp contrast to the "available information" they claim they had.

38. The only available information they had was from the Petitioner but they had began to falsify and omit the facts. The Department acted in bad faith and unfairly by falsifying its "Claim of Status Report". The Respondent used their discretionary power to act arbitrary and capricious.

39. The Department had intentionally made contradictory statements in their "Claim of Status Report" against the Petitioner in order to disqualify him from this Act. One example is when the Department acted with bias towards the Petitioner and constructed false facts such as claiming the Petitioner "never had facts". The Department ignores the Petitioner's written statements which supported the legal presumption he left the Employer through no fault of his own.

40. Another example, is when the Employer told Petitioner on November 5, 2014, around 9:00AM, that he was to receive a paycut after he was demoted but did not yet say exactly how much. The Petitioner informs the Examiner and she records the statement in portion in the "Claim of Status Report".

Then the Examiner, with malice and prejudice, writes "Clmt admits he wasn't told if it was a paycut...". There was no contrary information to write that and it was made in contradiction with the intent to unjustly disqualify Petitioner's claim for benefits.

VI.
RESPONDENT ACTED WITH PREDJUDICE BY DENYING PETITIONER'S SUBSTANTIAL RIGHTS & EXCLUDING UNDISPUTED FACTS IN THE APPEAL PROCESS

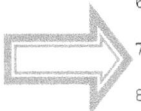

41. The Respondent has further acted with reckless disregard for the truth and undisputed facts herein. On or around January 14, 2015, Petitioner appeared in person at the Inglewood Office of Appeals (herein "Inglewood Office").

42. The Petitioner requested to an ALJ for witnesses and/or evidence to "subpoena and/or noticed to attend and produce documents", Exhibit 8, in support of his claim.

43. The ALJ presiding stated to Petitioner that the "Employer is not even a party to the action", he did not think that a video could be played at the hearing, and said "this is not a place for free discovery", as if any evidence of violations in employment, labor, and safety were not relevant to intolerability and credibility.

44. The ALJ substantially prejudiced the Petitioner by declaring the Employer "not a party to the action" and opposed the Petitioner's request in Exhibit 8. The ALJ further failed to offer a fair hearing on the matter regarding the relevance of any key witnesses and evidence requested. The ALJ simply wrote his legal reason in the right hand corner of the application in blue ink in Exhibit 8 and made a note in his file folder.

45. Exhibit 8 was scribed "Denied Er not a party no contrary evidence [signature]". The ALJ substantially prejudiced the Petitioner, acted unjust, and erred in this legal matter. The ALJ used his discretionary power to substantially prejudice the Petitioner.

46. This substantial prejudice of denying a right to direct and/or supplemental evidence in support of this case was unjust and unfair; especially when the Employer was automatically opted-out by virtue of the Respondent.

47. The request was denied but if granted, the Petitioner could have compelled the Employer's "most knowledgeable person". Petitioner was denied the opportunity to have impeached the Employer on their credibility by examination of the most knowledgeable person, documents, and video in their possession.

48. The Respondent unfairly and prejudicially denied his "Application and Declaration For Subpoena Duces Tecum/Notice To Attend And/or Produce", attached herein as "Exhibit 8". The Petitioner should have been allowed to call a key witness, examine additional documents, and video footage in support of Petitioner's lawful claim.

49. The supplemental evidence in the Employer's possession would have impeached their credibility with regard to discrimination and retaliation, also coupled with Labor Law and OSHA violations, supported by additional evidence reserved for impeachment; showed substantial good cause and through no fault of his own, did Petitioner become unemployed.

50. In this request the Petitioner was unfairly denied by the Respondent the right to access a key witness. The opportunity to cross-examine the Employer with regard to these undisputed facts presented to Respondent.

51. The Petitioner had proffered proof to Respondent but they had omitted this fact in their alleged "findings of fact".

52. California law and public policy prohibit these type of adverse employment actions and arbitrary decisions within administrative agencies. The Respondent cannot incite, aid, nor abet the Employer's intentional deprivation of one's equal opportunities in employment. In California, government agencies must uphold California's legislative intent with regard to providing benefits to the unemployed.

//

Sex Discrimination

VII.
RESPONDENT ERRED, FALSIFIED AND EXCLUDED DIRECT EVIDENCE, AND ABUSED THEIR DISCRETION AS "FACT FINDERS"

53. Pursuant to the provision of Section §1328 of the Unemployment Insurance Code, the Petitioner was the only party lawfully appearing and submitting facts in this case.

54. The Petitioner duly filed an appeal with the Respondent and appeared by written declaration on January 20, 2014. Starting at "Exhibit 10".

55. The Petitioner knew Respondent was not acting objectively and fairly so he wrote the Director of the Department and the California legislature.

56. In this Action the Petitioner submitted his appeal papers by writing such as "Claimant Statement of Questions, Facts, and Information in Dispute" herein attached as "Exhibit 9 ".

57. The Petitioner's " Notice of Declaration and Memorandum of Points and Authorities", herein attached as "Exhibit 10". ALJ Kurz substantially prejudiced the Petitioner's direct evidence by changing the true facts without any objective contrary information presented by the Employer. The Petitioner had presented two lawful declarations, Exhibits 10 & 11, sub-Exhibit B, as direct evidence.

58. The Employer provided nothing in writing to the contrary. ALJ Kurz obscures the actual undisputed facts with intentionally omitting that Petitioner was a Shift Supervisor. The Petitioner had no disciplinary actions prior to his sexual harassment complaints and the Employer was under and/or just released from an "EEO Consent Decree".

59. ALJ Kurz, with no contrary evidence, omits the facts that the Petitioner was being transferred in violation of the CBA and California law. ALJ Kurz had no unbiased, nor objective contrary evidence supporting his decision.

60. The Respondent excludes the fact that the Employer's demoted the Petitioner. The Employer vowed to lower his wage in violation of California law but

Respondent excluded the fact from this case.

61. ALJ Kurz knew or should have known of these facts, as they were presented in Petitioner's moving papers. ALJ Kurz knew the Petitioner sought to subpoena additional evidence from the Employer, but Respondent failed to compel the Employer to rebut the Petitioner's direct evidence and undisputed facts. ALJ Kurz claims and concludes that the Petitioner simply did not like being transferred, got mad, and quit. ALJ Kurz further distorts the truth of this matter by intentionally hiding the fact that the Employer never investigated the sexual harassment at the time they transferred the Petitioner. ALJ Kurz abuses his discretion and constructs these false facts and untruths in order to protect the Department's libel and bias against Petitioner.

62. ALJ Kurz had no objective factual evidence presented from the Employer, nor did the Employer ever rebut the Petitioner's undisputed statement  of facts and declarations, as is required by <u>Unemployment Insurance Code Section § 1327, 1328, and 1256.2</u>.

63. A copy of the decision is attached hereto as "Exhibit 12" and made a part hereof. ALJ Kurz simply creates fiction by continuing to claim that an actual "investigation" took place, which it did not, as presupposed by the Department. ALJ Kurz falsely claims as "fact" that an investigation was "to play out", but this is an outright fabrication and falsely presumed to cover-up the Department's arbitrary and malicious intentions against the Petitioner.

64. ALJ Kurz, adopts the 'blame the victim approach', and purposefully excludes the facts and ignores the Petitioner's lawful declarations. The Respondent omits the undisputed facts that the Petitioner was unlawfully being harassed.

65. The Respondent knew or should have known that he was intentionally deprived of his equal opportunities by the series of adverse actions.

66. The Respondent needed to blame the Petitioner and obscure the truth as an abuse of power and discretion for the sole purpose of denying him benefits.

Sex Discrimination

ALJ Kurz diverged and did not vigorously uphold California legislative public policy. ALJ Kurz may have been politically and prejudicially motivated to deny benefits herein. ALJ Kurz erroneously presumes and falsely concludes as a "finding of fact" that the Petitioner "voluntarily quit" without "good cause".

67. The Petitioner's undisputed facts submitted in a proper legal form was never rebutted by the Employer at any point, as is required by <u>Unemployment Code Sections § 1327,§ 1328, and § 1256</u>. ALJ Kurz recklessly disregards the law and objective fact finding. The Employer did not investigate the Petitioner's allegations of sexual harassment before nor at the time of transfer, thus failing to prevent harassment and take the necessary legal action thereof.

VIII.
THE RESPONDENT'S DECISION WAS NOT SUPPORTED BY THE UNCONTESTED FACTS & EVIDENCE

68. The Respondent disregarded the validity of the EEOC Complaint that the Petitioner duly filed against the Employer. Exhibit 4. The Respondent omitted this fact in order to disqualify him with bias and libel. The Respondent knew that the Petitioner had filed a bona fide EEOC Complaint but excluded it in their written decision.

69. The Respondent, never had a valid contested case presented to them with contrary evidence to support any written decision. ALJ Kurz simply created a fiction of "facts" in order to justify his written decision. This is a divergence against the legislative intent of the California legislature.

70. The Employer never provided any evidentiary statement(s), nor did the Employer verify in writing to rebut the legal presumption as required by law.

71. Therefore the questions beg, how does ALJ KURZ acting on behalf of the Respondent, know "the employer was investigating..." if the Employer was never required to have appeared in this action nor provided any written statement to rebut the real facts provided by the Petitioner? Why would ALJ KURZ write

that as fact? Where was the bridge between the 'raw evidence' and the decision of law? Should this practice at this agency be a public concern? Does ALJ Kurz always act with political bias and gender prejudice, by undertone, in his written decisions? Is this a widespread practice or an isolated case?

72. ALJ Kurz continues to fabricate the actual history of events, by claiming: "Instead of going with the transfer, allowing the investigation to play out, the claimant instead became upset, angry, and voluntarily quit". ALJ Kurz falsely constructs this "fact" in order to absolve the Respondent of their legal duties and obligations under California Unemployment Insurance Code Section 1256.

73. In affirming the Department's determination and ruling, ALJ Kurz abused his discretion, changed and constructed his own "facts" to conform to the Department's falsified "Claim of Status Report". ALJ Kurz had substantially prejudiced the rights of the Petitioner, acted with political bias and motive to not enforce the policy of equal employment opportunity for all Californians, especially for the Petitioner.

74. The Respondent had fabricated a "dispute of facts" and has acted in excess of their jurisdiction in concluding that the Petitioner "voluntary left his work without good cause". The Respondent knowingly and intentionally falsified facts and improperly excluded the Petitioner's statements and evidence. A copy of the decision is attached hereto as Petitioner "Exhibit 12".

IX.

THE RESPONDENT ABUSES ITS DISCRETION AND DOES NOT PROPERLY APPLY THE LAW TO THE UNDISPUTED EVIDENCE

75. As authorized by Section § 1336 of the Unemployment Insurance Code, Petitioner thereafter duly filed an appeal with the "California Unemployment Insurance Appeals Board" (herein "Board"), which on April 1, 2015, affirmed ALJ Kurz's decision and notified Petitioner accordingly

//

SEX DISCRIMINATION

76. In affirming the erroneous decision of ALJ Kurz, the Board, now as the Respondent, jointly abused its discretion, administrative power, and further diverged from California law and public policy; further acting in excess of its jurisdiction in the same manner as did ALJ Kurz and the Department. The Board simply rubberstamped ALJ Kurz's erroneous decision and excluded the undisputed evidence. The Board also excluded and omitted evidence and upheld the falsified "Claim of Status Report". The Respondent, as the Board, in its final decision continued to alter and change the "findings of fact".

77. The Respondent notes and changes ALJ Kurz's clerical errors, such as the Petitioner actual last day worked. The Respondent writes that the Petitioner "felt the new position was a 'demotion'". However, the Respondent intentionally omits and prejudicially excludes the undisputed fact that the Employer told the Petitioner that he was indeed demoted. Exhibit 1, 4, 5, 6, 10.

78. The Employer never presented not one shred of evidence in writing nor to the contrary of anything supporting the Respondent's erroneous decisions. The Respondent knew it was making unfounded allegations by consistently changing the facts in order to fit its erroneous decision. The Board acted unjustly by denying the undisputed facts and evidence of the unlawful adverse employment actions. The Respondent has acted in excess of its jurisdiction and discretion in order to further diminish the Petitioner's rights under California law.

79. This is truly not a contested case, according to the procedures proscribed in the Unemployment Insurance Code Section 1256. The Respondent is not only untruthful about the unlawful demotion but has knowingly prejudiced him in Exhibit 7, 8; and in his moving papers in "Exhibit's 4-6, 8-11". Even if additional documentary evidence would have been provided, the Respondent still would have acted arbitrary and capricious.

//

80. The Respondent has acted abusively in its discretion and the evidence does not support their findings or decision. The Respondent treated the Petitioner unfairly, causing harm and economic injury. The faulty and prejudicial reasoning forged by the Respondent against the Petitioner was done with malice, prejudice, and an intent to cause humiliation. The Respondent has acted with the intent to publically shame the Petitioner and incite the Employer to harbor discrimination.

PRAYER FOR RELIEF:

WHEREFORE, PETITIONER prays as follows:

1. That this Court issue a Writ of Mandate ordering Respondent Unemployment Insurance Appeals Board:

(a) To set aside its final decision affirming the decision of the administrative law judge, who affirmed the determination of the Director of Employment Development that the claimant voluntarily left his work without good cause; and is ineligible for unemployment compensation benefits, and to grant such benefits against the Employer's reserve account, or

(b) In the alternative, to show cause before this Court at a time and place to be fixed by the Court why it has not done so and directing it to file with this Court the record of all proceedings in this matter before the Respondent, Department and the administrative law judge;

2. That, after hearing on the order to show cause, this Court issue a preemptory writ of mandate to the same effect as the alternative writ except for the order to show cause;

(a) To issue a Statement of Decision pursuant to Code of Civ. Proc. § 632;

(b) compliance with Unemployment Insurance Code Section § 1329 and ordered to perform and produce the computation on the claim for certified weeks for payment to Petitioner;

3. For prejudgment interest and costs of suit herein incurred;

4. For such other and further relief as the court may deem proper.

-15-
PETITION FOR WRIT OF MANDATE

Sex Discrimination

Dated: 9/21/2015

_____ Petitioner in pro per

VERIFICATION

I, ▬▬▬▬▬▬ am the Plaintiff in the above-entitled action. I have read the foregoing complaint and know the contents thereof. The same is true of my own knowledge, except as to those matters which are therein alleged on information and belief, and as to those matters, I believe it to be true.

I declare under penalty of perjury under the laws of the State of California that the foregoing is true and correct, in Los Angeles, California, on September 21, 2015, Los Angeles, CA.

_____ Petitioner in pro per

Certificate of Word Count

The total number of words in this Petition and Points and Authorities (excluding exhibits and judicial notices) is 7003.

_____ Petitioner in pro per

Certificate of Interested Entities or Persons

This Petition for Writ of Mandate is being submitted on behalf of ▬▬▬▬▬ also known as ▬▬▬▬▬ and there are no known interested entities or persons on his behalf to his knowledge that must be listed under CRC rule 8.208.

THE ADMINISTRATIVE RECORD CERTIFIED BY THE EDD INCLUDING ALL PAPERS FILED DURING THE 1ST APPEAL

Table of Contents

1. Certification (1)
2. Department Determination (2-3)
3. Appeal to ALJ/Appeal Transmittal (4-48)
4. Notice of Hearing (49-50)
5. Register (51)
6. Transcript (52-54)
7. Exhibits (55-157)
8. ALJ's Decision (158-162)
9. Appeal to the Appeals Board (163-185)
10. Acknowledgement Letters (186-188)
11. Appeals Board Decision (189-192)

CERTIFICATE OF THE ADMINISTRATIVE RECORD

"A notary public or other officer completing this certificate verifies only the identity of the individual who signed the document to which this certificate is attached, and not the truthfulness, accuracy, or validity of that document."

CERTIFICATE OF RECORD

State of California)
) ss
County of Sacramento)

Kim Hickox, being duly sworn, deposes and says: That she is an Attorney with the California Unemployment Insurance Appeals Board.

That the attached administrative record was prepared from the original file of the Appeals Board and contains originals or copies of the records, documents, and other papers in the matter of Luke Edward Dumas. Appeals Board Case No. AO-380059.

Kim Hickox

Subscribed and sworn to (or affirmed) before me on this 21st day of January, 2016 by Kim Hickox, proved to me on the basis of satisfactory evidence to be the person(s) who appeared before me.

I certify under PENALTY OF PERJURY under the laws of the State of California that the foregoing paragraph is true and correct.

WITNESS my hand and official seal.

Signature Cathy L. Vandeleur

Sex Discrimination

NOTICE OF DETERMINATION & APPEAL FORM

```
EMPLOYMENT DEVELOPMENT DEPT
SAN BERNARDINO PAC
PO BOX 641
SAN BERNARDINO  CA 92402-0641
```

NOTICE OF DETERMINATION

```
                                  DATE MAILED        12/11/14
                                  BENEFIT YEAR BEGAN 03/30/14
```

```
              0410           EDD TELEPHONE NUMBERS:
                             ENGLISH      1-800-300-5616
                             SPANISH      1-800-326-8937
                             CANTONESE    1-800-547-3506
                             MANDARIN     1-866-303-0706
                             VIETNAMESE   1-800-547-2058
                             TTY          1-800-815-9387
```

SSA NUMBER

YOU ARE NOT ELIGIBLE TO RECEIVE BENEFITS UNDER CALIFORNIA UNEMPLOYMENT INSURANCE CODE SECTION 1256 BEGINNING 11/02/14 AND CONTINUING UNTIL YOU RETURN TO WORK AFTER THE DISQUALIFYING ACT AND EARN $2250.00 OR MORE IN BONA FIDE EMPLOYMENT, AND YOU CONTACT THE ABOVE OFFICE TO REOPEN YOUR CLAIM.

YOU QUIT YOUR LAST JOB WITH ABM ONSITE SERVICES BECAUSE YOU FELT THE WORKING CONDITIONS WERE INTOLERABLE. YOU DID NOT EXPLORE ALL REASONABLE SOLUTIONS BEFORE YOU QUIT. AFTER CONSIDERING AVAILABLE INFORMATION, THE DEPARTMENT FINDS THAT YOU DO NOT MEET THE LEGAL REQUIREMENTS FOR PAYMENT OF BENEFITS. SECTION 1256 PROVIDES - AN INDIVIDUAL IS DISQUALIFIED IF THE DEPARTMENT FINDS HE VOLUNTARILY QUIT HIS MOST RECENT WORK WITHOUT GOOD CAUSE OR WAS DISCHARGED FOR MISCONDUCT FROM HIS MOST RECENT WORK. SECTION 1260A PROVIDES - AN INDIVIDUAL DISQUALIFIED UNDER SECTION 1256 IS DISQUALIFIED UNTIL HE/SHE, SUBSEQUENT TO THE DISQUALIFYING ACT, PERFORMS SERVICES IN BONA FIDE EMPLOYMENT FOR WHICH HE/SHE RECEIVES REMUNERATION EQUAL TO OR IN EXCESS OF FIVE TIMES HIS OR HER WEEKLY BENEFIT AMOUNT.

APPEAL:

YOU HAVE THE RIGHT TO FILE AN APPEAL IF YOU DO NOT AGREE WITH ALL OR PART OF THIS DECISION.

TO APPEAL, YOU MUST DO ALL OF THE FOLLOWING:

A. COMPLETE THE ENCLOSED APPEAL FORM (DE1000M) OR WRITE A LETTER STATING THAT YOU WANT TO APPEAL THIS DECISION. IF YOU WRITE A LETTER TO APPEAL, EXPLAIN THE REASON WHY YOU DO NOT AGREE WITH THE DEPARTMENT'S DECISION. WRITE YOUR SOCIAL SECURITY NUMBER ON EACH DOCUMENT YOU SUBMIT TO THE DEPARTMENT. (TITLE 22, CALIFORNIA CODE OF REGULATIONS (CCR), SECTION 5008).

B. MAIL THE DE1000M OR YOUR LETTER TO THE ADDRESS OF THE OFFICE LISTED ON THE FIRST PAGE OF THIS DECISION.

Appeal Documents

C. FILE YOUR APPEAL WITHIN TWENTY (20) DAYS OF THE MAIL DATE OF THIS NOTICE OR NO LATER THAN 12/31/14.

YOUR HANDBOOK, "A GUIDE TO BENEFITS AND EMPLOYMENT SERVICES", GIVES MORE INFORMATION ABOUT APPEALS. IF YOU DO NOT HAVE A HANDBOOK, CONTACT THE OFFICE LISTED ON THE FIRST PAGE OF THIS NOTICE.

APPEAL INFORMATION:

WHEN YOUR APPEAL IS RECEIVED, YOUR CASE WILL BE REVIEWED. IF THE DECISION REMAINS THE SAME, WE WILL SEND YOUR APPEAL TO THE OFFICE OF APPEALS. IF YOU APPEAL AFTER THE 20 DAYS, YOU MUST INCLUDE THE REASON FOR THE DELAY. THE ADMINISTRATIVE LAW JUDGE WILL DETERMINE WHETHER YOU HAD GOOD CAUSE FOR THE DELAY. IF THE ADMINISTRATIVE LAW JUDGE DETERMINES YOU DID NOT HAVE GOOD CAUSE FOR SUBMITTING YOUR APPEAL LATE, YOUR APPEAL WILL BE DISMISSED.

THE OFFICE OF APPEALS WILL SEND YOU A LETTER WITH THE DATE, PLACE, AND TIME OF YOUR HEARING AND A PAMPHLET EXPLAINING APPEAL HEARING PROCEDURES. AT THE HEARING, THE ADMINISTRATIVE LAW JUDGE WILL LISTEN TO YOU, EXAMINE THE FACTS, AND MAKE A DECISION. YOU MAY HAVE A REPRESENTATIVE OR SOMEONE ELSE HELP YOU.

IF YOU ARE CLAIMING CONTINUING BENEFITS:

WHILE YOU WAIT FOR THE ADMINISTRATIVE LAW JUDGE'S DECISION, YOU MUST CONTINUE TO MAIL YOUR CLAIM FORMS TO THE EDD. IF YOU DO NOT RECEIVE CLAIM FORMS OR A FORM FROM THE OFFICE OF APPEALS, CONTACT THE OFFICE LISTED ON THE FIRST PAGE OF THIS NOTICE. IF THE ADMINISTRATIVE LAW JUDGE DECIDES YOU ARE ELIGIBLE FOR BENEFITS; WE CAN ONLY PAY BENEFITS IF CLAIM FORMS WERE RECEIVED FOR THAT WEEK.

OTHER SERVICES: CONTACT EDD FOR INFORMATION ABOUT (1) JOB REFERRALS, (2) DISABILITY INSURANCE, (3) OTHER EDD SERVICES (4) SERVICES OFFERED BY OTHER AGENCIES.
DE1080 CZ   REV. 1 (06-05)   (CLU)

Appeal Documents

Sex Discrimination

EDD APPEAL FORM

12/10/14
2682-
VQ

RECEIVED
EDD
SAN BERNARDINO #041
14 DEC 30 AM 9:37
APPEAL FORM

EDD Telephone Numbers:
ENGLISH 1-800-300-5616
SPANISH 1-800-326-8937
CANTONESE 1-800-547-3506
MANDARIN 1-866-303-0706
VIETNAMESE 1-800-547-2058
TTY (non-voice) 1-800-815-9387
website: www.edd.ca.gov

If you disagree with the Notice of Determination(s) and/or Determination(s)/Rulings by the EDD, you may appeal the decision(s) to the California Unemployment Insurance Appeals Board (CUIAB) by completing this form and explaining why you disagree. You must sign the form and return it to the EDD at the office address listed on the notice that you are appealing. **YOU HAVE 20 DAYS FROM THE MAIL DATE OF THE NOTICE TO FILE A TIMELY APPEAL.** If you appeal after the 20-day period, you must include the reason for the delay. The administrative law judge (ALJ) will determine whether you had good cause for the delay. If the ALJ determines you did not have good cause to submit your appeal late, your appeal will be dismissed.

CLAIMANTS: While your appeal is pending, **you must continue to certify for benefits**. If you are found eligible, you can be paid only for periods for which you have certified and have met all other eligibility requirements.

NOTE: Claimants for Disaster Unemployment Assistance (DUA) have 60 days to file an appeal. Employers appealing the *Notice of Determination or Assessment*, DE 3807, have 30 days to file an appeal.

SECTION I APPELLANT INFORMATION

INSTRUCTIONS: The following information must be provided by the Appellant (the claimant or employer who is appealing a notice), or by the authorized agent or representative of the Appellant. The signature of the Appellant or agent is required. Please use **BLACK INK** when filling out this form.

Claimant Name: ▓▓▓▓▓▓▓▓▓▓   Social Security Number:

Do you need a translator? ☐ Yes ☒ No   If yes, what language/dialect? _____

Appellant Address: _____
E-mail Address: _____

☒ I authorize the CUIAB to send confidential information regarding my appeal to the e-mail address listed above.
☐ I authorize the CUIAB to send confidential information regarding my appeal by text message or voice mail to the cell phone number listed above.

Complete this section for employer appeals only
Employer Account Number: _____   Agent Name (if applicable): _____
Agent Address: _____

SECTION II APPELLANT STATEMENT

INSTRUCTIONS: Explain the reason for your appeal and why you disagree with the decision(s). If required, attach additional pages to this form and write your name and Social Security number on each page.

I disag▓▓▓▓▓▓▓▓▓

Signature of Appellant or Agent: ▓▓▓▓▓▓   Date: 12/26/14

DE 1000M Rev. 7 (1-14)   - Versión en español en el dorso -   CU

Sex Discrimination

First Appeal Legal Argument to the EDD & CIUAB: The State of California Mandates Anti-Harassment

● RE: ●

TO: EMPLOYMENT DEVELOPMENT DEPARTMENT

From:

RE:

THE STATE OF CALIFORNIA MANDATES ANTI-HARASSMENT IN THE WORKPLACE AGAINST

EMPLOYEES BY NONEMPLOYEES

Sexual harassment is illegal in the workplace and harassment of employees is forbidden under California Law, see California Government Code Section §12940 (a),(h), (i), (j)(3), and (k). Employers have a duty, and are obligated to train their employees in sexual harassment prevention and procedures under California Government Code § 12950.1 (a).

Employers are liable for harassment by nonemployees and employees alike, see California Government Code Section§12940 (j) and (k). The California Constitution art I, §8 prohibits sex discrimination in employment. Title VII of the Civil Rights Act of 1964 (42 USC §§ 2000e-2000e-17) prohibits discrimination based on sex and has been construed to include sexual harassment, see Meritor Savings Bank v. Vinson (1986) 477 UA 57, 67, 106 S. Ct 2399. Whether an employee is a male or female, the California Legislature has strict mandates against harassment in the workplace by non-employees.

If ABM is going to operate in the State of California; ABM has the legal duty and obligation to take to preventative "immediate and corrective action" against sexual harassment in order to protect their employee, male, female, or transgender, even if it is alleged to have been committed by a non-employee. I have performed the legal duty and obligation to report unlawful harassment in the workplace to ABM.

ABM FAILED TO RESPOND TO MY COMPLAINT AND TO PREVENT HARASSMENT WITH IMMEDIATE RESPONSE AND CORRECTIVE ACTION

I made an oral complaint to ABM and a good faith effort to prevent the harassment that was occurring at work from October 6 to November 2, 2014, I promptly reported it to my immediate supervisor of the occurrence ("Exhibit A"), I was never contacted by Human Resources during that time, I was told it was going to be investigated but it was not.

On October 6, 2014, I initially first complained to my immediate supervisor, then on October the 10, 2014, I contacted the District Manager via email ("Exhibit A"), and I was led to believe by my immediate supervisor that my complaint would be investigated or

Privileged Communication & Confidential Information © 2014 Edward Dumas All rights reserved. No part of this publication may be reproduced or transmitted in any form or by any means, electronic or mechanical, including photocopy, recording or any other information storage and retrieval system without prior permission in writing from Edward Dumas.

corrected. Instead I was removed by the District Manager, whom is in charge of the entire region for the department I worked under. ABM termed "transfer", put me on termination notice via disciplinary action, and I was demoted from shift supervisor to lobby ambassador without being informed until I arrived at the new worksite. For a detailed account of harassment please refer to the Statement of Facts on page 8 of this appeal for benefits.

I believe I was discriminated because of my sex and/or gender and unlawfully sexually harassed at work; and ABM failed to take any "immediate and corrective action" against sexual harassment as is required by California law. This is contrary to what the California law and public policy mandates to employers and to what the contract terms are for employment between ABM and the Union. This adverse action was designed by ABM management to constructively terminate my employment with them for reporting sexual harassment.

The United States Equal Employment Opportunity Commission (EEOC) publishes guidelines stating that harassment based upon sex is a form of "discrimination". The EEOC Guidelines also give some examples of conduct which, in the agency's view, would give rise to liability for harassment. The Guideless are updated and revised periodically to reflect new developments in the law. The State of California has even stricter guidelines that are statutory law. Copy of EEOC guidelines can be obtained at http://www.eeoc.gov/policy/docs/harassment.html.

"Discrimination" refers to bias in the exercise of personnel management authority on behalf of the ABM, in which has taken some adverse action against me such as adverse job assignment, disciplinary action, promotion and/or demotion. In Roby, "Harassment" refers to the bias that is expressed or communicated through interpersonal relations in the workplace". Roby v. McKesson Corp. (2009) 47 Cal.4th 686, 706 [101 Cal.Rptr.3d 773, 787-788].

The Department must take notice that The California Fair Employment and Housing Act (FEHA) requires and mandates that ABM must take "all reasonable steps necessary to prevent discrimination and harassment from occurring", see California Government Code§ 12940(k). It is ABM's legal duty to perform reasonable steps as the means to explore reasonable solutions in order to prevent and correct harassment in the workplace.

The FEHA specifically prohibits "harassment" as well as "discrimination" at ABM under California Government Code § 12940(a)(h)(j); Discrimination and harassment based on sex, gender, and/or sexual orientation; and sexually harassing conduct under the FEHA

SEX DISCRIMINATION

The FEHA extends protection to independent contractors or persons providing services pursuant to a contract" as well as employees and job applicants.

The FEHA ban on harassment extends to all employers, even ABM, regardless of the number of employees working for the employer. The Department must consider and cannot ignore that California Government Code Section §12940 (a) prohibits "discrimination" in the terms, conditions, or privileges of employment on the basis of "sex", "gender", "gender identity", "gender expression" or "sexual orientation". California Government Code §12940(j)(1) prohibit "harassment" on the basis of "sex", "gender", gender identity," "gender expression" or "sexual orientation".

EXPLORING LEGAL SOLUTIONS AND ABM POLICY

Employer's Duty to Prevent Harassment means that ABM must take all reasonable steps to prevent harassment against me. An employer, like ABM is liable for failing "to take all necessary steps necessary to prevent discrimination and harassment from occurring." California Government Code §12940 (k); Weeks v. Baker & McKenzie (1998) 63 Cal.4th 1128, 1157; Doe v. Capital Cities (1996) 50 Cal.4th 1038, 1053; BAJI No. 2527(4th ed. 2000).

If the harassment has already occurred the duty to maintain a harassment free work environment requires the employer, such as ABM, to take remedial action not only change the harasser's behavior, but to deter potential harassers from unlawful conduct, see Intlekofer v. Turnage (9th Cir. 1992) 973 F2d 773, 778. ABM never took remedial action to change the harasser's unlawful conduct toward me. I followed ABM policy and was deprived equal opportunities in employment for complaining about sexual harassment.

ABM FAILS TO INSITUTE ITS OWN EQUAL EMPLOYMENT POLICY

ABM claims to have an "open door" policy when it comes to equal employment opportunities and/or sexual harassment ("Exhibit B"). According to ABM policy an employee must first discuss the situation with their immediate supervisor within a week of the occurrence who in turn will work with Human Resources to provide a solution or explanation. I did my duty in informing my immediate supervisor and did speak up within a week with my immediate supervisor at ABM. For a detailed account please refer to the "Statement of Facts".

As the harassment worsened and the problem persisted I contacted the District Manager which is also known as the Department or Branch Manager, who was supposed to investigate and provide me with a solution or explanation as claimed in ABM company policy. The ABM District Manager who is the acting Department or Branch Manager; did not conduct an investigation, I was never contacted, nor provided with a solution and explanation. I was led to believe there was going to be an investigation, solution and/or explanation. Instead I was treated unfairly and was issued a termination notice (first and final warning) and ABM demoted me for complaining about the sexual harassment.

Whether an employer like ABM has exercised reasonable care to prevent and correct the harassing conduct is determine by "whether the employee's actions as a whole established a reasonable mechanism for prevention and correct" Holly D. v. California Inst. of Technol. (9th Cir 2003) 339 F3d 1158, 1177. ABM never took reasonable care to prevent and correct the harassing behavior against me, in light of me providing notice of the harassment.

My actions to report and declare I was sexually harassed was a reasonable mechanism for prevention and correction. The Ninth Circuit has found that a common way of showing that an employer has established a "reasonable mechanism for prevention" is if the employer has promulgated an appropriate anti-harassment policy that includes a complaint procedure, *although proof of such a policy is not dispositive.* Burlington Indus. Inc. v. Ellerth (1998) 524 US 742, 765, 118 S. Ct. 2257; see, e.g., EEOC v. Hacienda Hotel (9th Cir. 1989) 881 F.2d. 1504, 1516.

I followed ABM's complaint procedure but they failed in instituting their own anti-harassment policy. An employer like ABM, as in Yates v. Avco Corp. (6th Cir 1987) F.2d 630, 635, an employer, who urged confidentiality, did not tell the complainant of his or her rights against harassment, and/or the steps the employer would take to protect their employee can subject the employer to increased liability. After I complained, ABM never consulted me about my rights nor how they would take steps to protect me, and any alleged protection was false and not executed.

The State of California Government Code Section 12940 et al clarifies that ABM should not have stigmatized or penalized me; ABM must have interviewed me and the alleged harasser; any necessary witnesses to the alleged occurences; ABM never communicated to me the progress and conclusion of "the investigation"; ABM has failed to make me whole; ABM has not taken steps to prevent future harassment and discrimination; ABM has not ensured me that there is no retaliation against the me. See Tayborn v. City & County of San Francisco (9th Cir. 2003) 341 F.3d 957, 960. ABM, as in Sarro v. City of Sacramento (1999) 78 F. Supp. 2d 1057, 1064, is now focusing much of their time on the most personal and private aspects of my life, rather than on the alleged harasser and harassment, ABM is not acting appropriately. ABM took no serious steps to show honor and respect for California Laws and the rights of its citizens.

GOOD CAUSE EXISTS FOR LEAVING ABM PURSUANT TO CALIFORNIA PUBLIC POLICY

With respect to ABM's failure to prevent and correct sexual harassment in the workplace, ABM cannot allow me to be sexually harassed in the workplace, that is against California law and public policy. This statute carries a 1 year statute of limitation and requires a government complaint before filing a lawsuit in Court. The Department should not take the side of ABM and presume false facts nor ignore the California Legislative Mandate against discrimination and harassment in the workplace. The Department should not assume that ABM under took an investigation into my complaint of sexual harassment; and the Department cannot ignore that there is ample evidence that I reported the sexual harassment.

ABM never did any investigation into my allegations of sexual harassment at work. ABM is playing both sides of the fence on this legal matter in the hope to absolve the corporation from any legal duty or obligation it had under law. I have since rescinded my signature on the erroneous written warning notice for 'conflict of interest' ("Exhibit D'). ABM has not honored my right to rescission and their breach and/or mistake of contract.

Pursuant to California Unemployment Insurance Code Section §1256.2 (a) states "Except as otherwise provided by subdivision (b), an individual who terminate his or her employment shall not be deemed to have left his or her most recent work without good cause if his or her employer deprived the individual of equal employment opportunities on any basis listed in subdivision (a) 12940 of the Government Code, as those basis are defined in Sections 12926 and 12926.1 of the Government Code."

Subdivision (b) (2) states "An individual who fails to make reasonable efforts to provide the employer with an opportunity to remove any unintentional deprivation of the individuals' equal employment opportunities." This subdivision will exempt subdivision (a); however the Department is acting as the alter ego of ABM in asserting that I failed to "explore all reasonable solutions..." ("Exhibit F"); the Department has falsely assumed that I did not make reasonable efforts to provide the employer with an opportunity to remove "any unintentional deprivation of the individual's equal employment opportunities."

ABM has intentionally deprived me of my equal opportunities and has failed to remedy, restore, and make me whole for the economic injury I have incurred. ABM has operated in bad faith and unlawfully; ABM is not being held accountable for violating California laws but should be held accordingly to due process for their noncompliance.

Privileged Communication & Confidential Information © 2014 Edward Dumas All rights reserved. No part of this publication may be reproduced or transmitted in any form or by any means, electronic or mechanical, including photocopy, recording or any other information storage and retrieval system without prior permission in writing from Edward Dumas.

In <u>Thomas v. California Employment Stabilization Commission</u> (1952) 39 Cal.2d 501 [247 P2.d 561] references that the unemployment insurance appeals board is a statutory agency with statewide jurisdiction but without constitutional authority to make final determinations of fact and the benefits provide for by the UI Act are 'property rights' and therefore anyone deprived of a property right by such administrative body is entitled to a limited trial de novo in the Superior Court.

In <u>Pratt v. Local 683, Film Technicians of The Motion Picture and Television Industries</u> (1968) 260 Cal.App.2d 545[67 Cal.Rptr. 483] the Court held that state CUIAB exercises discretionary administrative functions and does not exercise judicial powers in the sense that its decision on the question of whether any employee was or was not discharged for misconduct. The employee's right to receive unemployment insurance benefits should be determinative of her or his right to sue his employer in a court of law for breach of contract of employment. See also <u>Chrysler Corp. v. California Employment Stabilization Commission</u> (1953) 116 Cal.App.2d 8 [253 P.2d 68].

In <u>Pratt</u> the claimant was denied all his legal remedies, even at the trial court level; the Court of Appeals held the trial court reversed in part that decision. The Court also found all throughout the Unemployment Appeals process, the employer made false statements and misrepresentations to the government. ABM has followed the same pattern and the Department should not presume false facts nor assumptions, or become a proxy advocate for their defense to unlawful conduct against me.

Pursuant to <u>Unemployment Insurance Code § 1256</u> states "An individual is presumed to have been discharged for reasons other than misconduct in connection with his or her work and not to have voluntarily quit without good cause unless his or her employer has given written notice to the contrary to the department as provided in Section 1327, setting forth facts sufficient to overcome the presumption. The presumption provided by this section is rebuttable."

California statutes presumes that an individual has not voluntarily left his work without good cause is established to implement public policy upon payment of benefits to unemployed so as to reduce suffering caused thereby, presumption affects burden of proof in that it imposes upon parties against whom it operates, the employer and the department of human resources, burden of proving non existence of presumed fact, which means that to overcome presumption employee or department must prove by a preponderance of evidence that claimant quit without probable cause or was discharge for misconduct in connection with his work. <u>Perales v. Dept. of Human Resources Development</u> (1973) 32 Cal.App.3d 332 [108 Cal.Rptr. 167].

Privileged Communication & Confidential Information © 2014 Edward Dumas All rights reserved. No part of this publication may be reproduced or transmitted in any form or by any means, electronic or mechanical, including photocopy, recording or any other information storage and retrieval system without prior permission in writing from Edward Dumas.

SEX DISCRIMINATION

In Prescod v. California Unemployment Ins. Appeals Bd. (1976) 57 Cal.App.3d 29[127 Cal.Rptr. 540], where's ones work is made intolerable over period of time by discriminatory acts of employer, such as refusal to reinstate, demotion, or loss of promotional opportunity, there is "good cause'" for leaving employment. It is settled law in California that leaving one's employment because they oppose discrimination or harassment is good and just cause.

While harassing conduct need not occur in workplace in order to render employer liable under Fair Employment and Housing Act, it most occur in work related context. See Capitol City Foods, Inc. v. Superior Court (1992) 5 Cal.App.4th 1042 [7 Cal.Rptr.2d 418]. An employee is not required to use legal terms or buzzwords when opposing discrimination or harassment, see Yanowitz v. L'Oreal USA, Inc. (2005) 103 Cal.App.4th 1021[32 CalRptr.3d 436].

In Greene v. Pomona Unified School Dist. (1995) 32 Cal.App.4th 1216 [38 Cal.Rptr. 2d 770], the court held that there is no need to require unions to become involved with employees' claims of discrimination against their employer based on protected characteristics because employees have remedies available to them through Department of Fair Employment and Housing (DFEH) and the EEOC, as well as civil actions under the FEHA and under Title VII.

It is the legislative intent of the State of California and declared by Governor Arnold Schwarzenegger that "Equal employment opportunity for all individual is the policy of the State of California in all its activities. All state officials, managers, and supervisor shall vigorously enforce this policy."

ABM DID NOT PERFORM THE MANDATORY TRAINING OR EDUCATION IN HARASSMENT AS REQUIRED BY CALIFORNIA LAW

To the best of my knowledge and belief, ABM did not fully comply with California Government Code §12950.1 (a) and never provided me with at least two hours of classroom or other effective interactive training and education regarding sexual harassment to all supervisory employees in California, as the law requires. It is the employers duty to train and educate on how to prevent and correct sexual harassment in the workplace. It is the employees duty to report it promptly, in which I did. The sexual harassment never ceased and they failed to investigate the harassment that was occurring against me. ABM never provided the proper legal training as required, nor took immediate and corrective legal action. The disciplinary action is pretextual, invalid, and unexecutable pursuant to the union contract and California's Public Policy against Discrimination and Harassment.

Privileged Communication & Confidential Information © 2014 Edward Dumas All rights reserved. No part of this publication may be reproduced or transmitted in any form or by any means, electronic or mechanical, including photocopy, recording or any other information storage and retrieval system without prior permission in writing from Edward Dumas.

California Government Code §12950.1 (a) further requires for ABM to train all new supervisory employees within six months of their assumption of a supervisory position. The training and education required by this section shall include information and practical guidance regarding the federal and state statutory provisions concerning the prohibition against and the prevention and correction of sexual harassment and the remedies available to victims of sexual harassment in employment.

The State of California mandates that ABM must provide training and education that shall also include practical examples aimed at instructing supervisors in the prevention of harassment, discrimination and retaliation, and shall be presented by trainers or educators with knowledge and expertise in the prevention of harassment, discrimination, and retaliation. I believe ABM failed to provide this training to me as a shift supervisor; I do not recall receiving any anti-harassment training at ABM as required by the State of California.

California Government Code §12950.1 (d) states that even if the training and education required by this part of California law did not reach me it shall not result in and of itself in liability to ABM; and even if ABM complied with this section, it does not necessarily insulate ABM from liability for sexual harassment of any current or former employee.

California Government Code §12950.1 (f) states that the training and education required by this section is intend to establish and minimum threshold and should not discourage nor relieve any employer from providing for longer more frequent, or more elaborate training and education regarding workplace harassment or other forms of unlawful discrimination in order to meet its obligations to take all reasonable steps necessary to prevent and correct harassment and discrimination in the workplace.

 **RESERVATION OF RIGHTS AND RIGHT TO PRIVACY**

I reserves the right, upon completion of a lawful investigation and discovery, to tender and to file supplemental and amended allegations as may be appropriate under the applicable law. I further reserve the right to privacy as provided under California Article 1, Section 1, privacy. Shaffer v. Superior Court (1995) 33 Cal.App.4th 993 [39 Cal.Rptr.2d 506]. In Tylo v. Superior Court (1997) 55 Cal.App.4th 1379 [64 Cal.Rptr.2d 731]; Barrenda L. v. Superior Court (1998) 65 Cal.App.4th 794 [76 Cal.Rptr.2d 727]. In addition to the rights vested to me under The United States Constitution and Bill of Rights.

Pursuant to the California Civil of Civil Procedure § 2017.220 (a) states "In any civil action alleging conduct that constitutes sexual harassment...any party seeking discovery concerning the plaintiff's sexual conduct with individuals other than the alleged perpetrator shall establish specific facts showing that there is good cause for that discovery

Privileged Communication & Confidential Information © 2014 Edward Dumas All rights reserved. No part of this publication may be reproduced or transmitted in any form or by any means, electronic or mechanical, including photocopy, recording or any other information storage and retrieval system without prior permission in writing from Edward Dumas.

SEX DISCRIMINATION

concerning the plaintiff's sexual conduct with individuals other than the alleged perpetrator shall establish specific facts showing that there is good cause for that discovery and that the matter sought to be discovered is relevant to the subject matter of the action and reasonably calculated to lead to the discovery of admissible evidence. This showing shall be made by noticed motion, accompanied by a meeting and confer declaring under Section 2016.040, and shall not be made or considered by the court at an ex parte hearing."

ABM has demonstrated an intent to side-step this Civil Procedure and has misconstrued, misrepresented, and/or omitted the facts to The California Employment Development Department. ABM has acted as if it is above the rule of law and does not honor nor respect California Laws and Public Policy. ABM has treated me unfairly by law and by contract and is opposed to preventing harassment and discrimination in their workplace.

STATEMENT OF FACTS

* Sexual Harassment Incidents at ▉▉▉▉▉▉▉▉

January 27, 2014: After I was scheduled for a series of job interviews for a Security Officer position with ABM Scheduler ▉▉▉▉, ABM Manager ▉▉▉▉, and ABM District Manager ▉▉▉▉ I was hired to start as a Security Shift Supervisor and started working for ABM at the location known as ▉▉▉▉▉, Los Angeles, California, for $13.40 per hour, *and under a written contract with ABM management and SEIU Labor Organization.* The location is under business contract for security services between CALSTRS (CBRE acting agent) and ABM.

January 27, 2014 to October 5, 2014: I worked as a Shift Supervisor and Security Officer for *ABM* at ▉▉▉▉▉ I worked in the security division at this building with no disciplinary issues and was given customer compliments from time to time.

Sunday, October 5, 2014: I was harassed by a non-employee, named ▉▉▉▉ in where this person *demanded that if I did not* ▉▉▉▉▉▉▉▉▉▉ she would get me fired from my job. I did not accept her offer and told ▉▉▉▉ to leave me alone. (Exhibit A "Declaration of ▉▉▉▉").

Monday, October 6, 2014: *I had a complaint about someone harassing me in the building and I promptly notified my immediate supervisor,* ABM Manager ▉▉▉▉ ▉▉▉▉ did not leave me alone and became harassing toward me at work. 'Crank calls' at the security desk station *began to come through at various times,* ▉▉▉▉ spoke curse words at me *when she walked by, even whispering profanity to me* while I was working at the security desk.

Privileged Communication & Confidential Information © 2014 Edward Dumas All rights reserved. No part of this publication may be reproduced or transmitted in any form or by any means, electronic or mechanical, including photocopy, recording or any other information storage and retrieval system without prior permission in writing from Edward Dumas.

Tuesday, October 7, 2014: I continued receiving crank calls at *the* security desk. I notified Manager ▓▓▓ regarding the crank calls, curse words, and harassing behavior toward me by ▓▓▓. I was told to just document it by ABM Manager ▓▓▓ ▓▓▓ and I became increasingly more afraid of her.

Wednesday, October 8, 2014: I started regular work shift at 11:00PM, for a graveyard shift, and I was receiving multiple crank calls throughout the night. My co-worker, Security Officer ▓▓▓ noticed the strange behavior ▓▓▓ was exhibiting towards me throughout the workweek and on the graveyard shift. ▓▓▓ harassing behavior was negatively affecting me at the workplace.

Thursday, October 9, 2014: I, *again*, informed ABM Manager David Brown that building employee ▓▓▓ behavior toward me was just getting worse; as the crank calling persisted at the desk all throughout my shift, when she would appear at the security desk she would continue to use curse words at me, act strangely by saying that she's "cracking", "dying", "can't live", passing me notes in sexual nature, and looking at me in a strange manners. **I asked ABM Manager David ▓▓▓ to report the unlawful harassment to ABM Corporate**. I explained to ABM Manager David ▓▓▓ that if these incidents continue to go unreported then there can be major liabilities; I specifically stated to ABM Manager David ▓▓▓ that "...[W]e need to protect the client, ABM, and our jobs". I was feeling like the harasser's behavior was so intentional as to sabotage my job and work performance, I needed ABM to get more involved. ABM Manager David ▓▓▓ stated to me that he called ABM District Manager (▓▓▓ and/or ABM Security Director ▓▓▓ , his immediate supervisor, and informed me that the *ABM District Manager wants me to write a statement*.

Friday, October 10, 2014: **I wrote a statement about the incident** on October 5, 2014, I made a Declaration under penalty of perjury; I arrived at the worksite, **I emailed** the Declaration along with a note, attached as evidence, written to me by ▓▓▓ and **awaited a response from ABM. I never received a response nor call from ABM Human Resources or ABM Management**; *I was led to believe* that there was going to be an investigation. ABM Manager ▓▓▓ stated, "...the wheels are rolling...its starting...", thus leading me to believe that there was going to be *a prompt and fair investigation; to investigate my harassment complaint*.

October 11 to 16, 2014:

I kept reporting the harassing behavior by ▓▓▓ to my immediate supervisor and no one still spoke with me about my complaint. I was receiving multiple crank calls

SEX DISCRIMINATION

at the security desk where I was stationed; also, how building employee ▇▇▇ would speak curse words at me such as ▇▇▇ or would walk by the security desk and whisper to me "▇▇▇"; even as far as making suicidal insinuations at times when she would approach me by myself at the security desk. I felt awkward and simply stayed alert in case her behavior became physical. I attempted to give ABM Manager ▇▇▇ the two notes she gave me but he <u>ignored</u> reading the note(s).

When ▇▇▇ was present at the building, at the time I was working at the security desk, she had often and continued to speak curse words at me such as "▇▇▇, "you mother ▇▇▇", "son of a ▇▇▇, and "you're so full of shit". ▇▇▇ would pass me explicit sexual notes but I disregarded them because her behavior was unwelcomed.

<u>Friday, October 17, 2014:</u> I worked for the ABM Security Director ▇▇▇ worksite, with ABM District Manager ▇▇▇ and ABM Scheduler I ▇▇▇. I spoke with ▇▇▇ as to if she had knowledge of my complaint about possible sexual harassment at work; she stated that she was unaware of the situation. None of the above named Managers ever discussed nor investigated my concern or complaint regarding building employee ▇▇▇ behavior.

<u>Saturday: October 18, 2014 to Sunday, October 19, 2014:</u> I continued to receive crank calls and when building employee ▇▇▇ walked by, she would speak curse words at me. **No one from ABM Human Resources or ABM Management ever discussed or investigated** the harassment that was occurring.

<u>Monday, October 20, 2014:</u> I attended a building training meeting and ABM District Manager ▇▇▇ was present but did not speak with me in regards to my sexual harassment complaints against building employee ▇▇▇. No one from ABM ever **discussed nor investigated my complaint about what has become a hostile work environment.**

<u>Tuesday, October 21, 2014; Wednesday, October 22, 2014; Thursday, October 23, 2014:</u> I continued to receive crank calls and when building employee ▇▇▇ was present she would speak curse words at me; I asked my co-workers if anyone from the company has talked to them about my harassment concerns regarding ▇▇▇ behavior and verified that **no one from ABM has talked to them to investigate the basis of my claim of sex harassment.** Building employee ▇▇▇ began bothering other Security Officers on another shift, as I was informed.

Friday, October 24, 2014: Off

Saturday, October 25, 2014//Sunday, October 26, 2014: No one from ABM Human Resources or ABM Management ever called me nor discussed my complaint and concerns about building employee ▬▬▬ harassing me at work. I attempted to forward the letter(s) she was giving me but the ABM Manager ▬▬▬ did not want to read them.

Monday, October 27-28, 2014: (Company held a Meeting for a Fire Drill; Building was evacuated for a Fire Drill)

Wednesday October 29, 2014: I was receiving crank calls at work (Graveyard).

Thursday, October 30, 2014: After working from 11:00PM to 7:00AM, I received a phone call at home about 9:00AM from ABM Scheduler ▬▬▬ wanting to me to go an ABM corporate office for a meeting with ABM District Manager ▬▬▬ I inquired what kind of meeting would this be, if it is about the incidents, and if I would need my Union Representative, ▬▬▬ stated to me that "▬▬▬ thinks highly of you" and "your going to have to talk to him about that".

Friday, October 31, 2014: OFF

Saturday, November 1, 2014: I was receiving crank calls at the security desk.

Sunday, November 2, 2014: ▬▬▬ argued with me regarding keeping a Tenant's glass door closed and secure; co-worker ▬▬▬ was present.

Monday, November 3, 2014: I meet with ▬▬▬ and ▬▬▬ whom presented me with a first and final written warning for violating ABM's conflict of interest policy, told me that "the Union would not disagree with [us], it is better to have a job than no job...", and I was to be removed to another worksite or would not have employment with the company.

Tuesday, November 4, 2014: I experienced a loss of wages, as I would have worked my regularly scheduled shift. *I utilized the complaint procedure ABM had in place on October 6, 2014, which was to report it to my immediate supervisor, then to later write a statement, and wait for something to happen such as a transfer and/or training.* No one from ABM still has not talked to me about the harassment incidents that had occurred at ABM.

Wednesday, November 5, 2014: I arrived at the new worksite in where I was brought into ▬▬▬ office and he informed that I was demoted and that any mistake I make, "even a wrong look at the lady's" and I would be terminated. ▬▬▬ *stated to the effect* that I would start receiving lesser pay, I pressed this issue of a pay cut with him, and he stated that "he really does not know anything". I informed him at approximately

Privileged Communication & Confidential Information © 2014 Edward Dumas All rights reserved. No part of this publication may be reproduced or transmitted in any form or by any means, electronic or mechanical, including photocopy, recording or any other information storage and retrieval system without prior permission in writing from Edward Dumas.

SEX DISCRIMINATION

11:47AM that I am quitting ABM by "throwing in the towel" and will seek legal remedies and action.

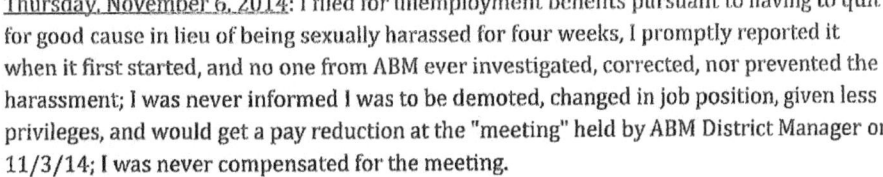

Thursday, November 6, 2014: I filed for unemployment benefits pursuant to having to quit for good cause in lieu of being sexually harassed for four weeks, I promptly reported it when it first started, and no one from ABM ever investigated, corrected, nor prevented the harassment; I was never informed I was to be demoted, changed in job position, given less privileges, and would get a pay reduction at the "meeting" held by ABM District Manager on 11/3/14; I was never compensated for the meeting.

November 10, 2014: I filed an intake with the EEOC.

November 26, 2014: I received a letter from the EEOC, per ▓▓▓▓▓▓ regarding my intake and a one page informational sheet ("Exhibit C").

November 27, 2014 to December 11, 2014: I am currently processing the EEOC complaint so I can move forward with securing my rights by Court in order to file a lawsuit, as needed. ("Exhibit G").

December 12-21, 2014: Interviewed by California EDD, the representative stated and questioned to me in that employers do not have a duty to protect their employees from harassment and falsely presumed that ABM did an investigation and took "immediate and corrective action" as is required by California Law. Benefits denied by EDD; EDD states "[I] did not explore all reasonable solutions before I quit" ("Exhibit F").

December 27, 2014: I am currently filing an appeal with the CUIAB.

The EDD, EEOC, & Superior Court Legal Forms

Privileged Communication & Confidential Information © 2014 Edward Dumas All rights reserved. No part of this publication may be reproduced or transmitted in any form or by any means, electronic or mechanical, including photocopy, recording or any other information storage and retrieval system without prior permission in writing from Edward Dumas.

SEX DISCRIMINATION

Subject: Fwd: ▮▮▮ s Declaration RE Quid Pro Quo Incident
From: ▮▮▮
To: ▮▮▮
Date: Monday, October 13, 2014 3:33 PM

---------- Forwarded message ----------
From: **800 Hope Security**
Date: Fri, Oct 10, 2014 at 10:21 AM
Subject: ▮▮▮ Declaration RE Quid Pro Quo Incident
To: ▮▮▮

Please find my attached Declaration regarding the incident of quid pro quo sex harassment I reported and Exhibit A for supporting evidence of such.

I apologize for any inconvenience I may have caused you.

Feel free to contact me for further investigation.

Truthfully,

▮▮▮

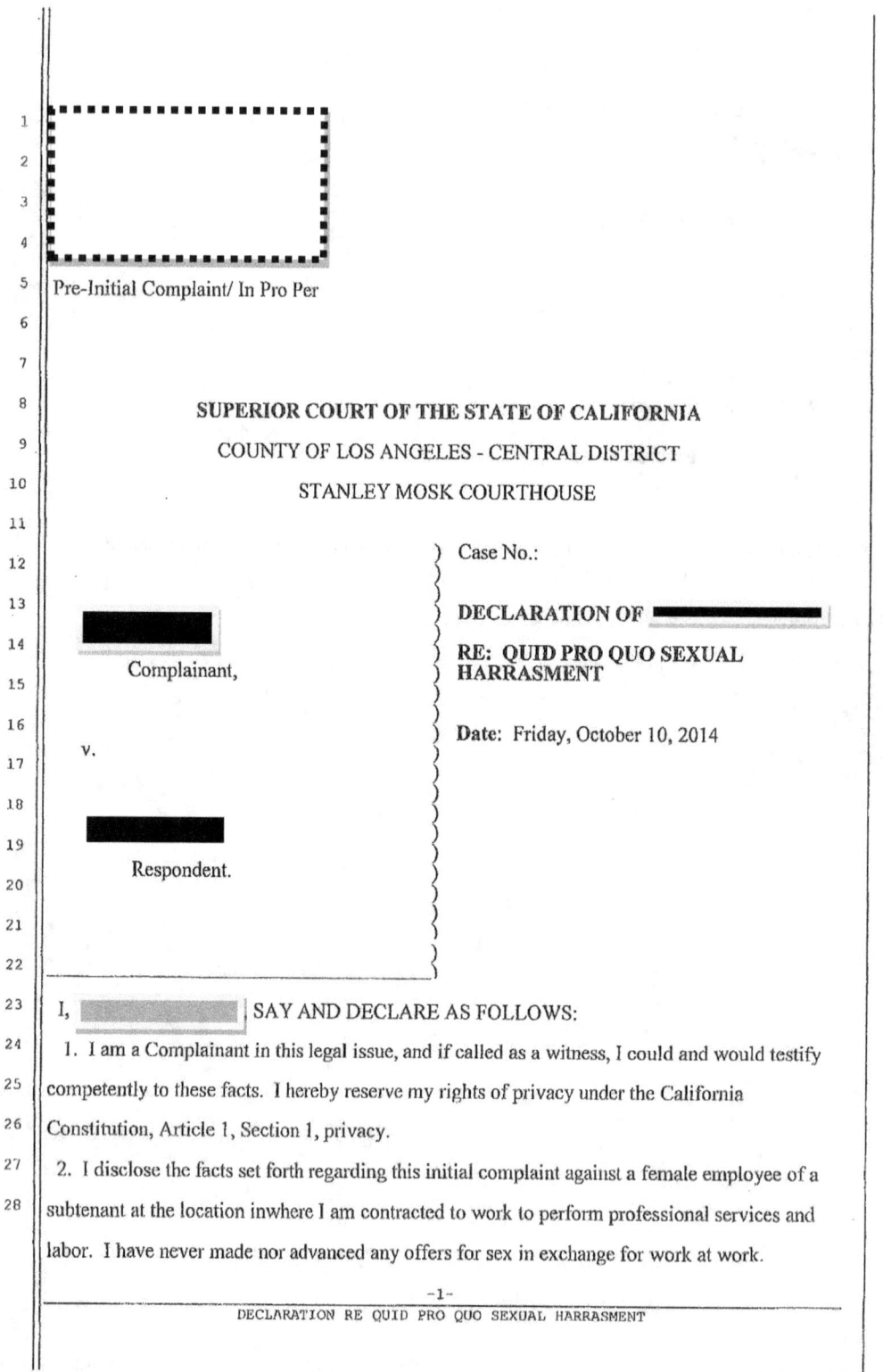

Pre-Initial Complaint/ In Pro Per

SUPERIOR COURT OF THE STATE OF CALIFORNIA

COUNTY OF LOS ANGELES - CENTRAL DISTRICT

STANLEY MOSK COURTHOUSE

Complainant, v. Respondent.	Case No.: DECLARATION OF ▇ RE: QUID PRO QUO SEXUAL HARRASMENT Date: Friday, October 10, 2014

I, ▇ SAY AND DECLARE AS FOLLOWS:

1. I am a Complainant in this legal issue, and if called as a witness, I could and would testify competently to these facts. I hereby reserve my rights of privacy under the California Constitution, Article 1, Section 1, privacy.

2. I disclose the facts set forth regarding this initial complaint against a female employee of a subtenant at the location inwhere I am contracted to work to perform professional services and labor. I have never made nor advanced any offers for sex in exchange for work at work.

-1-
DECLARATION RE QUID PRO QUO SEXUAL HARRASMENT

DECLARATION FOR PROOF OF SEXUAL HARRASSMENT IN THE WORKPLACE

SEX DISCRIMINATION

CLAIMS:

1. 3. The female employee is known as ▓▓▓ herein referred to as the "Respondent". The business the Respondent is employed at is known as '▓▓▓ (herein "▓▓▓"). ▓▓▓y operates and subcontracts its lease from the location inwhere I am contracted to perform professional services and labor.

5. 4. On October 5, 2014, at approximately 6:00PM (PST) I discussed in length with the Respondent ▓▓▓ outside of the workplace. The Respondent demanded terms and conditions to be set forth regarding ▓▓▓ outside of the workplace. I did not agree with the Respondent's terms and conditions, so I explained to the Respondent that I could not meet her expectations for the terms and conditions she demanded from me.

10. 5. The Respondent was angry and screaming at me so I started to walk away, as I started walking away from the Respondent she screamed and demanded that if I do not ▓▓▓ ▓▓▓, she will make sure that I am fired from my job at the location inwhere I provide my professional services and labor. I did not accept the Respondent's offer and told her that I did not want ▓▓▓ The Respondent starting to chase after me ▓▓▓ ▓▓▓.

16. 6. On October 6, 2014, at 3:00PM I arrived to my job and informed my immediate supervisor of the incident that occurred outside of the workplace. At 4:26PM the Respondent provided me with a typed letter, herein "Exhibit A". I have not had any personal contact with Respondent outside the workplace since I ran away from her on October 5, 2014.

I hereby declare under the penalty of perjury under laws of the State of California that the foregoing is true and correct, Executed in Los Angeles, California on October 10, 2014.

-2-
DECLARATION RE QUID PRO QUO SEXUAL HARRASMENT

PAGE 23 IS REDACTED FROM PUBLICATION

"EXHIBIT B"

FOR EDD LEGAL REVIEW

Privileged Communication & Confidential Information © 2014 Edward Dumas All rights reserved. No part of this publication may be reproduced or transmitted in any form or by any means, electronic or mechanical, including photocopy, recording or any other information storage and retrieval system without prior permission in writing from Edward Dumas.

SEX DISCRIMINATION

ABM INTERNAL COMPANY POLICY REGARDING EQUAL EMPLOYMENT

Equal Employment Opportunity ("EEO"): Policy Against Harassment in the Workplace

Purpose of this Policy

Professional behavior is expected and required of all ABM employees. The Company's intent is to provide all employees with a workplace environment consistent with ABM's core values of Respect, Fairness and Dignity. Employees who are respected and valued and who are not distracted by discrimination, harassment or other forms of unprofessional or unacceptable conduct can fully contribute their skills and talents to enhance ABM's performance. Accordingly, ABM does not tolerate workplace discrimination or harassment based on race, religion, gender, national origin, age, disability, sexual orientation, veteran or any other status protected by law.

This policy is designed to promote a culture of Respect, Fairness and Dignity. To achieve this goal, this policy prohibits both illegal conduct and unprofessional, offensive conduct that is disruptive to teamwork and productivity. This policy applies equally to interactions between ABM employees as well as interactions between ABM employees, customers, vendors, tenants and other third-parties.

Prohibited Conduct

Prohibited conduct includes offensive or derogatory verbal comments or jokes based on any personal characteristic unrelated to job performance. Obscene gestures, display of offensive or sexual visual material, unwanted sexual advances and physical touching or blocking of movement are also prohibited. Submission to sexual advances in order to get, keep or advance in a job, is a serious form of sexual harassment. If you are not sure if your conduct is appropriate for the workplace ask: "Would I want to see my behavior portrayed on the front page or the evening news?" If the answer is "no," then stop what you are doing. If you are unsure about the answer, you should contact Human Resources.

Employee Responsibilities

Speak Up: If you are offended by conduct in the workplace, we encourage you to respond immediately by objecting directly to the offender, which is often very effective. If you are uncomfortable objecting to the offender, or if the conduct continues, report the conduct using the Company's reporting procedures described below. Keep in mind that if you fail to respond to harassment by objecting or reporting it, ABM cannot help resolve the situation or address any misconduct. If you witness offensive conduct, report it using the reporting procedures below. Preferences based on familial or romantic relationships are not appropriate in ABM's workplace. If you see favoritism occurring, report it using the procedures below.

ABM takes seriously all concerns about employee treatment and maintaining a professional workplace environment and prohibits retaliation against individuals who report violations of this policy in good faith. If you observe or experience retaliation, please report it using the reporting procedures below. Retaliation is defined as any conduct or harm that would have the effect of discouraging an employee to make a complaint.

---

of underrepresented groups, to develop an Affirmative Action Program, and take extra steps for implementing those reasonable goals through outreach, recruitment, training, and other special activities and commitments.

Any goals that are established are not intended as rigid, inflexible quotas that must be met, but rather as targets reasonably attainable by applying every good faith effort in implementing these plans. The use of goals in the Company's plans is not intended to discriminate against any individual or group of individuals with respect to any employment opportunity for which they are qualified on the grounds that they are not the beneficiaries of Affirmative Action themselves. Nothing in the Company's Affirmative Action Plans is intended to sanction the discriminatory treatment of any person. Thus, the Company's plans have been developed in strict reliance upon the guidelines on Affirmative Action issued by the U.S. Dept. of Labor.

Equal Employment Opportunity: Open Door

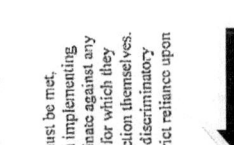

Suggestions for improving ABM are always welcome. At some time, employees may have a complaint, suggestion, or question about their job, working conditions or treatment they are receiving. Employee good-faith complaints, questions, and suggestions also are of concern to the Company. The Company has established an "open door" practice to promote effective communication between employees and management in resolving personal problems.

An employee who encounters problems concerning any aspect of employment by the Company is encouraged to:

1. First discuss the situation with their immediate supervisor within a week of the occurrence who will in turn work with Human Resources to provide a solution or explanation.

2. If the employee is not satisfied with the proposed solution, cannot discuss it with the immediate supervisor, or the problem persists, the employee should contact the Department or Branch Manager or the division's head of Human Resources, who will investigate and provide a solution or explanation.

3. If the problem persists, the employee may contact the ABM Industries' Human Resource Department or the Compliance Hotline at **1-877-253-7804** (abmhotline.ethicspoint.com).

The company encourages employees to bring the matter to Human Resources as soon as possible if they believe that their immediate supervisor has failed to resolve it.

This procedure, which the Company believes is important for both the employee and the Company, cannot guarantee that every problem will be resolved to the employee's satisfaction. However, ABM values employee observations and employees should feel free to raise issues of concern, in good faith, without fear of retaliation.

"EXHIBIT C"

SEX DISCRIMINATION

EEOC CORRESPONDENCE REGARDING FILING CHARGE(S)

U.S. EQUAL EMPLOYMENT OPPORTUNITY COMMISSION
Los Angeles District Office

255 E. Temple Street, 4th Floor
Los Angeles, CA 90012
Intake Information Group: (800) 669-4000
Intake Information Group TTY: (800) 669-6820
Los Angeles Status Line: (866) 408-8075
Los Angeles Direct Dial: (213) 894-1096
TTY (213) 894-1121
FAX (213) 894-1118

Date: November 20, 2014

Dear Mr.

Your correspondence (*letter, intake questionnaire other communication*) concerning allegations of employment discrimination by the Respondent named above has been received by our office and is in the process of being reviewed. The correspondence has been assigned the above-referenced charge number. We have also notified the Respondent that you are filing a charge, which the EEOC is required to do. Upon completion of the review you will be contacted regarding further processing.

Be advised, the EEOC is located in a U.S. Courthouse and anyone attempting to enter must present valid United States state or federal identification (state driver's license, state I.D. card, U.S. passport, or a similar document) to gain entrance into the building. If you do not have United States identification, please contact EEOC at (213) 894-1000 for additional information.

Sincerely,

CRTIU Supervisor

Office Hours: Monday – Friday, 8:00 a.m. – 4:30 p.m.
Website: www.eeoc.gov
Enclosure: Information Sheet for Charging Parties

"EXHIBIT D"

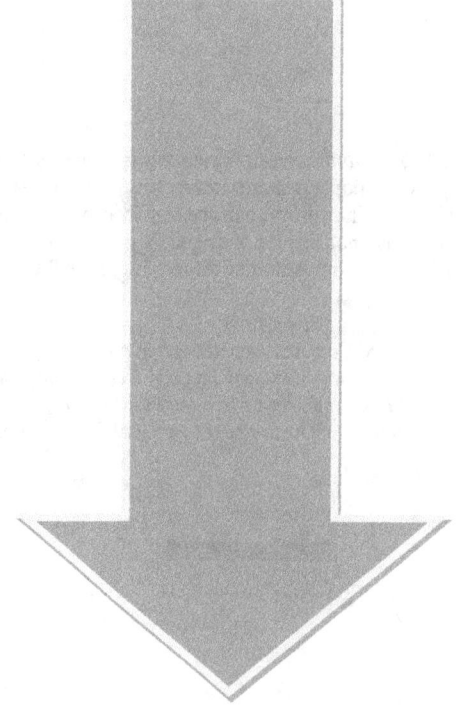

SEX DISCRIMINATION

Subject: Recission and Breach of Contract
From:
To:
Date: Monday, December 1, 2014 2:09 PM

I hereby rescind my signature on the Warning Notice that was issued to me on or around November 3, 2014, at approximately 2:00PM (PST), pursuant to the Los Angeles Master Collective Bargaining Agreement (Contract), Article 4, Discipline and Discharge, Section 4.2 herein states:

"Warning notices shall be issued within ten days after the Employer knew or should have known of the offense. A copy of the warning shall be sent to the Union. Each warning notice shall contain a place for the employee to sign to acknowledge receipt without admitting guilt."

Pursuant to Contract, the Warning Notice regarding the alleged "Conflict of Interest" was in fact a breach of contract because you failed, within ten days, as prescribed by Contract. Nevertheless, you knew I became friends with someone in the building; therefore the warning notice **is not valid and is hereby declared null and void.**

I further declare I was constructively terminated due to quid pro quo sexual harassment in the workplace and the failure to take corrective action to prevent such further harassment from occurring.
I experienced loss of wages, privileges and benefits, and was unjustly demoted for complaining about an employee from another company in the building sexually harassing me.

Please note that I complained to you about Ms. ███████ from ███████, sexually harassing me on October 6, 2014, I wrote a *Declaration, under penalty of perjury*, on October 10, 2014, and emailed it to you. I saw you in at least in two separate and distinct meetings throughout the month and you never discussed the sexual harassment complaint with me at all.

It was not until October 30, 2014, that I was notified by Ms. ███████ of a meeting desired by you in regards to "the incident", I inquired if this is a disciplinary meeting, if I would need my Union Representative at this meeting, and if this meeting would be compensated. Mrs. Garcia was silent and simply responded, "Gilbert thinks highly of you, you're going to have to talk to him when he is here."

I meet with you on November 3, 2014, with Ms. Garcia present but silent, at the scheduled meeting at 2:00PM in where you had me waiting for thirty to forty-five minutes in the lobby with no information, parking accommodation, or union representation. You stated a take or leave it demand, inwhere I would be transferred to a different location, inwhere I would be training and working with the 'Director of Security' OR I would not be employed.

1 of 2

12/26/2014 5:05 PM

I found the adverse action, new terms and conditions set forth unacceptable after learning that I was demoted, along with a potential pay-cut, and it has not been tolerable working for an employer who does not compensate correctly on a consistent basis. Therefore, please forward me a copy of timesheets from January 27, 2014 to November 5, 2014, for all the times I had worked, "clocked in", or "wrote in", whether it was by myself or someone else, for everyday I had worked.

Please attach this letter and my Declaration RE Quid Pro Quo Sexual Harassment to the Warning Notice, along with any other additional information you receive from the EEOC, as should be sent to the Union along with the original warning notice.

Feel free to contact me if you have any comments or questions at 213-███████

Sex Discrimination

"EXHIBIT E"

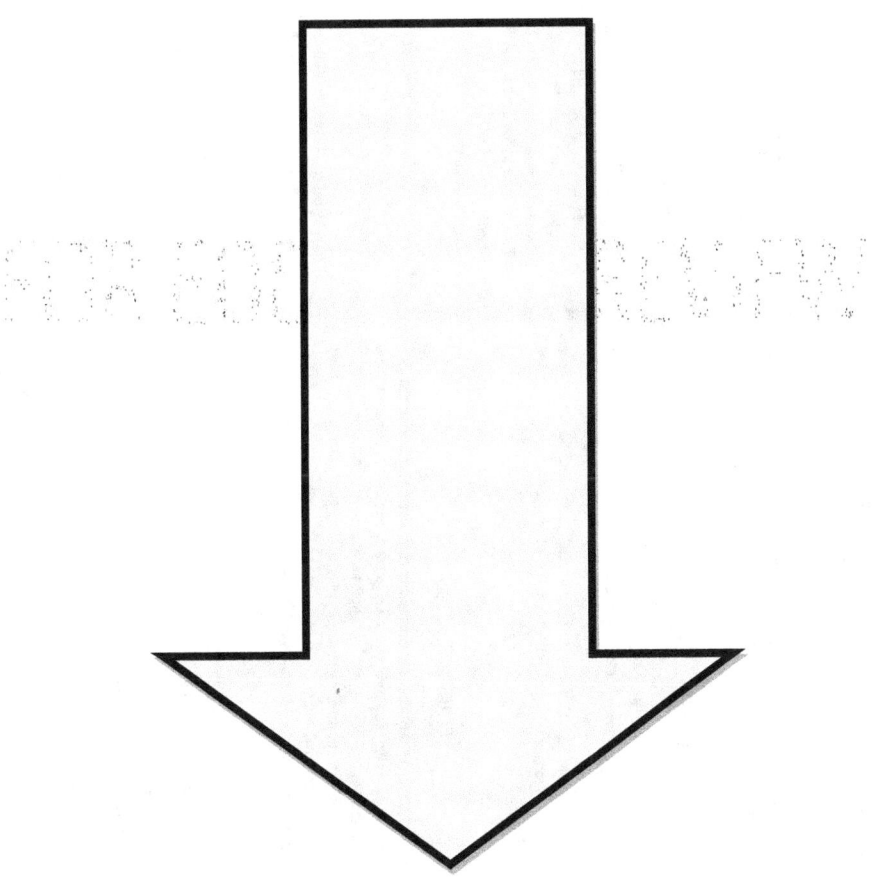

Privileged Communication & Confidential Information © 2014 Edward Dumas All rights reserved. No part of this publication may be reproduced or transmitted in any form or by any means, electronic or mechanical, including photocopy, recording or any other information storage and retrieval system without prior permission in writing from Edward Dumas.

deductions were made, together with a monthly list of the employees for whom it has deducted dues and on whose behalf it is remitting dues. The list shall include the first and last name of each employee, the total amount of dues which were deducted, and the Social Security number or other unique nine (9) digit employee identifier number associated with the individual employee.

All deduction authorization forms must be submitted to the Employer within six (6) months from the date the employee completed the form. The Employer will not process deduction authorization forms submitted in excess of six (6) months after their completion.

2.4 The Union will furnish the forms to be used for authorization. The Employer will furnish the Union with a duplicate copy of all signed authorizations, unless another procedure has been adopted.

2.5 The Union will completely defend and indemnify and hold the Employer free and harmless against any and all claims, damages, suits or other forms of liability whatsoever that shall arise out of or by reason of action taken by the Employer at the Union's request for the purpose of complying with any of the provisions of Article 2, including the Employer's termination of any employee for the failure to pay dues or an agency fee, including court costs and reasonable attorney fees. The Union shall have the right to select counsel to represent the Employer to contest, litigate, administer and/or settle any legal action with the Employer's consent, which shall not be unreasonably withheld.

ARTICLE 3 – NO DISCRIMINATION

The Union and the Employer agree they shall not discriminate in violation of federal or state law against any applicant or employee in hiring, promotions, assignments, suspensions, discharge, terms and conditions of employment, wages, training, recall or lay-off status, because of race, color, ancestry, religion, creed, national origin, age, sex, maternity status, sexual orientation, gender expression, veteran status, or against a qualified individual with a disability (defined by the Americans with Disabilities Act). No employee or applicant for employment covered by this Agreement shall be discriminated against because of membership in the Union or activities on behalf of the Union.

ARTICLE 4 – DISCIPLINE AND DISCHARGE

4.1 The Employer shall be free to discharge employees for refusal to obey lawful orders, incompetency, misrepresentation, intoxication, or any just cause. An employee who has not completed his or her probationary period may be disciplined or discharged without just cause and without recourse to the Grievance and Arbitration procedure set forth in Article 25.

4.2 The Employer shall be free to discipline any employee who commits an infraction, which, while not being sufficient to constitute just cause for discharge, is sufficient to warrant some lesser disciplinary action. However, no employee who has completed the probationary period will be discharged for offenses, which do not in and of themselves constitute just cause to discharge, unless the employee has progressed through the discipline process and been given the opportunity to correct his/her behavior.

Warning notices shall be issued within ten (10) days after the Employer knew or should have known of the offense. A copy of the warning shall be sent to the Union. Each warning notice shall contain a place for the employee to sign to acknowledge receipt without admitting guilt.

Warning or disciplinary notices may not be considered as a part of the Employer's discipline process after twelve (12) months and shall be no longer valid for the purpose of discipline.

4.3 In addition to those circumstances mentioned elsewhere in this Agreement, just cause circumstances for discharge shall include, but not be limited to, unlawful use or unlawful possession of controlled substances, intoxication, insubordination, theft, excessive absenteeism, gross negligence, failure to comply with reasonable rules, policies or directives promulgated by the Employer and clearly communicated to the employee (where such failure to comply constitutes serious misconduct or creates a safety concern), use of unnecessary force or disrespectful treatment of a tenant, visitor or employee and inability or unwillingness to be trained to fulfill existing or modified security needs of the Employer, the building owner or its tenants. The Union further understands and agrees that the Employer provides an important service to its tenants of a personalized nature to fulfill their security needs, as those needs are perceived by the Employer, the building owner and the tenants. Accordingly, the provisions of this Section shall be implemented and interpreted by the parties and by an arbitrator in arbitration proceedings so as to give significant consideration to such needs.

4.4 The Employer will discharge any employee who is denied registration or whose registration is canceled by the Department of Consumer Affairs of the State of California or any other governmental agency.

Employees who have renewed their registration and document this with a receipt or similar proof by the end of the BSIS grace period, but have not yet received their new registration cards, shall not be denied work, subject to BSIS regulations.

Any employee, who by reason of the requirements of his job assignment must pass a test prescribed by any governmental agency or obtain a permit from any governmental agency and is not able to pass the test to obtain such a permit, shall be removed from the job. The employee will then be offered the first available job for which the employee is qualified that becomes available within the same dispatch area. If the employee refuses the first available job for which the employee is qualified and which is located in his/her geographic area, he/she may be permanently removed from the payroll. Discharge under this Article for failure to possess a license, except as limited above in this Section, shall be without recourse to the Grievance Procedure of Article 25.

Sex Discrimination

"EXHIBIT F"

EMPLOYMENT DEVELOPMENT DEPT
SAN BERNARDINO PAC
PO BOX 641
SAN BERNARDINO CA 92402-0641

NOTICE OF DETERMINATION

DATE MAILED   12/11/14
BENEFIT YEAR BEGAN 03/30/14

0410

EDD TELEPHONE NUMBERS:
ENGLISH   1-800-300-5616
SPANISH   1-800-326-8937
CANTONESE   1-800-547-3506
MANDARIN   1-866-303-0706
VIETNAMESE   1-800-547-2058
TTY   1-800-815-9387

SSA NUMBER

YOU ARE NOT ELIGIBLE TO RECEIVE BENEFITS UNDER CALIFORNIA UNEMPLOYMENT INSURANCE CODE SECTION 1256 BEGINNING 11/02/14 AND CONTINUING UNTIL YOU RETURN TO WORK AFTER THE DISQUALIFYING ACT AND EARN $2250.00 OR MORE IN BONA FIDE EMPLOYMENT, AND YOU CONTACT THE ABOVE OFFICE TO REOPEN YOUR CLAIM.

YOU QUIT YOUR LAST JOB WITH ABM ONSITE SERVICES BECAUSE YOU FELT THE WORKING CONDITIONS WERE INTOLERABLE. YOU DID NOT EXPLORE ALL REASONABLE SOLUTIONS BEFORE YOU QUIT. AFTER CONSIDERING AVAILABLE INFORMATION, THE DEPARTMENT FINDS THAT YOU DO NOT MEET THE LEGAL REQUIREMENTS FOR PAYMENT OF BENEFITS. SECTION 1256 PROVIDES - AN INDIVIDUAL IS DISQUALIFIED IF THE DEPARTMENT FINDS HE VOLUNTARILY QUIT HIS MOST RECENT WORK WITHOUT GOOD CAUSE OR WAS DISCHARGED FOR MISCONDUCT FROM HIS MOST RECENT WORK. SECTION 1260A PROVIDES - AN INDIVIDUAL DISQUALIFIED UNDER SECTION 1256 IS DISQUALIFIED UNTIL HE/SHE, SUBSEQUENT TO THE DISQUALIFYING ACT, PERFORMS SERVICES IN BONA FIDE EMPLOYMENT FOR WHICH HE/SHE RECEIVES REMUNERATION EQUAL TO OR IN EXCESS OF FIVE TIMES HIS OR HER WEEKLY BENEFIT AMOUNT.

APPEAL:

YOU HAVE THE RIGHT TO FILE AN APPEAL IF YOU DO NOT AGREE WITH ALL OR PART OF THIS DECISION.

TO APPEAL, YOU MUST DO ALL OF THE FOLLOWING:

A. COMPLETE THE ENCLOSED APPEAL FORM (DE1000M) OR WRITE A LETTER STATING THAT YOU WANT TO APPEAL THIS DECISION. IF YOU WRITE A LETTER TO APPEAL, EXPLAIN THE REASON WHY YOU DO NOT AGREE WITH THE DEPARTMENT'S DECISION. WRITE YOUR SOCIAL SECURITY NUMBER ON EACH DOCUMENT YOU SUBMIT TO THE DEPARTMENT. (TITLE 22, CALIFORNIA CODE OF REGULATIONS (CCR), SECTION 5008).

SEX DISCRIMINATION

B. MAIL THE DE1000M OR YOUR LETTER TO THE ADDRESS OF THE OFFICE LISTED ON THE FIRST PAGE OF THIS DECISION.

C. FILE YOUR APPEAL WITHIN TWENTY (20) DAYS OF THE MAIL DATE OF THIS NOTICE OR NO LATER THAN 12/31/14.

YOUR HANDBOOK, "A GUIDE TO BENEFITS AND EMPLOYMENT SERVICES", GIVES MORE INFORMATION ABOUT APPEALS. IF YOU DO NOT HAVE A HANDBOOK, CONTACT THE OFFICE LISTED ON THE FIRST PAGE OF THIS NOTICE.

APPEAL INFORMATION:

WHEN YOUR APPEAL IS RECEIVED, YOUR CASE WILL BE REVIEWED. IF THE DECISION REMAINS THE SAME, WE WILL SEND YOUR APPEAL TO THE OFFICE OF APPEALS. IF YOU APPEAL AFTER THE 20 DAYS, YOU MUST INCLUDE THE REASON FOR THE DELAY. THE ADMINISTRATIVE LAW JUDGE WILL DETERMINE WHETHER YOU HAD GOOD CAUSE FOR THE DELAY. IF THE ADMINISTRATIVE LAW JUDGE DETERMINES YOU DID NOT HAVE GOOD CAUSE FOR SUBMITTING YOUR APPEAL LATE, YOUR APPEAL WILL BE DISMISSED.

THE OFFICE OF APPEALS WILL SEND YOU A LETTER WITH THE DATE, PLACE, AND TIME OF YOUR HEARING AND A PAMPHLET EXPLAINING APPEAL HEARING PROCEDURES. AT THE HEARING, THE ADMINISTRATIVE LAW JUDGE WILL LISTEN TO YOU, EXAMINE THE FACTS, AND MAKE A DECISION. YOU MAY HAVE A REPRESENTATIVE OR SOMEONE ELSE HELP YOU.

IF YOU ARE CLAIMING CONTINUING BENEFITS:

WHILE YOU WAIT FOR THE ADMINISTRATIVE LAW JUDGE'S DECISION, YOU MUST CONTINUE TO MAIL YOUR CLAIM FORMS TO THE EDD. IF YOU DO NOT RECEIVE CLAIM FORMS OR A FORM FROM THE OFFICE OF APPEALS, CONTACT THE OFFICE LISTED ON THE FIRST PAGE OF THIS NOTICE. IF THE ADMINISTRATIVE LAW JUDGE DECIDES YOU ARE ELIGIBLE FOR BENEFITS; WE CAN ONLY PAY BENEFITS IF CLAIM FORMS WERE RECEIVED FOR THAT WEEK.

OTHER SERVICES: CONTACT EDD FOR INFORMATION ABOUT (1) JOB REFERRALS, (2) DISABILITY INSURANCE, (3) OTHER EDD SERVICES (4) SERVICES OFFERED BY OTHER AGENCIES.

DE1080 CZ   REV. 1 (06-05)   (CLU)

"EXHIBIT G"

Privileged Communication & Confidential Information © 2014 Edward Dumas All rights reserved. No part of this publication may be reproduced or transmitted in any form or by any means, electronic or mechanical, including photocopy, recording or any other information storage and retrieval system without prior permission in writing from Edward Dumas.

SEX DISCRIMINATION

U.S. Equal Employment Opportunity Commission
Los Angeles District Office

255 E. Temple St. 4th
Los Angeles, CA 90012

(213) 894-1096
TTY (213) 894-1121
Fax: (213) 894-1118

Respondent: ABM
EEOC Charge No.:
FEPA Charge No.:

December 16, 2014

This is with reference to your recent written correspondence or intake questionnaire in which you alleged employment discrimination by the above-named respondent. The information provided indicates that the matter complained of is subject to the statute(s) checked off below:

[X] Title VII of the Civil Rights Act of 1964 (Title VII)

[ ] The Age Discrimination in Employment Act (ADEA)

[ ] The Americans with Disabilities Act (ADA)

[ ] The Equal Pay Act (EPA)

[ ] The Genetic Information Nondiscrimination Act (GINA)

The attached EEOC Form 5, Charge of Discrimination, is a summary of your claims based on the information you provided. Because the document that you submitted to us constitutes a charge of employment discrimination, we have complied with the law and notified the employer that you filed a charge.

To enable proper handling of this action by the Commission you should:

(1) Review the enclosed charge form and make corrections.

(2) Sign and date the charge in the bottom left hand block where I have made an "X". For purposes of meeting the deadline for filing a charge, the date of your original signed document will be retained as the original filing date.

(3) Return the signed charge to this office.

Please sign and return the charge within thirty (30) days from the date of this letter. Under EEOC procedures, if we do not hear from you within 30 days or receive your signed charge within 30 days, we are authorized to dismiss your charge and issue you a right to sue letter allowing you to pursue the matter in federal court. Please be aware that after we receive your signed Form 5, the EEOC will send a copy of the charge to California Department Of Fair Employment & Housing 2218 Kausen Drive Suite 100 Elk Grove, CA 95758 as required by our procedures. If that agency processes the charge, it may require the charge to be signed before a notary public or an agency official.

Please use the "EEOC Charge No." listed at the top of this letter whenever you call us about this charge. Please also notify this office of any change in address or of any prolonged absence from home. Failure to cooperate in this matter may lead to dismissal of the charge.

Please also read the enclosed brochure, "What You Should Know Before You File A Charge With EEOC," for answers to frequently asked questions about employee rights and the EEOC process. If you have any questions, please call me at the number listed below. If you have to call long distance, please call collect.

Sincerely,

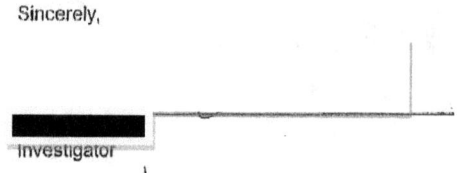

Investigator

Office Hours: Monday – Friday, 8:00 a.m. - 4:30 p.m.
www.eeoc.gov

Enclosure(s)
    Copy of EEOC Form 5, Charge of Discrimination
    Copy of EEOC Uniform Brochure, "What You Should Know Before You File A Charge With EEOC."

"EXHIBIT H"

The EDD, EEOC, & Superior Court Legal Forms

LABOR COMMISSIONER, STATE OF CALIFORNIA

BUREAU OF FIELD ENFORCEMENT
STATE OF CALIFORNIA-DEPARTMENT OF INDUSTRIAL RELATIONS
DIVISION OF LABOR STANDARDS ENFORCEMENT

OFFICE USE ONLY
TAKEN BY: _____ DATE FILED: _____ INDUSTRY: _____

Please print legibly or type. Fill out this form if you would like to report a widespread violation of workplace laws (e.g., wage and hour, child labor, workers' compensation, or recordkeeping laws) by an employer that affects all or a group of employees working for the employer. If you are claiming only unpaid wages on behalf of yourself and do not wish to report a widespread violation of the law by your employer that also affects other workers, then fill out the DLSE Form 1 (Initial Report or Claim) to file an individual wage claim, instead of this form.

REPORT OF LABOR LAW VIOLATION

SECTION 1. REPORTING PARTY (INDIVIDUAL OR REPRESENTATIVE)

NAME OF REPORTING PARTY: ▇▇▇▇▇▇▇ IF INTERPRETER IS NEEDED, INDICATE LANGUAGE: _____
ADDRESS: _____ CITY: _____ STATE: CA ZIP: _____
HOME PHONE: ( ) _____ CELL/OTHER PHONE: ( ) _____ E-MAIL (if available): _____

If you are represented by a lawyer or other advocate, enter your ADVOCATE and ORGANIZATION information:
NAME: N/A _____ ORGANIZATION NAME: _____
ADDRESS: _____ CITY: _____ STATE: _____ ZIP: _____
HOME PHONE: ( ) _____ CELL/OTHER PHONE: ( ) _____ E-MAIL (if available): _____

SECTION 2. EMPLOYER REPORTED

EMPLOYER BUSINESS NAME: ABM
ADDRESS: 1150 S. Olive Street, 19th Floor   CITY: Los Angeles   STATE: CA   ZIP: 90015
PHONE: (213) 284-7600   TYPE OF BUSINESS: Security Services, Facility Services   TOTAL EMPLOYEES: 107,000
ENTITY TYPE: ✓ CORPORATION   INDIVIDUAL   PARTNERSHIP   LLC   LLP   OTHER (explain): _____
OWNER'S NAME: N/A   NAME AND JOB TITLE OF PERSON IN CHARGE: Gilbert Naranjo, District Manager

	ADDRESS CITY, STATE, ZIP	EMPLOYER STILL OPERATING THERE?	BUSINESS HOURS	TOTAL EMPLOYEES
EMPLOYER'S MAIN WORK LOCATION	▇▇▇▇▇▇▇	✓ YES NO UNKNOWN	9-5p	
OTHER WORK LOCATION (if any, whether or not you worked there)	▇▇▇▇▇▇▇	✓ YES NO UNKNOWN	8-5p	
OTHER WORK LOCATION (if any, whether or not you worked there)	▇▇▇▇▇▇▇	✓ YES NO UNKNOWN		

IS THE EMPLOYER COVERED BY WORKERS' COMPENSATION INSURANCE? ✓ YES · NO   UNKNOWN
IS THERE A UNION CONTRACT? ✓ YES   NO   DID YOUR JOB INVOLVE PUBLIC WORKS? YES ✓ NO
EMPLOYER'S VEHICLE LICENSE PLATE NUMBER: _____

SECTION 3. WORK HOURS AND WAGES

DO YOU OR DID YOU WORK FOR THE EMPLOYER? (YES) NO   IF "YES":
   DATE OF HIRE: 01 / 27 / 14   LAST DAY OF WORK (if applicable): 11 / 05 / 15   ✓ QUIT   FIRED   STILL EMPLOYED

DID THE EMPLOYER DESIGNATE WHAT TIME THE WORKDAY BEGAN FOR EMPLOYEES? ✓ YES   NO   DON'T KNOW   IF "YES":
   WHAT TIME DID THE EMPLOYER DESIGNATE? SUN/12 ✓ AM   PM

DID THE EMPLOYER DESIGNATE WHICH DAY OF THE WEEK THE WORKWEEK BEGAN? ✓ YES   NO   DON'T KNOW   IF "YES":
   WHAT DAY DID THE EMPLOYER DESIGNATE? (SUNDAY)   MONDAY   TUESDAY   WEDNESDAY   THURSDAY   FRIDAY   SATURDAY

WHAT IS THE NORMAL OR STANDARD WORK SCHEDULE FOR EMPLOYEES DURING THE WEEK? PROVIDE YOUR BEST ESTIMATE OF THE START AND END TIMES AND NUMBER OF HOURS WORKED FOR EACH WORK DAY. (If employees did not work standard schedules, skip to the next question.)

SUNDAY	START TIME: ___ AM PM	END TIME: ___ AM PM	HOURS WORKED: ___			
MONDAY	START TIME: ___ AM PM	END TIME: ___ AM PM	HOURS WORKED: ___			
TUESDAY	START TIME: ___ AM PM	END TIME: ___ AM PM	HOURS WORKED: ___	TOTAL HOURS		
WEDNESDAY	START TIME: ___ AM PM	END TIME: ___ AM PM	HOURS WORKED: ___	WORKED PER		
THURSDAY	START TIME: ___ AM PM	END TIME: ___ AM PM	HOURS WORKED: ___	WEEK:		
FRIDAY	START TIME: ___ AM PM	END TIME: ___ AM PM	HOURS WORKED: ___			
SATURDAY	START TIME: ___ AM PM	END TIME: ___ AM PM	HOURS WORKED: ___			

BOFE 1 (Rev. 11/2012)   Page 1 of 3

SEX DISCRIMINATION

SECTION 3. WORK HOURS AND WAGES (continued)

DO EMPLOYEES WORK DIFFERENT SCHEDULES OR IRREGULAR HOURS SO YOU CANNOT PROVIDE A STANDARD WORK SCHEDULE? ✓ YES   NO

IF "YES," BRIEFLY DESCRIBE THE DIFFERENT SCHEDULES OR IRREGULAR WORK HOURS AS BEST AS YOU CAN: _____

WHEN IS THE NORMAL OR STANDARD SCHEDULED MEAL PERIOD FOR EMPLOYEES?
START TIME: _____ AM PM   END TIME: _____ AM PM   THERE IS NO STANDARD SCHEDULED MEAL PERIOD

WHAT IS THE AVERAGE LENGTH OF TIME FOR AN EMPLOYEE'S MEAL PERIOD? 30   MINUTES   HOURS

WHO SET THE WORK SCHEDULE? (FULL NAME AND JOB TITLE/POSITION): MARILYN GARCIA, SCHEDULER

WHAT DAY IS PAY DAY?   DAILY
WEEKLY ON _____   ✓ BI-WEEKLY ON (Once every two weeks) FRIDAY
MONTHLY ON _____   SEMI-MONTHLY ON (Twice a month) _____

WHO PAYS EMPLOYEES? (FULL NAME AND JOB TITLE/POSITION): UNKNOWN

ARE EMPLOYEES PAID BY THE HOUR? ✓ YES   NO   IF "YES," HOW MUCH? $_____ PER HOUR
VARIES (EXPLAIN): Pay structures vary throughout the corporation.

ARE EMPLOYEES PAID A FIXED AMOUNT OF WAGES (OR SALARY), REGARDLESS OF THE NUMBER OF HOURS WORKED? ✓ YES   NO
IF "YES," HOW MUCH? $_____ PER DAY   PER WEEK   EVERY 2 WEEKS   SEMI-MONTHLY   MONTHLY
VARIES (EXPLAIN): Varies on position and location of the employee per se.

ARE EMPLOYEES PAID BY PIECE RATE?   YES   NO   IF "YES," HOW MUCH? $_____ PER (Describe Unit) _____
PIECE RATES VARY (EXPLAIN): DON'T KNOW

HOW ARE EMPLOYEES PAID? ✓ CHECK   CASH
BOTH CHECK & CASH   OTHER METHOD (EXPLAIN): _____
✓ METHOD OF PAYMENT VARIES PER EMPLOYEE OR JOB POSITION (EXPLAIN): GIFTS AND BONUSES ARE PROVIDED.

IF EMPLOYEES ARE PAID IN CASH, DOES THE EMPLOYER KEEP CASH PAYMENT RECORDS OR LOGS?   YES   NO   ✓ DON'T KNOW

DOES THE EMPLOYER KEEP TIME RECORDS OF HOURS WORKED BY EMPLOYEES?   YES   NO   ✓ DON'T KNOW

WHAT LANGUAGES ARE SPOKEN BY EMPLOYEES? ✓ ENGLISH ✓ SPANISH   MIXTEC   TRIQUE   CANTONESE   MANDARIN   KOREAN
VIETNAMESE   TAGALOG   CAMBODIAN   HMONG   THAI   PUNJABI   HINDI   RUSSIAN   OTHER: _____

SECTION 4. SUSPECTED VIOLATIONS OF EMPLOYER

The boxes below describe conduct by an employer that violates the law. Please put a check mark in the box(es) if the employer engages in, or any employee or employees have experienced, any of the following violations:

☐ NO WORKERS' COMPENSATION INSURANCE	☐ CHILD LABOR VIOLATIONS:
	☐ No valid work permit(s)
	☐ No valid entertainment work permit(s)
	☐ Minor(s) work excessive or prohibited hours
	☐ Minor(s) work in hazardous conditions
	Estimated number of minors affected: _____

☑ MINIMUM WAGE VIOLATIONS:	☑ OVERTIME VIOLATIONS:
☐ Paid below minimum wage	☐ Not paid daily overtime for hours worked over 8 hours per day (or 10 hours per day for farmworkers)
☐ Not paid at all for overtime hours worked	☑ Not paid weekly overtime for hours worked over 40 hours per week
☑ Not paid for all hours worked, including unpaid travel time and try-out time	☑ Not paid double time for hours worked over 12 hours per day
☐ Paycheck issued with insufficient funds	☐ Not paid overtime for working on the 7th consecutive workday in a workweek
☐ Asked employee to pay back wages paid	
☑ No split shift premium pay	
Estimated number of employees affected: _____	Estimated number of employees affected: _____

BOFE 1 (Rev. 11/2012)   Page 2 of 3

SECTION 4 - SUSPECTED VIOLATIONS OF EMPLOYER (continued)

[✓] OTHER UNPAID WAGES:
- [ ] Wages are not paid at the contracted rate
- [✓] No reporting time premium pay
- [✓] No premium pay for missing meal or rest periods

Estimated number of employees affected: _____

[ ] PAY STUB VIOLATIONS:
- [ ] Paid by check or cash without an itemized wage deduction statement
- [ ] Itemized wage deduction statement provided but not accurate and/or incomplete
- [ ] Itemized wage deduction statement not provided at least semi-monthly

Estimated number of employees affected: _____

[ ] MEAL PERIOD VIOLATIONS:
- [ ] 30-minute off-duty meal period not provided by the end of the 5th hour of work
- [ ] Second 30-minute off-duty meal period not provided when working more than 10 hours
- [ ] Meal period provided but less than 30 minutes

Estimated number of employees affected: _____

[ ] REST BREAK VIOLATIONS:
- [ ] For work days between 3.5 hours and up to 6 hours per day, not allowed to take a 10-minute rest break
- [ ] For work days of more than 6 hours and up to 10 hours per day, not allowed to take two 10-minute rest breaks
- [ ] For work days of more than 10 hours and up to 14 hours per day, not allowed to take three 10-minute rest breaks

Estimated number of employees affected: _____

[✓] PAY DATE VIOLATIONS:
- [ ] No fixed pay date
- [✓] Late payment of wages

Estimated number of employees affected: _____

[✓] RECORD KEEPING VIOLATIONS:
- [✓] Daily time records are not kept or inaccurate
- [✓] Payroll records are not kept or inaccurate
- [✓] No notice to new hires (under Labor Code Section 2810.5)

[✓] BUSINESS EXPENSE VIOLATIONS:
- [✓] Uniforms not reimbursed or illegally charged to employees
- [ ] Tools, supplies or equipment not reimbursed or illegally charged to employees
- [ ] Illegal charges for cash shortages, breakage, or loss of equipment

Estimated number of employees affected: _____

[✓] FAILURE TO POST:
- [✓] Applicable Industrial Welfare Commission Order not posted
- [ ] Minimum Wage Order 2001 not posted
- [✓] Pay day notice not posted
- [ ] Workers' compensation insurance notice not posted
- [ ] Rate of compensation not posted (for farmworkers only)

[ ] MISCLASSIFICATION:
- [ ] Employees misclassified as independent contractors
- [ ] Salaried employees misclassified as exempt employees

Estimated number of employees affected: _____

[ ] LICENSING/REGISTRATION VIOLATIONS:
- [ ] Unlicensed construction contractor
- [ ] Contracted with unlicensed construction contractor
- [ ] Unlicensed farm labor contractor
- [ ] Unregistered garment contractor or manufacturer
- [ ] Unregistered car wash

[ ] FAILURE TO PROVIDE LACTATION ACCOMMODATIONS

Estimated number of employees affected: _____

[✓] OTHER VIOLATIONS (briefly explain):
Failure to provide suitable Seats, pursuant to IWC 4-2001, § 14.Seats

Estimated number of employees affected: _____

Please provide any other information about your complaint that you believe is important for the Labor Commissioner to know:
Time records are often altered and changed. Other employees have experienced late payment of wages and not paid for all hours worked; it is unknown to me how many are affected; I was told by my immediate Supervisor that "...there is no overtime to be paid, even if you have to stay overtime" when my relief was late.

Please provide the following information for any minors under the age of 18 who work for the employer:

FULL NAME (first and last name, and any "nick" names)	AGE	JOB POSITION/ TYPE OF WORK PERFORMED	NORMAL WORK SCHEDULE	HOW WAS THE MINOR PAID (by check, in cash, both cash and check, or other method?

MAY YOUR NAME BE USED IN AN INVESTIGATION? [ ] YES [✓] NO
DO YOU WANT DLSE TO KEEP YOUR NAME AND CONTACT INFORMATION CONFIDENTIAL? * [✓] YES [ ] NO

I HEREBY CERTIFY THAT THE INFORMATION ABOVE IS A TRUE STATEMENT TO THE BEST OF MY KNOWLEDGE.
SIGNED: ███████████████████ DATE: 11/20/2014
PRINT NAME: Edward Dumas

* DLSE will maintain confidentiality as appropriate in each case and to the extent provided for under the law. Information may need to be released in some cases.

Sex Discrimination

"EXHIBIT I"

DECEMBER 17, 2014

(Additional, Other, and Confidential Information)

I am writing in response to my interview with the *California Employment Development Department* on December 12, 2014. I hold that pursuant to California law, ABM should not be allowed take the position that a Corporation can let an employee be sexually harassed at work and not take any reasonable steps to prevent it.

In my interview on 12/10/14 at approximately 9:30AM, the interviewer assumed that my former employer, ABM, conducted an investigation into my sexual harassment allegations at work, with no factual basis to form that assumption. I explained that there was no investigation; I was removed or constructively transferred to another location four weeks after I had complained about someone constantly sexually harassing me at work; ABM failed to take "*immediate* and appropriate corrective action" according to what the law states and mandates to covered employers (see **Government Code § 12940(j)(1)**). Please note "immediate" is a legal requirement for employers to instantly take any reasonable steps to stop harassment.

ABM's District Manager's decision to remove me was executed four weeks later after I initially complained about sexual harassment to him and I consistently inquired if anyone was going to investigate the unlawful harassment or the harasser. ABM did nothing and took no steps to prevent the unlawful harassment from occurring during my work shifts. ABM took me off work or constructively suspended me for one day on 11/4/14 before removing me to another location and demoting me to another position four weeks after I complained about sexual harassment at work, in addition to a final notice, seasoned for wrongful termination.

Employers operating in California are obligated to take immediate action against harassment in the workplace and, moreover, are to provide anti-harassment training to new supervisors within the first six months of new hire. I was never provided that particular training as a newly hired supervisor which is required and mandated by law. (see **California Government Code §12950.1**)

It is settled law in California that if any covered employer fails in their duty to prevent or correct unlawful harassment, then they are liable for harassment that has occurred at the workplace. Pursuant to California law, specifically see **Government Code § 12940(j)(1)**, which makes it unlawful for employers to allow:

"... harassment of an employee, an applicant, or a person providing services pursuant to a contract by an employee, other than an agent or supervisor, shall be unlawful if the entity, or its agents or supervisors, knows or should have known of this conduct and fails to take immediate and appropriate corrective action. An employer may also be responsible for the acts of nonemployees, with respect to sexual harassment of employees, applicants, or persons providing services pursuant to a contract in the workplace, where the employer, or its agents or supervisors, knows or should have known of the conduct and fails to take immediate and appropriate corrective action. In reviewing cases involving the acts

SEX DISCRIMINATION

of nonemployees, the extent of the employer's control and any other legal responsibility that the employer may have with respect to the conduct of those non employees shall be considered. <u>An entity shall take all reasonable steps to prevent harassment from occurring.</u> Loss of tangible job benefits shall not be necessary in order to establish harassment."

Furthermore, pursuant to the <u>**California Attorney General's Office, Civil Rights Handbook, Third Edition, 2001, states on page 30**</u>: "...under Unemployment Insurance Code section 1256.7, you also have good cause to quit your job if you are sexually harassed by your employer [footnote]. Accordingly, if you are discriminated against on any of the basis set forth in section 125.2 or are sexually harassed, you may not be disqualified from receiving unemployment insurance benefits if you quit your job."

The Attorney General goes on to state how one must meet all other requirements to be eligible for unemployment and for more information regarding my rights to contact your Department for assistance. This is problematic because in my interview the Department took the position that some type of sexual harassment is legal and the employer did a good job in removing me after being sexually harassed at work for four weeks.

<u>I am very concerned because accordingly</u> the **California Attorney General** <u>goes on to state further on</u> **page 30**:

"It is very important to note that if you do quit your job because you have been discriminated against by your employer and file a claim for unemployment insurance benefits, your employer may appeal any EDD determination that you should receive benefits. If this occurs, you may wish to seek the advice of an attorney. Under California law, if you should subsequently lose your unemployment insurance case, your employer may then be able to use that decision against you in any subsequent discrimination case which you might file with some other governmental agency or in court. In other words, a loss in the unemployment insurance case may prevent you from prevailing in another forum under a different set of laws."

In addition, ABM does not fully comply with California Labor Code provisions; please find a confidential copy of the Labor Violation Report as supporting evidence for good cause; please find a copy of the EEOC correspondence as supporting evidence for my initial government complaint for good cause.

Feel free to contact me if you have any comments or questions at   or Email me at

Truthfully,

Privileged Communication & Confidential Information © 2014 Edward Dumas

All rights reserved. No part of this publication may be reproduced or transmitted in any form or by any means, electronic or mechanical, including photocopy, recording or any other information storage and retrieval system without prior permission in writing from Edward Dumas.

The EDD, EEOC, & Superior Court Legal Forms

```
12/18/2014                    07:46:47 PM

            Sales Receipt
Product      Sale    Unit     Final
Description  Qty     Price    Price

SAN BERNARDINO, CA  92402      $.70
Zone-1
First-Class Mail® Letter
 0 lb. 1.30 oz.
* Expected Delivery Day Monday,
December 22.
    Nonmachinable 1st Class    $.21
                              =======
Issue Postage:                 $.91

$.49 Stamp         1    $.49   $.49

Total:
                              =======
                               $1.40
Paid by:
MasterCard                     $1.40
    Account #:   ------------
    Approval #:    07242Z
    Transaction #:    631
23-902500982-99

SSK Transaction #:     219
USPS® #               054155-9550

            Thanks.
     It's a pleasure to serve you.

ALL SALES FINAL ON STAMPS AND POSTAGE.
REFUNDS FOR GUARANTEED SERVICES ONLY.

*****************************
*    Note: Priority Mail Express™   *
* refund restrictions in effect for *
*    mailing dates Dec. 22-25.      *
*             ***                   *
*****************************
```

U.S. POSTAGE $.49
90714
Date of sale
12/18/14
06   2500
208205332

Sex Discrimination

The EDD, EEOC, & Superior Court Legal Forms

Appeal Transmittal

```
SLU220M              APPEAL TRANSMITTAL           PAGE 1 OF 2    DATE: 12/30/14
                                                                 TIME: 14:04:56

TO: ING OAP              *** TIMELY ***

CLMNT SSN:
      NAME:
      BYB/CED:    03 30 14
      PGM CD:     A            CLM HOLDING FO: 0410

DEPT REP: N (N/Y)    CLMNT REP: N (N/Y)    NOTIFY AAO: ___    CSI: __

REFER TO FORMER CASE(s):

DEPT REQUESTS: ( _ ) NOTICE TO ATTEND  ( _ ) SUBPOENA  ( _ ) TELEPHONE HEARING
      NAME: _____      PH:( ___ ) ___ ____
      ADDRESS: _____
      CITY: _____ STATE: __ ZIP: _____ ____

REASON FOR REQUEST: _____
DEPT REPRESENTATIVE: L ROBINSON                FO: 0410


SLU210M              APPEAL PROCESS              DATE: 12/30/14
                                                 TIME: 14:04:43
FO: 0410        CLAIM HOLDING FO: 0410     REQUESTOR: L ROBINSON
BYB/CED: 03/30/14    PGM CD: A             APPEAL DATE: 12 / 29 / 14
CLMNT SSN:
      NAME:
      IN CARE OF: _____
      ADDRESS:
      CITY:                   STATE:      ZIP:
      PHONE:        (    )

ER ACCT:              ER NAME:
      REP/IN CARE OF:
      ADDRESS:
      CITY:                   STATE:      ZIP:

SECTIONS:    1256

INTERPRETER: N (N/Y)   LANGUAGE:
APPELLANT: C           ER FS: N (N/Y)            DI SUSP: ___
                       MM  DD  YY  WK              MM  DD  YY  RSN
      6315    6315CC  X 713  /   /         OP __ / __ / __  __

Document              pgs  Date
DE1000/1000DC(IB-101) 43   12 26 14
*ENVELOPE POSTMARKED       12 29 14
DE1080                02   12 11 14
CLAIM RECORD          1    12 30 14
CLAIM NOTES           01   12 30 14
DE 2403               3    12 10 14
```

RECEIVED
DEC 3 1 2014
INGLEWOOD OFFICE OF APPEALS

Appeal Documents

Sex Discrimination

NOTICE OF HEARING BEFORE ADMINISTRATIVE LAW JUDGE

CALIFORNIA UNEMPLOYMENT INSURANCE APPEALS BOARD

Michael Kurz
Administrative Law Judge

NOTICE OF HEARING

Case No [redacted]

Claimant-Appellant

HEARING TIME and PLACE
DATE: Tuesday, January 20, 2015
TIME: 2:30 PM
PLACE: 4300 Long Beach Blvd - #500
Long Beach CA 90807

Located near the corner of Long Beach Blvd. and W. San Antonio Dr.

EDD: 0410

* If an interpreter or reasonable accommodation for a disability is needed, call the phone number below immediately. Si necesita un intérprete llame el numero de telefono abajo inmediatamente.

* Bring all documents and witnesses necessary to support your case. *Evidence is rarely accepted after the hearing.*

* Arrive 15 minutes early to review the appeal file.

* The hearing room is in a secured facility. You may be screened.

* IMPORTANT: Read the enclosed 'Hearing Information' pamphlet.

THE FOLLOWING ISSUES WILL BE CONSIDERED AT THE HEARING (Section references are to the Unemployment Insurance Code unless otherwise noted):

1256   Did the claimant voluntarily leave his or her most recent employment without good cause. Was the claimant discharged for misconduct connected with his or her most recent work. (See UI sections 1256, 1256.1, 1256.2, 1256.5)

Direct questions to:

INGLEWOOD OFFICE OF APPEALS
Telephone: (310) 337-4302
Fax: (310) 337-4392

Date Mailed: 01/08/2015

INGLEWOOD OFFICE OF APPEALS
9800 South La Cienega Blvd - Ste 901
INGLEWOOD, CA 90301-0000
Telephone: (310) 337-4302
Fax: (310) 337-4392

NAMES AND ADDRESSES OF PARTIES / REPRESENTATIVES

SEX DISCRIMINATION

REGISTER – Office of Appeals

MAILING RECORD	CLAIMANT	CLT REP	EMPLOYER	ER REP	EDD	OTHER-SPECIFY
HEARING NOTICE & APPEAL PAMPHLET	YH JAN 0 8 2015					
HEARING NOTICE REMAILED						
PHONE DOCS & INSTRUCTIONS						
SUBPOENA SDT - NTA						
DECISION & DE 6401	1/28/15					
DECISION REMAILED						
DIGITAL HEARING COPY						
OTHER						
MAIL ADDITIONAL:	TO:					

Interpreter: _____ DATE NOTIFIED: _____

PARTY/WITNESS NAME:	APPEARING FOR CL / ER/PET / EDD	INTERP	Capacity REP / WIT / OBS	Hearing No. 1 / 2 / 3

IF DISMISSAL for UNTIMELY APPEAL, or DENIAL OF REOPENING, was all evidence on these issues taken at the START of the hearing?

HRS	YES	NO
1		
2		
3		

DATE	FROM	INFORMATION
1/27/15	HH	Dismissed w/ clt. Denied subpoena as Er not a party.

EDD & CUIAB'S ADMINISTRATIVE LAW JUDGE MICHAEL KURZ'S DISCRIMINATORY LEGAL DECISION NEGATING THE CIVIL AND LEGAL RIGHTS OF THE DISCRIMINATED EMPLOYEE AT ABM INDUSTRIES

```
         CALIFORNIA UNEMPLOYMENT INSURANCE APPEALS BOARD

In the Matter of:              Case No.: [redacted]
[redacted]
       Claimant-Appellant      TRANSCRIPT OF HEARING

                                       BEFORE

                               MICHAEL KURZ
                               ADMINISTRATIVE LAW JUDGE

                               Audio Recording
                               REPORTER

                               Sherry Rider
                               TRANSCRIBER (1/20/16)
```

Time(s) and Place(s) of Hearing

January 20, 2015
Long Beach, California

Appearances: Page

For the Claimant: [redacted], Claimant
                         (by written declaration)

Sex Discrimination

```
 1              P R O C E E D I N G S
 2
 3      BY THE ADMINISTRATIVE LAW JUDGE:   All right.  We're on
 4  the record in case ▇▇▇▇ in the matter of ▇▇▇▇
 5      Mr. ▇▇▇ has appeared by a written declaration.
 6      We're on the record now to go ahead and mark and accept
 7  exhibits into evidence.
 8      I'm going to start with the file at this time now.
 9      Exhibit No. 1 is a six page document called view
10  eligibility decision.  View eligibility decision.  Exhibit
11  No. 2 is the claim notes.  It's two pages.  Exhibit 3 is the
12  claim information sheet.  It's two pages.  Exhibit No. 4 is
13  the record of claim status interview regarding voluntarily
14  quitting.  Exhibit No. 5 is the determination appealed from.
15  Exhibit No. 6 is the envelope that the appeal came in.
16  Exhibit No. 7 is a receipt from Lakewood Post Office.
17  Exhibit No. 8 is the -- is the 8$^{th}$ exhibit.  (unclear)
18  Exhibits A through H are marked as Exhibit No. 8.  So it's
19  8A through H.  Exhibit No. 9 is the -- is the appeal.  And
20  it's one, two, three, four, five (inaudible).  It's 14
21  pages.  That's Exhibit No. 9.  Exhibit No. 10 is the appeals
22  transmittal document.  Exhibit 11 is the notice of today's
23  hearing.  That's actually scheduled January 21$^{st}$.  Exhibit
24  No. 12 is a document called notice of appearance by written
25  declaration.  And it's also got -- the declaration appears
26  to be 11 pages.  And then it's got Exhibits 1 -- 1 through 6
27  attached to it.  So the declaration in Exhibits 1 through 6
```

1 are Exhibit No. 12 for today's purposes. Exhibit No. 13 is
2 a point in support of claimant's appeal. It's a memorandum
3 and it consists of four pages. And then Exhibit No. 14 is a
4 claimant statement of question, fact and information in
5 dispute. The document is (unclear) here. And it consists
6 of six, seven, eight -- eight pages. I'm sorry, nine pages.
7 And Exhibit No. 15 is a statement of evidence to introduced
8 re: deprived of equal employment opportunities.
9   All right. These 15 exhibits and their sub exhibits
10 are all admitted into evidence at this time.
11   There being no further business we are off the record.
12   (HEARING CONCLUDED)

Sex Discrimination

CLAIMANT

THE STATE OF CALIFORNIA
EMPLOYMENT DEVELOPMENT DEPARTMENT
UNEMPLOYMENT INSURANCE APPEALS BOARD

███████, Claimant, v. ABM, Respondent.	CASE NO.: ███████ **NOTICE OF APPEARANCE BY WRITTEN DECLARATION** **MEMORANDUM OF POINTS AND AUTHORITIES** Administrative Law Judge: Judge Michael Kurz **Time:** 2:30PM **Date:** January 20, 2015 **Location:** Long Beach Office

DECLARATION

I, ███████, ALSO KNOWN AS ███████, IN THIS LEGAL MATTER, DECLARE AND SAY AS FOLLOWS:

1. I am a party to this legal matter and am over the age of 18, and if called as a witness I can testify competently to the facts set forth in the Declaration. I a duly licensed Unarmed

security guard in good standing, issued to me by the State of California.

2. I have gone through live scan and verified background checks for this privilege of providing security and investigative services in this specific area of licensure.

I. STATEMENT OF FACTS

1. In the month for January of 2014, I was interviewed for a job to be a Security Guard with ABM Scheduler ███████, ABM Post Commander ███████, and ABM upper level District Manager ███████.

2. ███████ is in charge of ABM's Region for the entire Los Angeles Area, as well as other Counties in California, his position is just below the Regional Vice President of ABM for this entire region and division, to the best of my knowledge and understanding, ███████ is the upper level manager who directly oversees the security and engineering departments throughout Southern California for this entire region for ABM.

3. I was screened and hired to be trained by ABM as a Security Shift Supervisor at the location known as ███████████████████████████, for $13.40 per hour. I never received any written disciplinary action prior to this event and was praised many times for my work performance by ABM and some of its clients' agents.

4. There were no substantial trainings, videos, and/or instructions on how to report and handle claims of sexual harassment at ABM. The written policies and instructions with regard to ABM's sexual harassment policy was limited to one to two pages each in one single handout and one single 'service' handbook that was issued to me at a nonpaid new hire orientation on January 25, 2014.

5. I was directed by ███████ to report to ███████, who became my immediate supervisor at this building. The security staff is unionized, requires a business-suit to be worn for uniform also known as "soft profile", and the building is not open to the public at this location.

6. From January 27, 2014 to October 5, 2014, I worked as a Security Shift Supervisor for ABM at 800 S. Hope Street. I worked in the security division at this building with no written warnings or disciplinary action(s) prior to, and was given customer and management compliments from time to time. I observed, reported, and discussed suspicious activity,

Sex Discrimination

1 suspicious individuals, and safety issues at this location. I delegated and directed another
2 Security Officer at this location, I assisted the Police, BID security, and other duties as assigned
3 with no disciplinary advisory notices prior to me reporting the sexual harassment incidents.

4   7. ABM has a "consensual relationship policy" that permits its employees to have
5 interpersonal relationships that have arose out of its business environment. It is not uncommon
6 at ABM for its employees to have acquaintances, friendships, and romantic relationships
7 between employees, clients, and contractors outside the workplace.

8   8. I became acquaintances with a person referred herein as "JANE DOE", whom had worked
9 for another company at 800 S. Hope. JANE DOE began making unreasonable demands to me
10 by making sexual advances directly towards me at work, and I began to feel very uncomfortable
11 with this type of behavior toward me at work.

12   9. On October 5, 2014, JANE DOE demanded from me that if I ▬▬▬▬▬ she
13 would get me fired from my job. I did not accept JANE DOE's offer, asked her to cease, and
14 I told this person to just leave me alone. See my Decl. in Exhibit 1.

15   10. On October 6, 2014, I notified my supervisor ▬▬▬ that I took this as a serious issue
16 and reported it as a "quid pro quo harassment incident". To the best of my knowledge I had a
17 duty to complain about a nonemployee of ABM harassing me at work.

18   11. JANE DOE became tense, highly aggressive, and harassing to me at work, even so far as
19 saying that she was "looking me up on the internet", as if she wanted to find out where I was
20 living. This became uncomfortable and disturbing toward me. JANE DOE's behavior seemed
21 so unreal as if someone was paying this person to do this on purpose or as a practical joke.

22   12. I considered filing a restraining order against JANE DOE but was not sure if
23 that was the best approach to this delicate issue especially since she physically worked there
24 and had access by way of employment. I already believed that there was no imminent threat of
25 violence by JANE DOE, just harassment, and expected ABM to have a professional solution.
26 I believe I was fulfilling my legal and material duty to report what was occurring to BROWN
27 and he led me to believe that ABM's upper level manager ▬▬▬ was going to help me.
28 //

-3-
DECLARATION
RE:

13. I began receiving 'prank calls' at the security desk station, of which there was no history of someone ever prank calling there in such a massive amount of times and not saying a word on the other line. I believed that this was JANE DOE prank calling me in order to negatively affect my work performance and to cause annoyance and embarrassment during my shift.

14. The prank calls began to come through at various times throughout the day and upcoming days, JANE DOE spoke curse words at me when she walked by, even whispering profanity to me while I was working at the security desk. I was bothered by this very much, and just wanted to remain professional and wait for ABM's investigative results.

15. On Tuesday, October 7, 2014, I continued receiving prank calls at the security desk in which I believed was JANE DOE, my harasser. I notified ▓▓▓▓ regarding the prank calls, curse words, and harassing behavior toward me.

16. ▓▓▓▓ told me to document it and as I did, but he did not want to assist me further; so I put it forth through in ABM's computer reporting system, known as "ODR" or "Auditmatic". This computer based system sends those reports to ABM lower, mid, and upper level managers such as ▓▓▓▓, ▓▓▓▓, and ▓▓▓▓ See Exhibit 2.

17. Although I became increasingly more uncomfortable, afraid, and felt harassed by JANE DOE; ▓▓▓▓N insisted that there would be an investigation by ABM. I believed I would be protected, receive some kind of counseling, training, and transfer in accordance with the Los Angeles Master Collective Bargaining Agreement. See Exhibit 3. On October 8, 2014, I started my regular work shift at 11:00PM, for a graveyard shift, and I was receiving multiple prank calls throughout the night.

18. On, October 9, 2014, I, again, informed ABM Manager ▓▓▓▓ that JANE DOE's behavior toward me was just getting worse. As the prank calling persisted at the desk throughout my shift, JANE DOE would appear at the security desk and continue to use curse words at me on the one hand and then in front of other persons act friendly on the other hand.

19. JANE DOE passed me notes in sexual nature in which I did not accept and threw away. The note had sexual terms regarding a "PROs" and "CONS" list in reference to a sexual relationship with her; she had listed many 'pros' such oral sex and for 'cons' there stated "none".

-4-
DECLARATION
RE:

SEX DISCRIMINATION

20. I regret throwing away that specific note for evidentiary purposes. Regardless, I did ██████ o have a ████████████████ I informed JANE DOE that I threw away her ████ to me because her behavior was not welcome and completely inappropriate at work.

21. On October 9, 2014, I asked and told ██████ to report w███ perceived to be the unlawful harassment by JANE DOE to ABM Corporate, in other words it was me telling ███████ do something more.

22. I specifically stated that "you have to go to ████████████". I further explained to ████████ that if these incidents go unreported then there can be major liabilities for the client, ABM, and myself; I specifically stated to ███████ that "...[W]e need to protect the client, ABM, and our jobs". I believed that I was fulfilling my legal duty as instructed by ABM regarding incidents like this. I believed I was following ABM's chain of command.

23. I was also feeling like JANE DOE's harassing behavior was so intentional as to sabotage my job and work performance, it felt like as if someone was paying this person to destroy my life, that's how powerless I continued to feel in my job.

24. ██████ stated to me that he called ███████ and ███████ and informed me that ███████ wants me to write a statement. ███████, is an upper level member of management, just below the Vice President, and the immediate supervisor to ███████ who is a mid to upper level manager also known as the "Security Director" for the CBRE portfolio. See Exhibit 4.

25. On October 10, 2014, I wrote the statement about the sexual harassment incident that occurred on October 5, 2014, I made a Declaration under penalty of perjury about the incident. I emailed ███████tion along with a note, attached as evidence, written to me by JANE DOE. For the record I did not respond to her note, did not understand it, and awaited a response from ABM with regards to the note.

26. I truly believed that there was going to be an investigation by ABM. ███████ specifically stated to me, "...the wheels are rolling...its starting...",thus leading me to believe that there was going to be a prompt and fair investigation.

-5-
DECLARATION

27. From October 11 to 16, 2014, I kept reporting the harassing behavior by JANE DOE to BROWN and no one from ABM spoke with me about my complaint. I was still receiving multiple prank calls at the security desk where I was stationed.

28. JANE DOE would still speak curse words at me such as ▮▮▮▮ or would walk by the security desk and whisper to me ▮▮▮▮"; even as far as making ▮▮▮▮ insinuations at times. I believed that this type of behavior was meant to annoy, embarrass, and humiliate me because I had declined her ▮▮▮▮ advances.

29. I still did not believe she posed any immediate threat to herself or others because I also observed her showing signs of not being genuine; and I observed her harassing behavior as means to humiliate and embarrass me, while inhibiting my work performance.

30. For example, JANE DOE stated that she was 'sick', 'dying of a disease', 'sick with multiple diseases', and just might 'end it all' and then later cursing me out about it. This made me feel harassed, embarrassed, and not wanting to be there anymore. However, when DOE's co-worker would walk by her in the lobby or hallway, I observed her attitude and demeanor change very differently toward that person, I felt singled out by JANE DOE.

31. I was being pursued by JANE DOE so aggressively, I keep telling her that it was unwelcome and inappropriate behavior. No matter what I could or could not say, I just felt powerless against it and I seriously thought help was coming from ABM.

32. From October 18 to October 19, 2014: I continued to receive crank calls at the security desk and when JANE DOE walked by, she would continue to speak curse words at me.

33. October 20, 2014, I attended a building training meeting and upper level ABM District Manager J▮▮▮▮ D was present but did not speak with me in regards to my sexual harassment complaints; he was patronizing the client's agent and appeared too busy for me.

34. From October 21, 2014, October 22, 2014, and October 23, 2014, I continued to receive prank calls and curse words directed toward me by my harasser, JANE DOE.

35. I asked my co-workers if anyone from the company has talked to them about my harassment concerns regarding JANE DOE's behavior. It was later verified that no one from ABM has talked to them to investigate anything.

-6-
DECLARATION

Sex Discrimination

36. On October 25, 2014 and October 26, 2014, No one from ABM ever called me nor discussed my complaint and concerns about my harasser. I attempted to forward the letter(s) she was giving me but ▮▮▮▮ still did not want to read them or get involved.

37. On October 30, 2014, After being available from 11:00PM to 7:00AM as I was working for ABM, I received a phone call at home after work about 9:00AM from ▮▮▮▮. ▮▮▮▮ stated that ▮▮▮▮ wanted me to come to the ABM Corporate office.

38. I asked ▮▮▮▮ as to what kind of meeting would this be, if it is about the incidents. I asked ▮▮▮▮ if this was a disciplinary meeting; I asked her about my union representation at this meeting such as if I would need my union representative for this meeting, and if I would be compensated for this meeting.

39. ▮▮▮▮ stated to me that "▮▮▮▮ thinks highly of you" and "your going to have to talk to him about that". I was confused as to the purpose of this meeting.

40. On November 1, 2014, I was receiving more prank calls at the security desk; On November 2, 2014, at around 3:30PM JANE DOE argued and scolded me at the security desk, with regards to keeping the main tenant's glass door closed and secure.

41. It was my impression that JANE DOE was constantly ease dropping on me at the security desk and would stay during after hours at the building. JANE DOE would continue to stay in the building throughout my work shifts, even throughout the middle of the night on my graveyard shifts, although her company did not operate in its offices during those business hours.

42. On Monday, November 3, 2014, ▮▮▮▮ had called and told me to meet with ▮▮▮▮ at 2:00PM at his office on South Olive Street. I arrived for the meeting with ▮▮▮▮ and ▮▮▮▮ whom left me waiting in their Lobby for about 40 minutes.

43. ▮▮▮▮ presented me with a first and final written warning for violating ABM's conflict of interest policy and for fraternization. ▮▮▮▮ told me that "the Union would not disagree with them, it is better to have a job than no job, and they really had no other job for me...". If I wanted to be employed by ABM still, then I had to be removed or "transferred" to another worksite, so he said.

//

44. I felt coerced and intimidated because ▮▮▮ represents that the Union and him never have any grievances, mediations or arbitrations. ▮▮▮ specifically stated in the month of around August to September of 2014 that ABM has "Zero" grievances with the Union...none ever leading up to arbitration". ▮▮▮ never informed me that I was going to be demoted and threatened with a paycut, as was stated by ▮▮▮ in his meeting with me at around 9:00AM on November 5, 2014.

45. On November 5, 2014, I arrived at the new worksite in where I was brought into ▮▮▮'s office around 9:00AM and he informed me in person, that I was demoted from my Shift Supervisor position and I was now a "Lobby Ambassador" and that any mistake I make, "even a wrong look at the lady's" and I would be terminated.

46. ▮▮▮ stated to the effect, around 11:40AM, that I would start receiving lesser pay, I pressed this issue of a pay cut with him, and he stated that he really did not know. I knew from previous experience that ▮▮▮ would sometimes falsify reports for ABM and his responses to my question reflected his tendency to lie.

47. For example, ▮▮▮ was exposed at a training meeting by one of his subordinates for falsifying a report that had to do with process servers delivering court papers in the building. After realizing that I was working with someone who is known to falsify reports in order to escape professional responsibility, I felt that I was never going to have an opportunity to be promoted at ABM anymore for a higher position in the company.

48. I then wanted to discuss and inform ▮▮▮ how I was feeling about what was happening to my job with ABM. ▮▮▮ made reference to the demotion being my fault and I would be receiving less pay now. So at approximately 11:47AM I informed him that I am quitting ABM. ▮▮▮'s office had since falsified this timesheet to state that I left at 11:00AM. See Exhibit 5.

-8-
DECLARATION

SEX DISCRIMINATION

50. I really did not understand why the disparate treatment was directed toward me; until I found out later that ABM has organizational compliance issues and problems with Federal and State employment laws.

51. I was never informed in the meeting with ▮▮▮▮ that I was to be demoted, changed in job position, given less privileges, and would get a pay reduction. The pay cut or reduction was specifically mentioned by ▮▮▮▮ to me on November 5, 2014, around 11:40AM.

52. On about November 10, 2014, I filed an intake with the EEOC. On November 26, 2014, I received a letter from the EEOC regarding my intake and a one page informational sheet. The EEOC has received my Charge of Discrimination on January 16, 2015, and is currently processing this government complaint for the discrimination against me reporting harassment in violation of Title VII. See Exhibit b.

53. I intend on filing a lawsuit against ABM once I receive my right to sue letter. I also intend on informing or "whistleblowing" to the California Department of Fair Housing and Employment agency that ABM is not in compliance with anti-harassment training laws mandated by the State of California.

54. ABM has discriminated against me because of my protected characteristics such as my sex and gender; and for a male complaining about sexual harassment against a female.

55. There is a double standard at ABM and in society with regard to this type of reverse discrimination and harassment, not rooted in law, but in culture and philosophy.

56. On December 30, 2014, I sent about 15 pages consisting of a written statement of these incidents, copy of the first declaration, and exhibits. On a letter dated on 12/30/14 after "review" our decision remains the same; and stated my case is transferred to the Inglewood Office of Appeals.

57. I made repeated demands for reinstatement at ABM, for ABM to send my complaint to the Union, and I had contacted the Union and the NLRB, in order to seek reinstatement with legal protection. The Union Representative deferred me to the EEOC and the California Labor Commissioner's Office, in which I have filed two complaints. The Union Representative also deferred me to a 'hotline' but it was an automated message so I hung up. I have never heard

-9-
DECLARATION

back from the Union despite entering my information on to their website.

58. I reasonably utilized the complaint procedure ABM had in place for me. I followed ABM's steps and where it broke down was at the fault of ABM. The employer was misleading me, did not investigate the matter, and then ended up demoting me for reporting it.

59. ABM has acted unreasonably and was not to 'ambush and punish' me with a first and final written warning for reporting sexual harassment because of my sex and gender, and ABM's problems with government agencies with regards to this issue.

60. ABM upper level management knew and should have known that I had reported harassment since October 10, 2014, and did nothing to help me.

61. I am a California citizen and taxpayer in good standing. I would still be working full-time with benefits and paying my taxes but for ABM's discriminatory conduct in this situation. I would not be asking for the safety net of unemployment insurance but for ABM's discriminatory conduct toward me.

62. It was ABM's intent to separate me from the company for reporting harassment and has made me feel that I was wrong in reporting it. This should not be the case, because it is embarrassing and humiliating in and of itself for any person to be going through this issue.

63. I have asked ABM to restore me to my job several times, (not at the same location of course); I do not want to be on unemployment, I want to be working, but ABM has shown no intent or interest to honor my legal rights by reinstating and making me whole again.

64. I have no personal car and have to be limited to public transportation despite the rising cost of Metro and Transit services in Los Angeles County. I have already spent time and money trying to prepare for this appeal. I need my time and money to find new and suitable employment since ABM is not reinstating me back to my job with the company.

65. There was no reason for me to have left ABM but for their unreasonable discriminatory conduct and adverse employment actions against me. I made it an effort to keep my job and shield the company from liability but I was no longer allowed equal opportunities at ABM by upper level management. ABM has showed no intent on removing the intentional deprivation of equal employment opportunities in their organization.

-10-
DECLARATION

SEX DISCRIMINATION

66. ABM did not reprimand and transfer me within the scope of the terms and conditions set forth within the Los Angeles Master Collective Bargaining Agreement. The transfer and removal of me to another worksite was not even in accordance with the CBA, see Exhibit 3.

67. I believed this action was a pretext and punishment for reporting sexual harassment in the workplace because ABM has been subjected to a Court Decree regarding sexual harassment and discrimination.

68. Since ABM's Consent Decree has expired, and the now nonexistence of a third party EEO monitor; ABM has reverted back to its unfair discriminatory practices again. (Please see U.S. EEOC v. ABM Industries, Inc. and ABM Janitorial Services, Inc., et al., Case No. 1:07 CV 01428 LJO JLT).

69. ABM has not disputed the facts set forth herein and their causing me to quit for good and just cause. I was never discharged for misconduct; and despite my efforts to keep my position, ABM was not willing to resolve its discriminatory practices and did not care if I was harassed at work.

70. The facts herein set forth are undisputed to this date and ABM has not presented any sufficient, substantial, nor convincing evidence to rebut this Declaration.

VERIFICATION

I, ▓▓▓▓▓▓▓▓▓▓▓▓▓▓, am the CLAIMANT in the above-entitled action. I have read the foregoing and know the contents thereof. The same is true of my own knowledge, except as to those matters which are therein alleged on information and belief, and as to those matters, I believe it to be true. I declare under penalty of perjury under the laws of the State of California that the foregoing is true and correct, in

-11-
DECLARATION

EXHIBIT 1

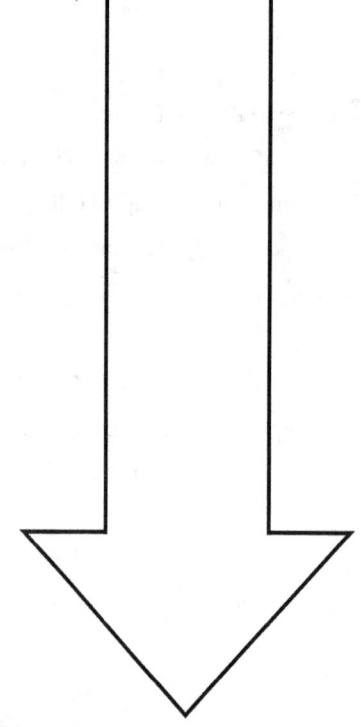

Sex Discrimination

Pre-Initial Complaint/ In Pro Per

SUPERIOR COURT OF THE STATE OF CALIFORNIA

COUNTY OF LOS ANGELES - CENTRAL DISTRICT

STANLEY MOSK COURTHOUSE

Complainant, v. Respondent.	Case No.: **DECLARATION OF** ▮ RE: QUID PRO QUO SEXUAL HARRASMENT Date: Friday, October ▮

I, ▮, SAY AND DECLARE AS FOLLOWS:

1. I am a Complainant in this legal issue, and if called as a witness, I could and would testify competently to these facts. I hereby reserve my rights of privacy under the California Constitution, Article 1, Section 1, privacy.

2. I disclose the facts set forth regarding this initial complaint against a female employee of a subtenant at the location inwhere I am contracted to work to perform professional services and labor. I have never made nor advanced any offers for sex in exchange for work at work.

-1-

DECLARATION RE QUID PRO QUO SEXUAL HARRASMENT

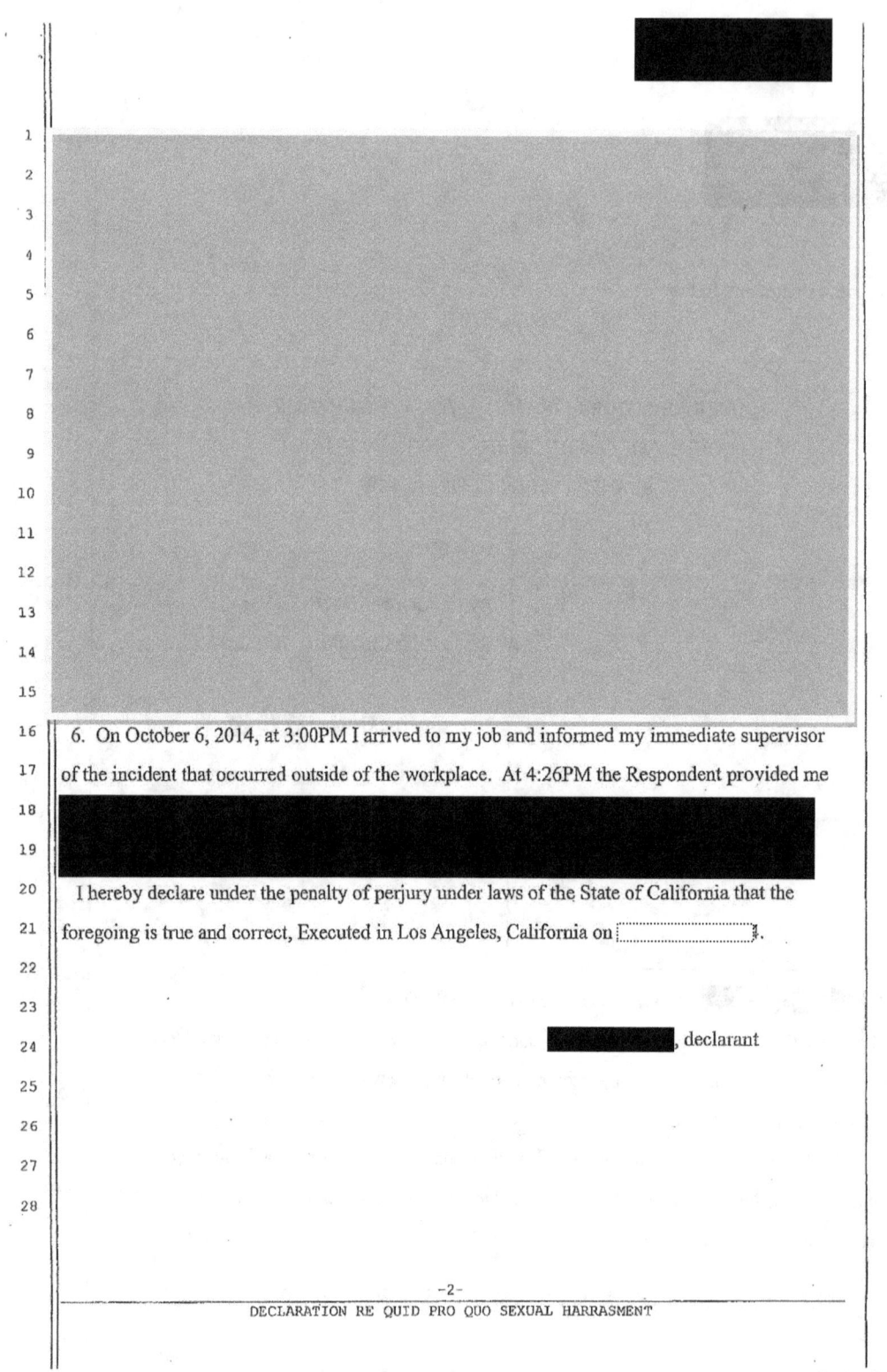

6. On October 6, 2014, at 3:00PM I arrived to my job and informed my immediate supervisor of the incident that occurred outside of the workplace. At 4:26PM the Respondent provided me

I hereby declare under the penalty of perjury under laws of the State of California that the foregoing is true and correct, Executed in Los Angeles, California on ▢.

▢, declarant

DECLARATION RE QUID PRO QUO SEXUAL HARRASMENT

SEX DISCRIMINATION

Subject: Fwd ▓▓▓ Declaration RE Quid Pro Quo Incident
From: ▓▓▓▓▓▓▓▓
To: ▓▓▓▓▓▓
Date: Monday, October 13, 2014 3:33 PM

---------- Forwarded message ----------
From ▓▓▓▓▓
Date: Fri, Oct 10, 2014 at 10:21 AM
Subject: ▓▓▓ Declaration RE Quid Pro Quo Incident
To: ▓▓▓▓▓▓▓▓▓▓▓▓

Please find my attached Declaration regarding the incident of quid pro quo sex harassment I reported and Exhibit A for supporting evidence of such.

I apologize for any inconvenience I may have caused you.

Feel free to contact me for further investigation.

Truthfully,

▓▓▓▓▓▓

Subject: Fwd ▓▓▓ Declaration RE Quid Pro Quo Incident
From: ▓▓▓▓▓▓▓▓▓▓
To: ▓▓▓▓▓▓▓▓▓▓
Date: Monday, October 13, 2014 3:33 PM

---------- Forwarded message ----------
From: ▓▓▓▓▓▓▓▓▓▓
Date: Fri, Oct 10, 2014 at 10:21 AM
Subject: ▓▓▓▓ Declaration RE Quid Pro Quo Incident
To: ▓▓▓▓▓▓▓▓▓▓

Please find my attached Declaration regarding the incident of quid pro quo sex harassment I reported and Exhibit A for supporting evidence of such.

I apologize for any inconvenience I may have caused you.

Feel free to contact me for further investigation.

Truthfully,

▓▓▓▓▓▓▓▓▓▓

* PAGE 72 IS REDACTED *

EXHIBIT 2

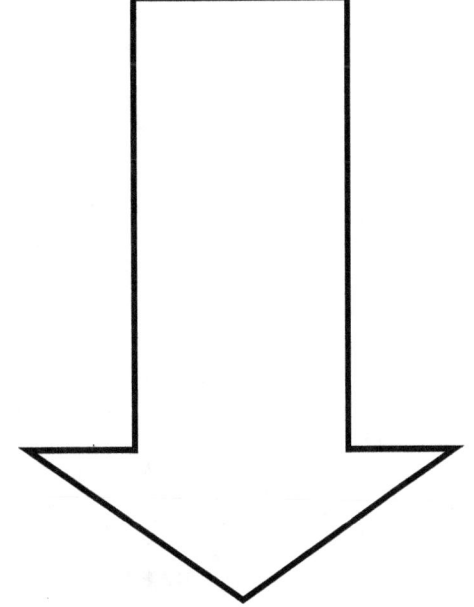

Activity Log

		800 S. Hope
		10/6/2014 16:46:15 PDT
		10/6/2014 16:50:27 PDT
1	Activity Date and Time	10/6/2014 16:26:15 PDT
4	On / Off Property	On Property
5	Choose current Activity category?	Officer Response
6	Officer Name:	■■■
7	What Action was Taken?	Other - type in
8	Comments or Other Details for Notes	Received note (4) from ■■■ employee ■■■ regarding non-business; filed.
9	Do you need to take a picture?	No

SEX DISCRIMINATION

Activity Log

21089502
800 S. Hope
10/11/2014 8:20:51 PDT
10/11/2014 0:32:22 PDT

1	Activity Date and Time	10/11/2014 8:20:51 PDT
4	On / Off Property	On Property
5	Choose current Activity category?	Officer Response
6	Officer Name:	[redacted]
7	What Action was Taken?	Communication
8	Comments or Other Details for Notes	[redacted] asked me a the security desk if I would be willing to work under her for [redacted] the owner of Freeway, to do part-time work, I declined.
9	Do you need to take a picture?	No

The EDD, EEOC, & Superior Court Legal Forms

21108122
800 S. Hope
10/13/2014 20:41:10 PDT
10/13/2014 20:40:23 PDT

Activity Log

1	Activity Date and Time	10/13/2014 18:41:09 PDT
4	On / Off Property	On Property
5	Choose current Activity category?	Officer Observation
6	What did you Observe?	Suspicious Activity
7	Comments or Other Details for Notes	Respondent, from my previous complaint/report; was at the security desk and used some curse words at me and attempted to argue with me regarding non-business.
8	Do you need to take a picture?	No

EXHIBIT 3

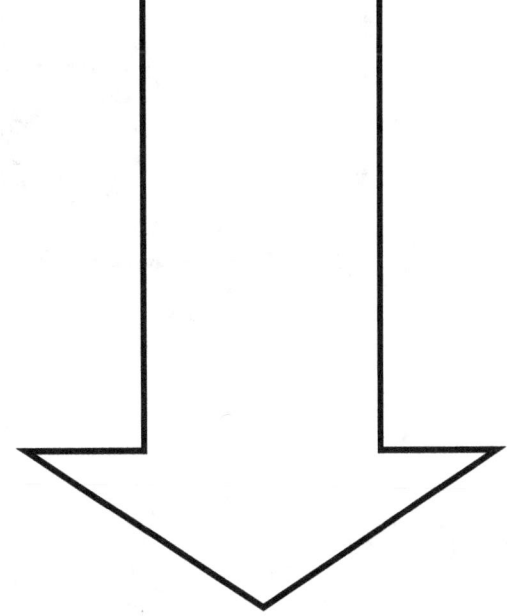

LOS ANGELES MASTER COLLECTIVE BARGAINING AGREEMENT

between

Security Employers

and

Service Employees International Union, United Service Workers West (SEIU-USWW)

Effective
June 22, 2013 through June 30, 2017

Sex Discrimination

TABLE OF CONTENTS

ARTICLE		PAGE
	PREAMBLE	3
1)	RECOGNITION	3-4
2)	UNION SECURITY	4-5
3)	NO DISCRIMINATION	5
4)	DISCIPLINE & DISCHARGE	5-7
5)	NO STRIKES/NO LOCKOUTS	7-8
6)	UNION REPRESENTATIVES	8-9
7)	TRAINING	9
8)	PROBATIONARY PERIOD	9-10
9)	SENIORITY	10-11
10)	JOB VACANCIES & CAREER ADVANCEMENT	11-12
11)	SCHEDULING	12
12)	WAGES	12-14
13)	WORKWEEK	14-16
14)	HOLIDAYS	16-17
15)	UNIFORMS	17-18
16)	FARES & TRAVEL	18
17)	VACATION	18-20
18)	SICK LEAVE	20-21
19)	HEALTH & WELFARE	21-23
20)	RETIREMENT	23
21)	PAY PERIODS	24
22)	BIDDING PROCEDURES	24-27
23)	LEAVE OF ABSENCE	28
24)	GENERAL CONDITIONS/RULES	28-29
25)	GRIEVANCE & ARBITRATION PROCEDURE	29-33
26)	MOST FAVORED NATIONS	33-34
27)	MANAGEMENT RIGHTS	34-35
28)	WAIVER	36
29)	INDIVIDUAL LEGAL RIGHTS	36
30)	DURATION & TERMINATION	37
	APPENDIX A – Geographic Definition of Tiers	38
	APPENDIX B – Plan Description	39
	APPENDIX C – Site-Specific Collective Bargaining Agreements	40
	APPENDIX D – Holiday Dates	41
	(Side Letter on Exclusions and additional Employer signature following Appendix D)	

Employers Signatory to

Los Angeles Master

Collective Bargaining Agreement

ABM Security Services
AlliedBarton Security Services
G4S Secure Solutions (USA) Inc.
Securitas Security Services USA, Inc.
Universal Protection Services
Guard-Systems, Inc.
Los Angeles Downtown Private Security

24.2 The Employer shall furnish to the Union copies of rules and regulations of general applicability to all employees, as well as any changes made thereto. This Section 2 shall not apply to rules applicable to a specific job site or post.

24.3 The Employer will establish stated call periods for each shift so as to minimize inconvenience to employees. Changes necessitated by seniority, changes in clients' needs, last minute orders, or other emergencies are recognized as exceptions.

24.4 The Employer shall comply with all applicable federal and Cal/OSHA laws and regulations pertaining to occupational health and safety, including the Hazardous Substance Information and Training Act.

ARTICLE 25
GRIEVANCE AND ARBITRATION PROCEDURE

25.1 During the term of this Agreement, all disputes and grievances shall be settled as quickly as possible by the Grievance Procedure provided herein except that the Employer may obtain injunctive relief from a Court to enforce Article 5 – No Strike/No Lockout. For the purpose of this Agreement, a grievance is defined as a difference of opinion between the Employer and the Union regarding only the meaning or application of this Agreement, presented to the Employer in writing within fourteen (14) days after it occurred, or when the employee or Union became aware of it, or should have become aware of it.

25.2 An employee and/or Union Representative may consult directly with his or her Supervisor on a matter that does not necessarily constitute a grievance. In any case, where an employee is not satisfied with respect to the disposition of a matter regarding the meaning or application of any provision of this Agreement, on which he or she has informally consulted with their Supervisor, the Union may submit the complaint as a grievance. The grievance will state, in addition to the employee's version of the facts, the specific portion of the Agreement allegedly violated, the date the alleged violation occurred and signed by the employee and the Union representative. If the grievance is filed on behalf of more than one employee, it may be signed by a Union representative.

STEP 1 – Employer's Designated Representative

The grievance shall first be submitted by the Union to the Employer's designated representative by fax, mail or electronic mail, and signed by the Union official, within fourteen (14) days from the date of the occurrence of the incident, or when the employee or Union became aware of it, or should have become aware of it. Such Employer designated representative shall, within seven (7) days after receiving the grievance, render his or her decision in writing

STEP 2 – Employer's Designated Manager or His or Her Appointed Representative

If the grievance has not been settled or answered during the above specific number of days under the above procedure, the Union may submit the grievance to the Employer's designated Manager or his or her appointed representative by fax, mail or electronic mail within seven (7) days after receipt of the initial decision in Step 1 by the Employer's representative. The Employer's designated Manager or his or her appointed representative shall, within seven (7) days after the receipt of the grievance, render a decision in writing by fax, mail or electronic mail to the Union. If requested, the designated Manager or his or her appointed representative will meet with the grievant(s) and/or appropriate Union representative(s) for the purpose of reviewing the matter. The Employer's designated Manager or his or her appointed representative responding at this Step Two shall be a person at a higher level within the Employer's organizational structure than the Employer's designated representative at Step 1.

The meeting shall be held on a mutually agreeable date within thirty (30) days following the request by the Union. If the grievance has not been resolved at the meeting held at this Step 2, the parties may agree to submit the grievance to a mediator of the Los Angeles, California office of the Federal Mediation and Conciliation Service (FMCS) as set forth in Step 3. If no agreement has been reached by the parties to submit the grievance to a mediator of the Los Angeles, California of the FMCS, within 7 days after the meeting held at Step2, the Union may proceed to Step 4 – Arbitration, as set forth herein.

STEP 3 – Mediation By the Federal Mediation and Conciliation Service (FMCS)

If the grievance has not been settled under the above procedure, the parties may agree to submit the grievance to a mediator of the Los Angeles, California office of the FMCS. If the parties agree to submit the grievance to a mediator, either or both parties shall make a written request to the FMCS Los Angeles office by fax, mail or electronic mail within seven (7) days after the meeting held at Step 2. The first available mediator shall meet with the parties and the affected employee to assist and offer advisory opinions in an effort to help them reach an agreement that resolves the grievance. If neither party requests mediation within the seven (7) day period, the Union may proceed to arbitration as set forth below in Step 4.

Without affecting the time lines set forth herein, the parties may also agree to request a specific mediator. It is the intention of the parties that the Step 3 mediation would be used for significant cases (e.g., suspensions, terminations and class grievances) and when there is a reasonable chance of resolution with the mediator's assistance.

STEP 4 - Arbitration

The Union may advance the grievance to Step 4 – Arbitration by making a written demand for arbitration by fax, mail or electronic mail to the FMCS, with a copy to the other party's representative, a) within twenty (20) days following the date the mediation was held at Step 3, or b) within thirty (30) days after the date the meeting was held at Step 2 if the parties did not agree to submit the grievance to a mediator of the FMCS.

The party making a demand for arbitration shall request the FMCS to provide the Employer and the Union with a list of seven (7) persons who are qualified and willing to act as arbitrators. Within fifteen (15) days of receipt of the Panel of Arbitrators from the FMCS, either party must

PREAMBLE

This Agreement is entered into effective June 22, 2013, between Service Employees International Union, United Service Workers West (SEIU-USWW) (successor to SEIU Local 2006/SOULA, hereinafter referred to as the "Union") and the following Employers:

ABM Security Services	(hereinafter "ABM")
AlliedBarton Security Services	(hereinafter "AlliedBarton")
G4S Secure Solutions (USA) Inc.	(hereinafter "G4S")
Securitas Security Services USA, Inc.	(hereinafter "Securitas")
Universal Protection Services	(hereinafter "Universal")
Guard-Systems, Inc.	(hereinafter "Guard-Systems")

Los Angeles Downtown Private Security

Other Employers may be added to this Preamble if (a) such Employers sign on to identical terms as provided in this Agreement, and (b) such Employers consent to the inclusion of their names in this Preamble.

In entering into this Agreement, the Union and the Employers recognize that the single greatest threat to their continued success is the proliferation of non-union competition in the security industry. As such, it is imperative that the Union and the Employers work together to preserve union jobs by supplying clients with the best possible security services. To this end, the Union and the Employers agree to resolve their problems through the procedures provided for in this contract and not by taking internal disputes to the customer for resolution. Only by cooperation and understanding each other's needs and the realities of the market place, can both the Union and the Employers prosper. Other security Employers may become signatories to this Agreement during its term, provided it is understood that under no circumstances shall any Employer or group of Employers be considered a multi-Employer bargaining unit.

ARTICLE 1
RECOGNITION

e Employer recognizes the Union as the exclusive bargaining representative for all of its non-supervisory full time and regular part time Security Officers employed by it at the single tenant, multi-tenant and flex office buildings and office parks of 75,000 square feet or greater in Los Angeles County in the State of California, but excluding all other employees including Security Officers employed in or at one of the following facilities: a) warehouse, b) public sector, c) industrial/manufacturing, d) distribution/logistics, e) retail, f) educational (K-12 and institutions of higher education), g) banking, but not administrative offices or branches housed in a commercial office building covered by this Agreement, h) medical office buildings, defined as facilities and buildings owned by health care companies which are used for patient care, i) hotels /lodging, and j) individuals who qualify as supervisors under Section 2(11) of the National Labor Relations Act, as amended. ("Act"). For the purposes of this Agreement, "security officer" shall have the same definition as "guard" under the Act.

Effective June 22, 2013, the Sunset Bronson and Sunset Gower Studios will be covered under this agreement and will be treated as covered accounts so long as the studios are being serviced by a union contractor at the time of bid.

ARTICLE 2
UNION SECURITY

2.1 It shall be a condition of employment that all employees of the Employer covered by this Agreement who are members of the Union in good standing on the effective date of this Agreement shall remain members in good standing and those who are not members on the effective date of this Agreement shall, on the thirtieth day following the effective date of this Agreement, become and remain members in good standing in the Union. It shall also be a condition of employment that all employees covered by this Agreement and hired on or after its effective date shall, on the thirtieth day following the beginning of such employment, become and remain members in good standing in the Union.

Membership in the Union shall be available to each employee on the same terms and conditions generally applicable to other members of the Union and shall not be denied or terminated for reasons other than the failure of such employee to tender the periodic dues and the initiation fee uniformly required as a condition of acquiring or retaining membership.

The Employer shall make known to any new hire their obligations under this provision, and present such new hire at that time, union membership materials including a membership application and voluntary payroll deduction authorization.

2.2 On a monthly basis, the Employer shall notify the Union of new hires and terminations providing name, Social Security number, work location and known address and telephone number. The Employer will notify the Union of known changes of phone numbers. Upon written request by the Union to the Employer's local designated representative, the Employer shall send by electronic mail a list of employee's names, their phone numbers and work locations to a designated representative of the Union, not more often than every six (6) months. It is understood that this list will include all employees covered under this Agreement.

2.3 The Employer agrees to deduct from the payrolls all initiation fees and periodic dues as required by the Union and voluntary contributions to the Union's Committee on Political Education ("COPE") Fund, Property Services Civic Engagement (PSCE) Fund, American Dream Fund (ADF), or any other authorized Political Action Fund, upon presentation by the Union or the employee of individual authorizations as required by law, signed by the employees directing the Employer to make such deductions from the employee's pay period each month and remit same to Union.

The Employer shall remit such fees, dues and voluntary contributions to the Union by no later than the twentieth (20th) day of the calendar month following the calendar month in which such deductions were made, together with a monthly list of the employees for whom it has deducted dues and on whose behalf it is remitting dues. The list shall include the first and last name of each employee, the total amount of dues which were deducted, and the Social Security number or other unique nine (9) digit employee identifier number associated with the individual employee.

All deduction authorization forms must be submitted to the Employer within six (6) months from the date the employee completed the form. The Employer will not process deduction authorization forms submitted in excess of six (6) months after their completion.

2.4 The Union will furnish the forms to be used for authorization. The Employer will furnish the Union with a duplicate copy of all signed authorizations, unless another procedure has been adopted.

2.5 The Union will completely defend and indemnify and hold the Employer free and harmless against any and all claims, damages, suits or other forms of liability whatsoever that shall arise out of or by reason of action taken by the Employer at the Union's request for the purpose of complying with any of the provisions of Article 2, including the Employer's termination of any employee for the failure to pay dues or an agency fee, including court costs and reasonable attorney fees. The Union shall have the right to select counsel to represent the Employer to contest, litigate, administer and/or settle any legal action with the Employer's consent, which shall not be unreasonably withheld.

ARTICLE 3
NO DISCRIMINATION

The Union and the Employer agree they shall not discriminate in violation of federal or state law against any applicant or employee in hiring, promotions, assignments, suspensions, discharge, terms and conditions of employment, wages, training, recall or lay-off status, because of race, color, ancestry, religion, creed, national origin, age, sex, maternity status, sexual orientation, gender expression, veteran status, or against a qualified individual with a disability (defined by the Americans i Disabilities Act). No employee or applicant for employment covered by this Agreement shall be discriminated against because of membership in the Union or activities on behalf of the Union.

ARTICLE 4
DISCIPLINE AND DISCHARGE

4.1 The Employer shall be free to discharge employees for refusal to obey lawful orders, incompetency, misrepresentation, intoxication, or any just cause. An employee who has not completed his or her probationary period may be disciplined or discharged without just cause and without recourse to the Grievance and Arbitration procedure set forth in Article 25.

4.2 The Employer shall be free to discipline any employee who commits an infraction, which, while not being sufficient to constitute just cause for discharge, is sufficient to warrant some lesser disciplinary action. However, no employee who has completed the probationary period will be discharged for offenses, which do not in and of themselves constitute just cause for discharge unless the employee has progressed through the discipline process and been given the opportunity to correct his/her behavior.

Warning notices shall be issued within ten (10) days after the Employer knew or should have known of the offense. A copy of the warning shall be sent to the Union. Each warning notice shall contain a place for the employee to sign to acknowledge receipt without admitting guilt.

Warning or disciplinary notices may not be considered as a part of the Employer's discipline process after twelve (12) months and shall be no longer valid for the purpose of discipline.

4.3 In addition to those circumstances mentioned elsewhere in this Agreement, just cause circumstances for discharge shall include, but not be limited to, unlawful use or unlawful possession of controlled substances, intoxication, insubordination, theft, excessive absenteeism, gross negligence, failure to comply with reasonable rules, policies or directives promulgated by the Employer and clearly communicated to the employee (where such failure to comply constitutes serious misconduct or creates a safety concern), use of unnecessary force or disrespectful treatment of a tenant; visitor or employee and inability or unwillingness to be trained to fulfill existing or modified security needs of the Employer, the building owner or its tenants. The Union further understands and agrees that the Employer provides an important service to its tenants of a personalized nature to fulfill their security needs, as those needs are perceived by the Employer, the building owner and the tenants. Accordingly, the provisions of this Section shall be implemented and interpreted by the parties and by an arbitrator in arbitration proceedings so as to give significant consideration to such needs.

4.4 The Employer will discharge any employee who is denied registration or whose registration is canceled by the Department of Consumer Affairs of the State of California or any other governmental agency.

Employees who have renewed their registration and document this with a receipt or similar proof by the end of the BSIS grace period, but have not yet received their new registration cards, shall not be denied work, subject to BSIS regulations.

Any employee, who by reason of the requirements of his job assignment must pass a test prescribed by any governmental agency or obtain a permit from any governmental agency and is not able to pass the test to obtain such a permit, shall be removed from the job. The employee will then be offered the first available job for which the employee is qualified that becomes available within the same dispatch area. If the employee refuses the first available job for which the employee is qualified and which is located in his/her geographic area, he/she may be permanently removed from the payroll. Discharge under this Article for failure to possess a license, except as limited above in this Section, shall be without recourse to the Grievance Procedure of Article 25.

SEX DISCRIMINATION

performance or to any grievance concerning the employee (as those phrases are defined by state law), shall follow the following procedure: submit a written request to the Employer's Human Resources Department (1) specifying the personnel and/or payroll information and time periods desired; and (2) indicating thereon whether the employee, during his/her unpaid non-working time, or his/her named designated representative, will inspect such records at a mutually convenient time, or pick up copies at the Employer's premises, or whether he/she desires to have electronic copies e-mailed to the e-mail address provided on his/her written request, and (3) if the employee or his/her representative elects to pick up copies of the documents at the Employer's premises, he/she first remits cash or a check made payable to the Employer for the cost of actual reproduction of the records (at the rate $0.10 per page); however this payment shall not be required from the Union when the copies are produced pursuant to the grievance/arbitration procedure. A former employee may receive a copy of said documents by mail if he/she also first reimburse the Employer for actual postal expenses.

Nothing herein shall require the Employer to produce any document that is exempt or excluded from disclosure or production by any law. If a grievance has been submitted by the Union as set forth in Section 25.2, or if any formal legal proceeding is commenced that relates to a personnel matter against the Employer involving the employee or former employee, the right to inspect or copy personnel records which relate to such grievance or legal proceeding ceases during the pendency of the grievance and/or legal proceeding.

ARTICLE 26
MOST FAVORED NATIONS

26.1 If during the term of this Agreement, the Union enters into or honors an agreement or understanding with another Employer or group of Employers employing security officers working in similar facilities as covered by this Agreement that provides for more favorable hours, wages and/or terms and conditions of employment (as that phrase has been defined under the National Labor Relations Act, as amended) than those set forth in this Master Agreement, any Employer bound by this Master Agreement shall be entitled to said more favorable hours, wages and/or terms and conditions upon request. To effectuate this Article of the parties' Master Agreement, the Union agrees to disclose the existence of any written or oral agreement or understanding it has or may have with any other Employer. The foregoing does not apply to the situations addressed in Sections 22.5(b) and 22.6(e) above.

26.2 If the Employer believes that the Union has entered into or is honoring an agreement or understanding that is more favorable as defined herein, the Employer shall notify the Union and the parties shall meet and confer to discuss such within the next 72 hours.

26.3 If the matter has not been resolved within 72 hours of notification to the Union, the Employer may request a list of seven (7) persons from the Federal Mediation and Conciliation Service. The parties will select an arbitrator using an alternate striking method. From that point forward,

the issue shall be handled and processed in accordance with Step 4, paragraph 4 and the subsequent provisions of the Grievance and Arbitration Procedure set forth in Article 25.

26.4 The arbitrator shall decide the issue of whether or not the Union has entered into or is honoring an agreement or understanding with another Employer or group of Employers employing security officers working in similar facilities as covered by this Agreement that would allow the Employer to be granted similar conditions as defined in Section 1 above.

ARTICLE 27
MANAGEMENT RIGHTS

27.1 Subject to the terms of this Agreement, the Employer shall have the exclusive right to manage and direct the workforce covered by this Agreement. Among the exclusive rights of management, but not intended as a wholly inclusive list of them are; the right to plan, direct and control all operations performed at the various locations served by the Employer; to direct and schedule the workforce; to determine the methods, procedures, equipment, operations and or services to be utilized and, or provided or to discontinue their performance by the employees of the Employer and, or subcontract the same; to transfer, or relocate any or all of the operations of the business to any location or discontinue such operations, by sale or otherwise in whole or in part at any time; to establish, increase or decrease the number of work shifts, their starting and ending times, determine the work duties of employees; promulgate, post and enforce reasonable rules and regulations governing the conduct and acts of employees during working hours; to require that duties other than normally assigned be performed; select supervisory employees; train employees; discontinue or reorganize or combine any part of the organization; to promote and demote employees consistent with the needs of the business; to discipline, suspend and discharge for just cause; to relieve employees from duty for lack of work or any other legitimate reason; to cease acting as a contractor at any location or cease performing certain functions at any locations, even though employees at that location may be terminated or relieved from duty as a result. In no case will this Article be used for the purpose of unlawfully discriminating against any employees.

27.2 The foregoing statements of management rights and Employer functions are not all inclusive, but indicate the type of matters or rights, which belong to and are inherent in management, and shall not be construed in any way to exclude other Employer functions and rights not specifically enumerated. Any of the rights, power or authority the Employer had when there was no Agreement are retained by the Employer and may be exercised without prior notice to or consultation with the Union except those specifically abridged or modified by this Agreement and any supplementary subsequent agreement which may be made and executed by the parties.

27.3 The Union recognizes that the Employer provides a service of critical importance to the customer and that this Agreement shall be interpreted so as to give primary consideration to grievance, that issue shall be resolved by a neutral arbitrator selected in accordance with Step 4 of Section 2 of this Article.

25.9 The Union and the Employer intend that the grievance and arbitration provisions in the Collective Bargaining Agreement shall be the exclusive method of resolving all disputes between the Employer and the Union and the employees covered by this agreement unless otherwise set forth or required under applicable law. Such disputes include "wage and hour claims or disputes," which shall include statutory claims over the payment of wages for all time worked, uniform maintenance, training time, rest and meal periods, overtime pay, vacation pay, and all other wage hour related matters. The parties agree that any employee's or employees' wage and hour claims or disputes relative to a violation of wage and hour law shall be resolved through the arbitration process provided for in this Agreement to the extent permitted by law and the employees (by and through the Union) shall have access to the arbitration provision in this Agreement for the purpose of resolving any wage and hour claims or disputes.

25.10 Regarding wage and hour claims or disputes:

a. The Union has the exclusive right to assert collective or class action grievances or grievances on behalf of more than one employee. All such grievances shall be initiated and processed in accordance with the standard provisions of the grievance and arbitration procedure, except as provided herein. The employees (by and through the union) shall be provided all substantive rights and remedies available under applicable law including the applicable statute of limitations.

b. Where the Union chooses not to assert a grievance under Section (a) above, an employee may assert claims or disputes to the Department of Labor or through a civil action on behalf of himself or herself individually concerning a wage and hour claim or dispute and the employee shall be provided all substantive rights and remedies that they would otherwise be entitled to under applicable law. As set forth in paragraph 25.10(a) an individual cannot pursue class and/or collective wage and hour claims or disputes to the Department of Labor or through civil litigation.

25.11 These provisions are not intended to limit or curtail employees' individual rights. To the contrary, it is the goal of the Employer to swiftly and fairly address and resolve employee concerns. In no event shall this Article or this agreement be read to construe a waiver of individual rights to pursue discrimination claims through administrative proceedings or civil actions.

25.12 The Employer and the Union agree to work swiftly and cooperatively to resolve and remediate, if necessary, any disputes that arise.

25.13 An employee covered by this Agreement who desires to inspect and/or receive copies of payroll records related to him/her, and/or personnel records relating to the employee's

32

---

contact the other for the purpose of selecting an arbitrator. Without waiving any of the time limits herein, if the parties mutually agree, they may select an arbitrator without use of the FMCS. If a party does not respond in writing within fifteen (15) days to a written demand from the other party to select an arbitrator from the Panel of Arbitrators sent to them by the FMCS, the party making the demand for arbitration shall have the right to unilaterally select the arbitrator from those names listed in the Panel unless the law permits the other party to refuse to proceed to arbitration.

25.3 Any grievance shall be considered withdrawn with prejudice if not filed and processed by the Union in strict accordance with the time limitations set forth above, unless time limits are extended or waived by mutual agreement in writing. Failure of the Employer to act within the time limit set forth in any Step shall entitle the Union to proceed to the next step of the grievance procedure.

25.4 The award of such arbitrator shall be in writing and shall be final and binding upon the Employer, the Union, and the employee or employees involved. The arbitrator shall consider and decide only the particular grievance presented in the written stipulation of the Employer and the Union. The arbitrator's decision shall be based solely upon an interpretation of the provisions of this Agreement. The arbitrator shall not have the right to amend, take away, modify, add to, change or disregard any of the provisions of this Agreement. The parties to the case shall share equally the expense of the arbitrator, including the hearing room and transcript incurred with the arbitration. The transcript taken at the Arbitration Hearing will constitute the official record of the Hearing. The party or parties requesting a copy of the transcript shall incur the cost of the transcript. Neither party shall be required to purchase a copy of the transcript. The Employer and the Union are only responsible for the wages and expenses of its own representatives and witnesses.

25.5 Grievances involving discharge or indefinite suspension must be presented directly to Step 2 of the grievance procedure. A grievance by the Employer against the Union must be presented directly to Step 4 of the Grievance Procedure and within seven (7) days of the Employer notifying the Union of its grievance in writing, the Employer shall request a list of potential arbitrators from the FMCS. Step 4, paragraph 1 shall not apply in the case of grievance filed by the Employer against the Union.

25.6 Without affecting any of the time limitations set forth herein, the Employer and the Union may settle the grievance.

25.7 In calculating time for purposes of this Article, Saturdays, Sundays and the Holidays cited in Article 14 shall not be counted. Time limits hereinabove mentioned may be modified, if desired, only in writing, by mutual agreement between the parties' designated representatives.

25.8 No more than one dispute may be submitted to any one arbitrator at the same hearing unless the parties agree to such in writing. If the Employer raises arbitrability as a defense to any

31

SEX DISCRIMINATION

ARTICLE 28
WAIVER

If any provisions of this Agreement or the application of such provision to any person or circumstances be ruled contrary to law, by any Federal or State Court or duly authorized agency, the remainder of this Agreement or the application of such provisions to other persons or circumstances shall not be affected thereby. The parties acknowledge that during the negotiations which resulted in this Agreement, each had the unlimited right and opportunity to make demands and proposals with respect to any subject or matter not removed by law from the area of collective bargaining and that the understandings and agreements arrived at by the parties after the exercise of that right and opportunity are set forth in this Agreement. Therefore, the Employer and the Union, for the life of this Agreement, each voluntarily and unqualifiedly waives the right, and each agrees that the other shall not be obligated to bargain collectively with respect to any subject or matter not specifically referred to or covered in this Agreement, even though such subjects or matters may have been within the knowledge or contemplation of either or both of the parties at the time they negotiated or signed this Agreement, except as required by law.

The wages and fringe benefits set forth in the Master Agreement, and any Appendices are minimum conditions, and the Employer may provide greater wages and/or fringe benefits in its sole discretion.

ARTICLE 29
INDIVIDUAL LEGAL RIGHTS

29.1 The Union is obligated to represent all employees without discrimination based upon national or ethnic origin. The Union is therefore obligated to protect employees against violations of their legal rights occurring in the workplace, including unreasonable search and seizure by a governmental agency.

29.2 In the event an issue arises involving the employment eligibility or social security number of an employee, the Employer shall promptly notify the employee in writing. Upon request, the Employer shall provide the Union with a copy of any correspondence or notice which the Employer receives regarding the immigration or work-authorization status of a bargaining unit employee.

29.3 If a question regarding an employee's immigration or work-authorization status arises and the employee takes leave to correct any immigration related problems or issues, the Employer, upon the employee's return, shall hire the employee into the next available job for which he or she is qualified.

29.4 Any lawful corrections in an employee's documentation, name, or social security number shall not be considered new employment or a break in service, and shall not be cause for adverse action.

---

customer needs and preferences, provided that the foregoing will not be construed to abrogate any rights under this Agreement.

27.4 Removal of Employees by Client Request

(a) If a customer demands that the Employer remove an employee from further employment at a location, the Employer shall have the right to comply with such demand.

However, unless the Employer has just cause to discharge the employee, the Employer will use its best efforts to place him/her in another job in same County not to exceed ten (10) miles from the job site from which he or she was removed, and schedule said employee with no loss of wages, seniority or benefits and with the same shift.

The Employer must have just cause to issue discipline to an employee removed from a job location based on client request.

Upon written request from the Union, a representative of the Employer (senior-level Employer representative at a level to be mutually agreed upon between the Union and each Employer upon the implementation of this Agreement), shall confirm in writing that the Employer received a request from the client to remove the employee.

(b) If the Employer is unable to place the officer in a comparable position as listed above, the employee will be considered laid off for lack of work and the Employer will not challenge the employee's claim for unemployment. Upon written request by the Union, the Employer shall document its efforts to place the employee in another job as set forth above.

(c) An employee removed from a job location due to client demand shall have the right to use accrued vacation time if the employee has not been placed in a new location as specified above within five (5) business days of the removal.

(d) If an employee who has been removed from a location declines another job with the Employer with the same wages, benefits, schedule and geographic area referenced above, the Employer shall have no further obligation toward that employee and the employee shall be considered a voluntary quit.

27.5 If the Employer subcontracts work covered by this Agreement, the Employer shall give thirty (30) days notice of such subcontracting, and upon request by the Union shall discuss the effects of such subcontracting.

ARTICLE 30
DURATION & TERMINATION

This Agreement shall become effective upon ratification of the Agreement, June 22, 2013, and shall remain in full force and effect through June 30, 2017, when it shall terminate and shall thereafter renew year to year, unless either party desires to modify or terminate this Agreement at the end of its term. Written notice must be provided to the other party at least sixty (60), prior to the expiration date in accordance with the National Labor Relations Act, as amended.

Service Employees International Union

Name: _Anton Hunnel_
Title: _Vice President_
SEIU USWW

Name: _MJ Ortho_
Title: _Bargaining Director_
SEIU-USWW

Name: _Jennifer Salkury_
Title: _VP, Midwest / So Calif._

Name: _Robert A Brandt_
Title: _Bargaining Com._
SEIU-USWW

Name: _Chris Cruz_
Title: _Bargaining Comm_
SEIU-USWW

Name: _Michael Granger_
Title: _Bargaining Committee_
SEIU-USWW

Name: _Bargaining Committee_
SEIU-USWW

Name:
Title:

Name:
Title:

Name: _____
Title: _____
Company: ABM Security Services

Name: _____
Title: Director, Labor Relations
Company: AlliedBarton Security Services

Name: _____
Title: Mn Compl- Lux Rel
Company: G4S Secure Solutions (USA) Inc.

Name: _____
Title: Vice President
Company: Securitas Security Services USA, Inc.

Name: _____
Title: VP-IR
Company: Universal Protection Services

Name: _____
Title: VP/GM
Company: Guard-Systems, Inc.

APPENDIX A
Geographic Definition of Tiers

1. **TIER 1(a) (Downtown Los Angeles, Century City)**

   (a) Downtown Los Angeles defined as follows: That area bounded on the north by a line extending along the Golden State Freeway to Alameda Street; on the east by Alameda Street; on the south by Santa Monica Freeway and on the west by a line extending along Hoover Street to Alvarado, then along Alvarado to Glendale Boulevard, and then along Glendale Boulevard to the Golden State Freeway; it shall also include the area bounded on the south by the north side of the 101 Freeway, on the east by the Los Angeles River, on the north by the south side of Caesar Chavez Blvd; and on the east by Alameda Street.

   (b) Century City area of the City of Los Angeles defined as follows: That area bounded on the north by Santa Monica Boulevard, on the east by Century Park East (including even numbers); on the south by Pico Boulevard and on the west by Beverly Glen.

2. **TIER 1(b) (Westside Area)**

   Tier 1(b) shall be defined as follows: that area bounded by a line from the Pacific Ocean on the west, Sunset Blvd. on the north until it meets North San Vicente Blvd, south or North San Vicente Blvd. to Robertson Blvd., south on Robertson Blvd. until it meets Interstate 10, west on Interstate 10 until it meets Interstate 405, south on Interstate 405 until it meets La Tijera Blvd., southwest on La Tijera Blvd. until it meets Manchester Blvd, then west along Manchester Blvd. to the Pacific Ocean, but not including addresses on Manchester Blvd.

3. **TIER 2 (Other Areas)**

   All geographic areas in Los Angeles County in the State of California which are not included in Tier 1(a) or Tier 1(b) as defined above.

EXHIBIT 4

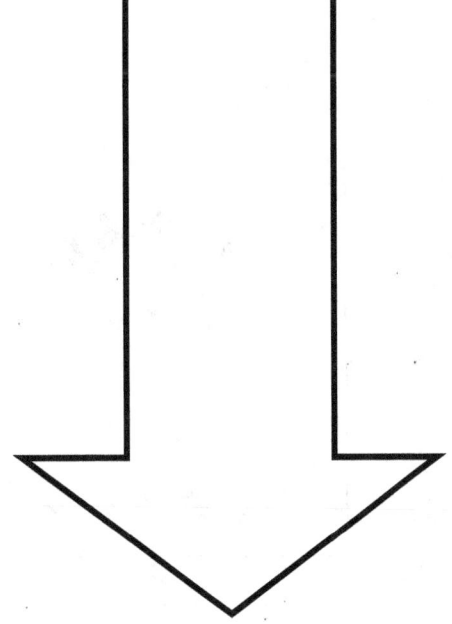

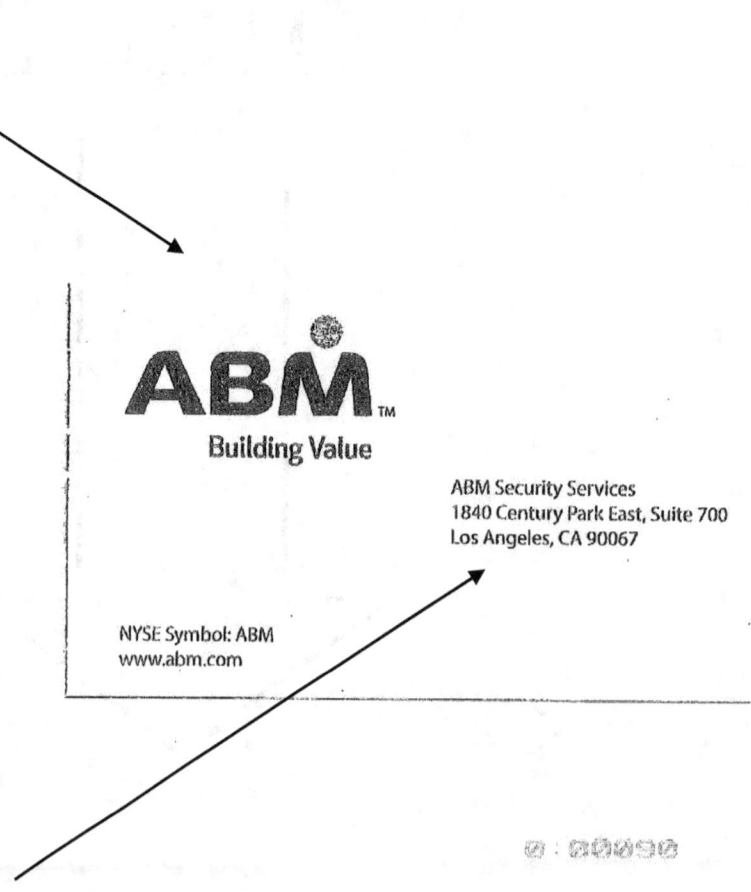

EXHIBIT 5

The EDD, EEOC, & Superior Court Legal Forms

ACCOUNT NAME: CBRE THE PLAZA					BASE-2		
JOB NUMBER: 15995		DAY: Wednesday			DATE: 11-05-14		
DATE	PRINT NAME	TIME IN	LUNCH OUT	LUNCH IN	TIME OUT	DEVIATION	SIGNATURE
DAY SHIFT (0700-1500)							
11-5-14	Brent Peterson	700	1150	1250	1500		
11-5-14	███████	0700			1100	TRAINING	███████
SWING SHIFT (1500-2300)							
11-5-14	███████	1500	2000	2030	2300		███████
Graveyard shift (2300-0700)							
11-6-14	███████	2300	0300	0330	0700		███████

1. This time sheet will be used for payroll back-up you must sign IN & OUT at the beginning of & end of each shift. Entries must be clearly printed. Do not pre-enter times.
2. All regular hours will be logged on a daily basis for each pay week. A separate time sheet must be prepared for each pay week or partial pay week in a pay period each pay week starts at 0001 hrs. on Saturday morning and ends 2400 hrs. Friday night.
3. Each work day begins at 0001 hrs. & ends at 2400 hrs. If your shift is 2300 hrs. to 0700 hrs. then sign-in at 2300 to 2400 hrs. on that day and enter 0001 to 0700 hrs on the next day
4. By initialing the time sheet, you are certifying that this is accurate account of the work hours during this pay period. You are also certifying that you the opportunity to take a 30 min. of paid non-work time that day and two rest periods. You also acknowledge having taken a 30 min. meal period for every 5 hours worked. If you are unable to take a meal period during a shift, you must indicate such on the day and shift you were unable to take a meal break.
5. All time sheets must be faxed to the branch payroll department three times each week, on Monday, Wednesday, Friday and 1st day of the month no later than 0800hrs. on these days. The site supervisor must review, validate and sign the completed Timesheets prior to faxing it to the branch office.

Supervisor's signature _____ Date: 11/6/14

EXHIBIT 6

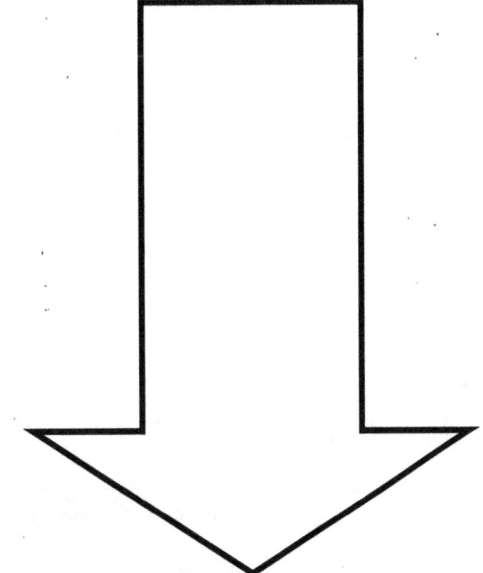

The EDD, EEOC, & Superior Court Legal Forms

EEOC CHARGE OF DISCRIMINATION

⬇

EEOC Form 5 (11/09)

CHARGE OF DISCRIMINATION This form is affected by the Privacy Act of 1974. See enclosed Privacy Act Statement and other information before completing this form.	Charge Presented To: ☐ FEPA ☒ EEOC	Agency(ies) Charge No(s):

California Department Of Fair Employment & Housing _____ and EEOC
State or local Agency, if any

Name (indicate Mr., Ms., Mrs.)	Home Phone (Incl. Area Code)	Date of Birth
███████████		

Street Address	City, State and ZIP Code

Named is the Employer, Labor Organization, Employment Agency, Apprenticeship Committee, or State or Local Government Agency That I Believe Discriminated Against Me or Others. *(If more than two, list under PARTICULARS below.)*

Name	No. Employees, Members	Phone No. (Include Area Code)
ABM INDUSTRIES	**500 or More**	**(213)** ███████

Street Address	City, State and ZIP Code
███████	Los Angeles, CA 90007

Name	No. Employees, Members	Phone No. (Include Area Code)

Street Address	City, State and ZIP Code

DISCRIMINATION BASED ON *(Check appropriate box(es).)*

☐ RACE ☐ COLOR ☒ SEX ☐ RELIGION ☐ NATIONAL ORIGIN
☐ RETALIATION ☐ AGE ☐ DISABILITY ☐ GENETIC INFORMATION
☐ OTHER *(Specify)*

DATE(S) DISCRIMINATION TOOK PLACE
Earliest _____ Latest _____

☐ CONTINUING ACTION

THE PARTICULARS ARE *(If additional paper is needed, attach extra sheet(s))*:

On or about ███████████, I believe I was disciplined because I reported sexual harassment in the workplace, in violation of Title VII of the Civil Rights Act of 1964, as amended.

I want this charge filed with both the EEOC and the State or local Agency, if any. I will advise the agencies if I change my address or phone number and I will cooperate fully with them in the processing of my charge in accordance with their procedures.	NOTARY – *When necessary for State and Local Agency Requirements*
I declare under penalty of perjury that the above is true and correct.	I swear or affirm that I have read the above charge and that it is true to the best of my knowledge, information and belief. SIGNATURE OF COMPLAINANT SUBSCRIBED AND SWORN TO BEFORE ME THIS DATE *(month, day, year)*
Date Charging Party Signature	

SEX DISCRIMINATION

MEMORANDUM OF POINTS AND AUTHORITIES IN SUPPORT OF CLAIMANT DUMAS' APPEAL FOR UNEMPLOYMENT INSURANCE BENEFITS

To The Office Of Unemployment Insurance Appeals Board, I, Claimant ▬, am entitled to unemployment insurance benefits for the foregoing reasons:

I. INTRODUCTION

1. Pursuant to the California Unemployment Insurance Code Section §1256.2 (a) states: "Except as otherwise provided by subdivision (b), an individual who terminates his or her employment shall not be deemed to have left his or her most recent work without good cause if his or her employer deprived the individual of equal employment opportunities on any basis listed in subdivision (a) § 12940 of the Government Code, as those basis are defined in Sections § 12926 and § 12926.1 of the Government Code."

2. ABM intentionally deprived me of equal opportunities in my employment within the company and has shown no intention of removing it. I, the Claimant, made reasonable efforts to provide ABM with the opportunity to remove the deprivation and reinstate me back to my position but ABM has refused to reinstate to this date despite my efforts.

3. The California statutes presume that an individual has not voluntarily left his work without good cause. This statute implements payment of benefits to the unemployed, as in this case, so as to reduce suffering caused by employers such as ABM.

4. ABM has the burden of rebutting the existence of a presumed fact, this means that to overcome this presumption of fact, ABM must prove by a preponderance of evidence that I quit without probable cause or was discharge for misconduct in connection with his work. Perales v. Dept. of Human Resources Development (1973) 32 Cal.App.3d 332 [108 Cal.Rptr. 167].

5. The Unemployment Insurance Code § 1256 states "An individual is presumed to have been discharged for reasons other than misconduct in connection with his or her work and not to have voluntarily quit without good cause unless his or her employer has given written notice to the

MEMORANDUM OF POINTS AND AUTHORITIES

contrary to the department as provided in Section 1327, setting forth facts sufficient to overcome the presumption. The presumption provided by this section is rebuttable."

6. ABM has not presented any written notice to the contrary, as I was informed that ABM is not a party to this action and there is no contrary evidence to dispute my Declarations, Statement of Evidence, and Exhibits.

II. ARGUMENT

7. Sexual harassment is illegal in the workplace and harassment of employees is forbidden under California Law under California Government Code Section §12940 (a), (h), (I), (j) (3); (k). Employers have a duty, and are obligated to train their employees in sexual harassment prevention and procedures under California Government Code § 12950.1 (a).

8. ABM operates in the State of California, therefore ABM has the legal duty and obligation to take to preventative "immediate and corrective action" against sexual harassment in order to protect their employee, male, female, or transgender, even if it is alleged to have been committed by a non-employee. I, the Claimant performed my legal duty and obligation to report the unlawful harassment in the workplace to ABM.

9. "Discrimination" refers to bias in the exercise of personnel management authority on behalf of the ABM, in which has taken some adverse action against me such as the adverse job assignment, disciplinary action, and/or demotion. In Roby, "Harassment" refers to the bias that is expressed or communicated through interpersonal relations in the workplace". Roby v. McKesson Corp. (2009) 47 Cal.4th 686, 706 [101 Cal.Rptr.3d 773, 787-788].

10. The California Fair Employment and Housing Act (FEHA) requires and mandates that ABM must take "all reasonable steps necessary to prevent discrimination and harassment from occurring", see California Government Code§ 12940(k). It is ABM's legal duty to perform reasonable steps as the means to explore reasonable solutions in order to prevent and correct harassment in the workplace.

11. As the harassment had already occurred, the duty to maintain a harassment free work environment required ABM to have taken remedial action, in which they did not; and not only change the harasser's behavior, but to have deterred potential harassers from unlawful conduct.

-2-
MEMORANDUM OF POINTS AND AUTHORITIES
RE: Case No.

SEX DISCRIMINATION

ABM never took remedial action to change the harasser's unlawful conduct toward me the Claimant. I, the Claimant followed ABM policy as he was instructed and was deprived equal opportunities in employment for complaining about sexual harassment.

12. An employer like ABM whom failed in instituting their own anti-harassment policy risks liability for any harassment in the workplace. For example, in Yates v. Avco Corp. (6th Cir. 1987) F.2d 630, 635. This type of negligence has subjected ABM to increased liability for depriving me of my equal employment opportunities and must be held accountable.

13. My right to receive unemployment insurance benefits should be determinative of my right to sue my former employer, such as in this case. Chrysler Corp. v. California Employment Stabilization Commission (1953) 116 Cal.App.2d 8 [253 P.2d 68].

14. The evidence set forth in Claimant's *Statement of Evidence to be Introduced* presented supports this legal reasoning, that the Claimant's right to receive insurance benefits can be determined on his right to sue for discrimination by ABM in violation of the FEHA and Title VII. Exhibit 6.

15. In Prescod v. California Unemployment Ins. Appeals Bd. (1976) 57 Cal.App.3d 29 [127 Cal.Rptr. 540], where's ones work is made intolerable over period of time by discriminatory acts of employer, such as refusal to reinstate, demotion, or loss of promotional opportunity, there is "good cause'" for leaving employment.

16. While harassing conduct need not occur in workplace in order to render employer liable under FEHA, it must occur in work related context. Capitol City Foods, Inc. v. Superior Court (1992) 5 Cal.App.4th 1042 [7 Cal.Rptr.2d 418]. An employee, such as me, is not required to use legal terms or buzzwords when opposing discrimination or harassment. Yanowitz v. L'Oreal USA, Inc. (2005) 103 Cal.App.4th 1021 [32 CalRptr.3d 436].

17. Although I contacted the union, the court held in Greene v. Pomona Unified School Dist. (1995) 32 Cal.App.4th 1216 [38 Cal.Rptr. 2d 770], that there is no need to require unions to become involved with employees' claims of discrimination against their employer based on protected characteristics because employees have remedies available to them through Department of Fair Employment and Housing (DFEH) and the EEOC, civil actions authorized

-3-
MEMORANDUM OF POINTS AND AUTHORITIES
RE: Case No.

under the FEHA and under Title VII.

18. Under California Government Code §12950.1 (a) it is the duty of employer to train and educate on how to prevent and correct sexual harassment in the workplace. It is the duty of employee to report it promptly, in which I did. ABM has deprived me the right to be free from discrimination and harassment in the workplace, and I am strongly opposed to harassment and discrimination in the workplace.

19. ABM has a history of ratifying harassment in the workplace and disciplining its employees for reporting it. Please see Ventura v. ABM Industries Inc. (2012) 212 Cal.4th 258 [150 Cal.Rptr.3d 861]. ABM, US SEC File Number 1-8929.

II. CONCLUSION

20. For these reasons, Claimant left his most recent employer, ABM, for good and just cause because he was deprived of equal opportunities and ABM failed to remove the deprivation. No misconduct as the basis for discharge has been alleged; and any misconduct alleged is pretextual and not in compliance with the Collective Bargaining Agreement. The first and final disciplinary advisory notice was a pretext to justify ABM's constructive termination of his employment for complaining about harassment in the workplace.

PRAYER FOR RELIEF:

WHEREFORE, and based on the foregoing, CLAIMANT prays to the Honorable Administrative Law Judge Michael Kurz, to please find:

1. Claimant left his most recent work for good cause; and
2. Claimant was not discharged from his most recent work for misconduct; and
3. Claimant is eligible for unemployment insurance benefits.

Dated: January 19, 2015   Respectfully submitted,

                                                                Claimant

Sex Discrimination

CLAIMANT

THE STATE OF CALIFORNIA
EMPLOYMENT DEVELOPMENT DEPARTMENT
UNEMPLOYMENT INSURANCE APPEALS BOARD

Claimant,	CASE NO.: ▓▓▓▓▓
	CLAIMANT STATEMENT OF QUESTION, FACTS, AND INFORMATION IN DISPUTE
v.	**RE RECORD OF CLAIM STATUS INTERVEIW VQ**
	Administrative Law Judge: Judge Michael Kurz
ABM,	**Time:** 2:30PM
Respondent.	**Date:** January 20, 2015
	Location: Long Beach Office

INTRODUCTION

1. The actual facts set forth herein are undisputed between the parties to this legal Action and other legal matters pending (Exhibit 6, Claimant's EEOC Charge).

-1-

CLAIMANT ▓▓▓ STATEMENT OF FACTS AND INFORMATION
IN DISPUTE RE RECORD OF CLAIM STATUS INTERVIEW VQ

2. The INTERVIEWER reporting in the "Record of Claim Status" was not present to witness the adverse employment actions taken against me for reporting harassment from 10/6/14 to 11/5/14. ABM, thus far, has not been a party to this legal Action but is aware of this hearing and has opportunity to respond on their own behalf.

3. ABM has not presented any evidence to contradict that I was harassed, discriminated, and deprived of equal opportunities at ABM from October 6, 2014 to November 5, 2014. I have knowledge and evidence of these facts, and if called as a witness in a sexual harassment and employment discrimination case, I can and will testify competently to those facts in order to rebut ABM.

QUESTION NO. 5:

4. The question of No. 5 in the 'Record of Claim Status' states "Potentially Disqualifying Facts VQ Reason' 'On 100514, I Reported someone sexually harassing me at ▓▓▓▓, I was Demoted and Given Less Terms'".

STATEMENT OF FACT IN DISPUTE

5. There is no factual dispute that I reported sexual harassment that was occurring against me in the workplace. There is no dispute that I reported it to lower, mid, and upper management at ABM.

6. There is no dispute to the fact that I was told by mid and upper level manager Security Director ▓▓▓▓▓▓▓▓▓ (see Exhibit 4) that I was in fact demoted from Security Shift Supervisor to Lobby Ambassador.

7. There is no factual dispute that I was given less terms as to what is set forth in the Los Angeles Master Collective Bargaining Agreement. (See Exhibit 3).

8. There is no dispute that sexual harassment is unlawful in the workplace and forbidden under California law. I reported the unlawful harassment that was occurring from October 6, 2014 to November 2, 2014, and nothing was done to resolve it by ABM.

9. I was told by ▓▓▓▓▓ that I was demoted. This is a fact that is not disputed by ABM, but only by the "INTERVIEWER".

-2-

CLAIMANT ▓▓▓▓ STATEMENT OF FACTS AND INFORMATION
IN DISPUTE RE RECORD OF CLAIM STATUS INTERVIEW VQ

Sex Discrimination

10. No one from ABM has produced any factual and legal evidence that I was not demoted by ABM management corporate team and certainly not documented in the "Record of Claim Status Interview VQ".

11. The employer has not disputed these facts and my evidence demonstrates by the preponderance of evidence before this agency, that I was deprived of equal opportunities at ABM for reporting sexual harassment, unjustly discriminated against, and left for good cause.

12. ABM allowed me, acting through its lower, mid, and upper level managers, to experience a type of discrimination, employers are not allowed to permit it at work. This discrimination and adverse employment actions were based on my sex and gender; especially for reporting sexual harassment in the workplace. (See Exhibit 6).

STATEMENT OF INFORMATION

13. The EDD website only allows approximately 100 characters to be submitted in the comment section of information to be entered into the website for the statement of information in question. Additional information has been made available to this governmental agency and was submitted on 12/30/14 as a first timely appeal to the adverse determination for benefits eligibility.

STATEMENT OF FACT

14. Record of Claim Status Interview states in pertinent part:

"HOW did clmt tell? Name ████████ Title DIRECTOR OF SECURITY
WHY(record the clmt's Primary Reason for quitting. Document specific dates and facts of FINAL INCIDENT: Clmt was sexually harassed at work. CLMT reported it the first time on 10/10/14 to ...his immediate supervisor nothing was done. Clmt wrote a statement on 10/10/14 ...to Director of Security and District Manager nothing was done. "CMT CANNOT DESCRIBE A VALID COMPELLING REASON FOR THE QUIT. ASKED HIM MULTIPLE TIMES".

//
//

STATEMENT OF ALLEGED FACT IN DISPUTE

15. The statement, entered as data on the Report Claim of Status, states that I "cannot describe a valid compelling reason for the quit." This should not be viewed as a fact of the "FINAL INCIDENT". The statement that I "cannot describe a valid compelling reason" is a conclusion of the "FINAL INCIDENT".

16. The INTERVIEWER was concluding that I was unable to give an account of words to reasonably to cause her or him to believe or agree; and that the statement I offered in explanation or justification was not rational and intelligent. The ending conclusion means that the INTERVIEWER was not convinced that I had good reason to leave ABM; it was a personal interpretation of me explaining the harassment and discrimination but even more so, that the INTERVIEWER subjectively presumed in the data that I was not even being rational.

17. This is a subjective conclusion of the facts, not the facts itself. Thus leading the way as to why the INTERVIEWER wanted me to produce a tangible picture, drawing, video, or image, independent of the perceived inability to explain a good reason for leaving ABM.

18. Regardless, of how I may or may not have been able to 'paint' a good enough picture for the INTERVIEWER, the conclusion of the FINAL INCIDENT is not based on undisputed nor disputed facts, but simply on personal judgment through interpersonal communication on the telephone with me, the Claimant.

19. Therefore, stating that I "cannot describe a valid compelling reason" is not a fact but a personal judgment or subjective assessment-of me uncomfortably communicating my work experience about the subject of sexual harassment in question.

20. for certain the INTERVIEWER and I were grounded in a definite misunderstanding as to why I had good and just cause to leave ABM for sexual harassment and discrimination.

21. The facts are not disputed, except for the INTERVIEWER's skepticism of this fact, as if I was lying in which I am not. My Declarations are direct evidence of these facts and cannot be ignored any longer.

//
//

CLAIMANT STATEMENT OF FACTS AND INFORMATION
IN DISPUTE RE RECORD OF CLAIM STATUS INTERVIEW VQ

Sex Discrimination

STATEMENT OF INFORMATION IN DISPUTE

22. Sexual harassment, discrimination, and retaliation for reporting sexual harassment is unlawful in the workplace, I ▇▇▇ and ▇▇▇ were well informed of me reporting harassment for 25 days. As the law uses and mandates the term "immediate", which generally means instant, without delay, and starting to do something fast.

23. These two managers, ▇▇▇ one upper level of ABM and the other mid to upper level of ABM did not act without delay or instantly, but had led me to believe acting through ▇▇▇ that they were investigating my complaint of harassment.

24. As the INTERVIEWER would not find a "valid" reason; because the interviewer did not believe me. I have told the truth in this matter, I told the truth that I was demoted and indeed threatened with a pay cut.

25. The INTERVIEWER stated to me in the interview, that they did not think that employers had the duty to stop harassment against their workers in the workplace. This truly sounded misplaced and appeared to be a double standard. This was frustrating, confusing, and extremely insensitive comment; particularly with regards to my experience with what I had gone through for 32 days at ABM with regards to harassment and discrimination.

26. This statement was never documented in the "Record of Claim Status Interview VQ".

QUESTION NO. 9:

27. "CLMT NEVER HAD FACTS SHOWING THAT HE WAS DEMOTED".

STATEMENT OF FACT IN DISPUTE

28. INTERVIEWER disputes and disbelieves that I was demoted. The INTERVIEWER has no authentic factual evidence to assume otherwise, only by subjective premise and conclusion. My witness statement was immediately disregarded and it is my legal contention is that the INTERVIEWER makes this entry as a false assumption.

29. The INTERVIEWER had referenced me to produce some kind of other tangible physical evidence not in my possession, with an assumption that there exists some kind of other "proof".

-5-

CLAIMANT ▇▇▇ STATEMENT OF FACTS AND INFORMATION
IN DISPUTE RE RECORD OF CLAIM STATUS INTERVIEW VQ

1 30. I provided my written statements, first declaration, and exhibits as proof. This evidence
2 submitted has been disregarded thus far.
3 31. The INTERVIEWER stated that they was going to ask ABM about my reasons for leaving,
4 the harassment investigation, and the demotion. There is no record in the "Record of Claim
5 Status Interview VQ", nor in any other document in my case file, that demonstrates the
6 INTERVIEWER followed up with those specific inquires to ABM.
7 32. The fact that I was told in person by ▮▮▮▮ is a valid showing of evidence.
8 The INTERVIEWER has not witnessed nor can dispute it and has disregarded my written
9 statements. I have facts showing that I was demoted, hence, my witness statement and my
10 appearance in this Appeal by written declaration.
11 33. The subjective assumption that material objects or documents that may or may not exist
12 should not be a precursor to my eligibility for benefits. Any material object(s) as part of that
13 fact, may have been able to help me prove, by having granted me to the requested subpoena of
14 the video footage.
15 34. Around January 15, 2015, I was denied the specific request, in addition to two more, for
16 the subpoena of this video by the Inglewood Office of Appeals.
17 35. My written declaration is direct evidence and testimony to the facts of this case and
18 should not be ignored or disbelieved, particularly absent any contrary evidence.

QUESTION NO. 10:

21 36. The INTERVIEWER stated that she or he would give the employer a call and ask about
22 the demotion and if they had conducted an investigation into my claims of sexual harassment
23 and discrimination.

STATMENT OF FACT

25 37. There are no facts currently in dispute, nor has arose prior to this administrative law
26 hearing.
27 //
28 //

-6-

CLAIMANT ▮▮▮▮ STATEMENT OF FACTS AND INFORMATION
IN DISPUTE RE RECORD OF CLAIM STATUS INTERVIEW VQ

Sex Discrimination

STATEMENT OF INFORMATION

38. There is no evidence that the INTERVIEWER had received additional or contrary information from ABM as to my reason for leaving ABM for good and just cause.

QUESTION NO. 11:

39. There is no information that has been documented as to obtaining Employer or Agent information from ABM in order to attempt to "Resolve Conflicting Information From Other Sources". There currently remains no conflicting information from other sources.

STATEMENT OF FACT

40. There are no facts currently in dispute between the parties, nor has there arose any prior disputes to this administrative law hearing.

STATEMENT OF INFORMATION

42. There is no evidence that the INTERVIEWER had received additional or contrary information as to my reason for leaving ABM for good and just cause.

QUESTION NO.13

44. In the "Summary of Material Facts and Reason For Decision":

    "CLMT ADMITS HE WASN'T TOLD IF IT WAS A PAY CUT AND HOW MUCH, AND HE ADMITS THAT HE DIDNT TALK TO UPPER MGMT UNTIL HE QUIT. CLMT DID NOT HAVE COMPLELLING REASON FOR THE QUIT AND DID NOT EXPLORE ALL REASONABLE ATERTIVES PRIOR TO QUITTING"

STATEMENT OF FACT IN DISPUTE

45. The terms ▇▇▇▇ stated that I would be making less money, less pay, and referenced a pay-cut for the demoting position with ABM is a fact. The fact that I was not told an exact dollar amount of how much by ▇▇▇▇ does not contradict this fact.

46. The INTERVIEWER misrepresents the material facts in order to disqualify me from being eligible for benefits. I specifically stated on the website that I was given less terms. This is a fact that cannot be disputed and has not been disputed by the real parties in interest such as my most recent employer ABM.

47. The INTERVIEWER logs and enters the statement, "He admits that he did not talk to upper management until he quit". This is not a complete statement of fact and the INTERVIEWER has misconstrued and misrepresented my words to be used against me in order to disqualify me for benefits.

48. The fact is that I had well informed ABM's lower, mid, and upper management team about the harassment. The fact that ABM discriminated against me for reporting it was unreasonable and ABM deprived me of equal opportunities at the company. This fact is not disputed by the employer in this case.

49. The first part "I did not talk to upper MGMT" is misleading and misplaced. The fact that I initiated communication to upper management since 10/10/14 specifically with regards to the harassment is referenced in my statement of question No. 9.

50. This fact can also be demonstrated in Exhibit __. The recipients of the 10/10/14 email with attachments was sent and received by ███████████.

51. The INTERVIEWER seems to be confused and unclear as to me "talk[ing] to upper MGMT, in one section the INTERVIEWER noted that I did on "101014" and then enters the data that I did not "up until I quit". This material fact obscures and omits essential facts, this statement of information was constructed by the INTERVIEWER in order to disqualify me from benefits.

STATEMENT OF INFORMATION IN DISPUTE

52. The statement of information in dispute that I did not talk to upper management until I quit, is contrary to the information I had provided in question No. 9.

54. The statement of facts regarding question No. 9 and the statement of facts in question No. 13 are in direct contradiction with each other. According to the INTERVIEWER on 101014, I informed ███████ and ███████, upper and mid level management members,

Sex Discrimination

but in question No. 13 the INTERVIEWER states that I did not "up until I quit".

55. These contradictions must be reconciled in favor of the Claimant because they are not rooted in fact and additional information has been available but ignored.

56. The real parties in interest are privy to the facts, not the INTERVIEWER whom had never witnessed any of these discriminatory events. The real parties in interest has presented valid information rebutting any presumption of other facts presumed by the INTERVIEWER in this case.

DATED: January 19, 2015

CLAIMANT

CLAIMANT

THE STATE OF CALIFORNIA

EMPLOYMENT DEVELOPMENT DEPARTMENT

UNEMPLOYMENT INSURANCE APPEALS BOARD

) CASE NO.: [ ]
)
▆▆▆▆▆▆▆▆▆) **STATEMENT OF EVIDENCE TO**
) **BE INTRODUCED**
    Claimant,)
) **RE DEPRIVED EQUAL EMPLOYMENT**
v.) **OPPORTUNITIES AT ABM**
)
) **Administrative Law Judge:**
ABM,)
)   Judge Michael Kurz
    Respondent.)
) **Time:** 2:30PM
)
) **Date:** January 20, 2015
)
) **Location:** Long Beach Office

CLAIMANT request permission to introduce documentary evidence and submits the following written statement of the nature and extent of the documents to be introduced at the hearing:

-1-
STATEMENT OF EVIDENCE TO BE INTRODUCED

SEX DISCRIMINATION

EXHIBIT 1
1. The first Declaration to ABM management on October 10, 2014, in regards to quid pro quo sexual harassment. Also attached is the email as proof that I had notified lower, mid, and upper management of ABM.

EXHIBIT 2
2. ABM "Auditmatic" or 'ODR' computer based software that makes reports or "activity log" of incidents or events, used in conjunction with Incident Reports. This automated windows based software, to the best of my knowledge, sends a copy of the activity log to ABM lower, mid, and upper management. I keep reporting the harassment as I was instructed.

EXHIBIT 3
3. The Los Angeles Master Collective Bargaining Agreement ("CBA") that is between ABM and SEIU-USWW, Local 721. The CBA sets forth disciplinary rules in Section 4.2. The CBA sets forht rules in 27.4 guiding the removal of an Employee from employment from one work location to another. ABM management did not conform or comply within the scope of the CBA with regards to my employment with them.

EXHIBIT 4
4. The business card of ABM Director of Security Mr. ▇▇▇▇▇▇ who is a member of mid and/or upper level management at ABM.

EXHIBIT 5
5. The time sheet of the location in where I was removed to, in noncompliance with the CBA. ABM falsified my timesheet to state that I worked until 11:00AM but in fact I worked until 11:47AM. I requested to the Office of Appeals in Inglewood to subpoena this video in ABM's possession but it was denied because they are not a party to this Action and has not submitted any contrary evidence.

//

EXHIBIT 6

6. The Charge of Discrimination that I had filed with the EEOC on January 16, 2015, in order to be allowed the right to sue for discriminating against me because of my sex and gender; and for disciplining me for reporting sexual harassment.

NATURE OF THE EVDENCE

1. The evidence to be introduced at the administrative hearing is "Article 4, Discipline and Discharge Section 4.2" of the Los Angeles Master Collective Bargaining Agreement between ABM and SEIU-USWW, which states in pertinent part "Warning notices shall be issued within ten (10) days after the Employer knew or should have known of the offense. A copy of the warning shall be sent to the Union. Each warning notice shall contain a place for the employee to sign to acknowledge receipt without admitting guilt".

2. In Article 4, Section 4.2, of the Collective Bargaining Agreement ("CBA") prohibits warning notices to be issued within ten days of the knowledge, such as in my case, the "conflict of interest and/or fraternization" should have been issued and discussed with me and my union representative by October 16, 2014.

DATED: January 19, 2015   Respectfully submitted,

By:

-3-
STATEMENT OF EVIDENCE TO BE INTRODUCED

SEX DISCRIMINATION

CALIFORNIA UNEMPLOYMENT INSURANCE APPEALS BOARD

Michael Kurz
Administrative Law Judge

NOTICE OF HEARING

Case No ■■■■■■

■■■■■■
Claimant-Appellant

HEARING TIME and PLACE
DATE: Tuesday, January 20, 2015
TIME: 2:30 PM
PLACE: 4300 Long Beach Blvd - #500
Long Beach CA 90807

Located near the corner of Long Beach Blvd. and W. San Antonio Dr.

EDD: 0410

* If an interpreter or reasonable accommodation for a disability is needed, call the phone number below immediately. Si necesita un intérprete llame el numero de telefono abajo inmediatamente.

* Bring all documents and witnesses necessary to support your case. *Evidence is rarely accepted after the hearing.*

* Arrive 15 minutes early to review the appeal file.

* The hearing room is in a secured facility. You may be screened.

* **IMPORTANT: Read the enclosed 'Hearing Information' pamphlet.**

THE FOLLOWING ISSUES WILL BE CONSIDERED AT THE HEARING (Section references are to the Unemployment Insurance Code unless otherwise noted):

➤ 1256   Did the claimant voluntarily leave his or her most recent employment without good cause. Was the claimant discharged for misconduct connected with his or her most recent work. (See UI sections 1256, 1256.1, 1256.2, 1256.5)

Direct questions to:

INGLEWOOD OFFICE OF APPEALS
Telephone: (310) 337-4302
Fax: (310) 337-4392

Date Mailed: 01/08/2015

INGLEWOOD OFFICE OF APPEALS
9800 South La Cienega Blvd - Ste 901
INGLEWOOD, CA 90301-0000
Telephone: (310) 337-4302
Fax: (310) 337-4392

NAMES AND ADDRESSES OF PARTIES / REPRESENTATIVES

SEX DISCRIMINATION

Appeal Transmittal

```
SLU220M              APPEAL TRANSMITTAL         PAGE 1 OF 2    DATE: 12/30/14
                                                               TIME: 14:04:56

TO: ING OAP              *** TIMELY ***

CLMNT SSN:
     NAME:              [redacted]         [redacted]
     BYB/CED:           03 30 14
     PGM CD:            A              CLM HOLDING FO: 0410

DEPT REP: N (N/Y)    CLMNT REP: N (N/Y)     NOTIFY AAO: ___    CSI: __

REFER TO FORMER CASE(s):

DEPT REQUESTS: ( _ ) NOTICE TO ATTEND  ( _ ) SUBPOENA  ( _ ) TELEPHONE HEARING
     NAME: _____        PH:( ___ ) ___ ____
     ADDRESS: _____
     CITY: _____ STATE: __ ZIP: _____

REASON FOR REQUEST: _____
DEPT REPRESENTATIVE:  L ROBINSON              FO:  0410

SLU210M              APPEAL PROCESS           DATE: 12/30/14
                                              TIME: 14:04:43
FO: 0410      CLAIM HOLDING FO: 0410    REQUESTOR: L ROBINSON
BYB/CED: 03/30/14   PGM CD: A           APPEAL DATE: 12 / 29 / 14
CLMNT SSN:
     NAME:              [redacted]         [redacted]
     IN CARE OF: _____
     ADDRESS:
     CITY:              STATE:   ZIP:
     PHONE:    (   )

ER ACCT:             ER NAME: _____
     REP/IN CARE OF:
     ADDRESS:
     CITY:              STATE:   ZIP:

SECTIONS:    1256

INTERPRETER: N (N/Y)  LANGUAGE:
APPELLANT: C         ER FS: N (N/Y)       DI SUSP: ___
             MM DD YY WK                    MM DD YY RSN
     6315    6315CC X 713  /  /         OP __ / __ / __ __

Document                  pgs  Date
DE1000/1000DC(IB-101)      43  12 26 14
*ENVELOPE POSTMARKED           12 29 14
DE1080                     02  12 11 14
CLAIM RECORD                1  12 30 14
CLAIM NOTES                01  12 30 14
DE 2403                     3  12 10 14
```

RECEIVED
DEC 3 1 2014
INGLEWOOD OFFICE OF APPEALS

Appeal Documents

12/10/14
2682
VQ

RECEIVED
EDD
SAN BERNARDINO #041

14 DEC 30 AM 9:34

APPEAL FORM

EDD Telephone Numbers:	
ENGLISH	1-800-300-5616
SPANISH	1-800-326-8937
CANTONESE	1-800-547-3506
MANDARIN	1-866-303-0706
VIETNAMESE	1-800-547-2058
TTY (non-voice)	1-800 815-9387
website: www.edd.ca.gov	

If you disagree with the Notice of Determination(s) and/or Determination(s)/Rulings by the EDD, you may appeal the decision(s) to the California Unemployment Insurance Appeals Board (CUIAB) by completing this form and explaining why you disagree. You must sign the form and return it to the EDD at the office address listed on the notice that you are appealing. **YOU HAVE 20 DAYS FROM THE MAIL DATE OF THE NOTICE TO FILE A TIMELY APPEAL.** If you appeal after the 20-day period, you must include the reason for the delay. The administrative law judge (ALJ) will determine whether you had good cause for the delay. If the ALJ determines you did not have good cause to submit your appeal late, your appeal will be dismissed.

CLAIMANTS: While your appeal is pending, **you must continue to certify for benefits**. If you are found eligible, you can be paid only for periods for which you have certified and have met all other eligibility requirements.

NOTE: Claimants for Disaster Unemployment Assistance (DUA) have 60 days to file an appeal. Employers appealing the *Notice of Determination or Assessment*, DE 3807, have 30 days to file an appeal.

SECTION I   APPELLANT INFORMATION

INSTRUCTIONS: The following information must be provided by the Appellant (the claimant or employer who is appealing a notice), or by the authorized agent or representative of the Appellant. The signature of the Appellant or agent is required. Please use **BLACK INK** when filling out this form.

Claimant Name: ▮▮▮▮▮▮▮▮▮▮   Social Security Number:

Do you need a translator? ☐ Yes ☑ No   If yes, what language/dialect? _____

Appellant Address: _____
   Street No., Apt. No., or P.O. Box
   City   State   ZIP Code

Telephone No.: (   )
Fax No.: (   )

E-mail Address: _____   Cell Phone No.:

☑ I authorize the CUIAB to send confidential information regarding my appeal to the e-mail address listed above.

☐ I authorize the CUIAB to send confidential information regarding my appeal by text message or voice mail to the cell phone number listed above.

Complete this section for employer appeals only

Employer Account Number: _____   Agent Name (if applicable): _____

Agent Address: _____
   Street No., Apt. No., or P.O. Box   City   State   ZIP Code

SECTION II   APPELLANT STATEMENT

INSTRUCTIONS: Explain the reason for your appeal and why you disagree with the decision(s). If required, attach additional pages to this form and write your name and Social Security number on each page.

I disagree with the determination in the notice dated 12/21/14 because

_____
_____
_____
_____
_____

Signature of Appellant or Agent: _____   Date: 12/26/14

DE 1000M Rev. 7 (1-14)   - Versión en español en el dorso -   CU

Sex Discrimination

RE:

TO: EMPLOYMENT DEVELOPMENT DEPARTMENT

From: ▓▓▓▓▓▓▓▓▓

RE:

THE STATE OF CALIFORNIA MANDATES ANTI-HARASSMENT IN THE WORKPLACE AGAINST

EMPLOYEES BY NONEMPLOYEES

Sexual harassment is illegal in the workplace and harassment of employees is forbidden under California Law, see California Government Code Section §12940 (a),(h), (i), (j)(3), and (k). Employers have a duty, and are obligated to train their employees in sexual harassment prevention and procedures under California Government Code § 12950.1 (a).

Employers are liable for harassment by nonemployees and employees alike, see California Government Code Section§12940 (j) and (k). The California Constitution art I, §8 prohibits sex discrimination in employment. Title VII of the Civil Rights Act of 1964 (42 USC §§ 2000e-2000e-17) prohibits discrimination based on sex and has been construed to include sexual harassment, see Meritor Savings Bank v. Vinson (1986) 477 UA 57, 67, 106 S. Ct 2399. Whether an employee is a male or female, the California Legislature has strict mandates against harassment in the workplace by non-employees.

If ABM is going to operate in the State of California; ABM has the legal duty and obligation to take to preventative "immediate and corrective action" against sexual harassment in order to protect their employee, male, female, or transgender, even if it is alleged to have been committed by a non-employee. I have performed the legal duty and obligation to report unlawful harassment in the workplace to ABM.

ABM FAILED TO RESPOND TO MY COMPLAINT AND TO PREVENT HARASSMENT WITH IMMEDIATE RESPONSE AND CORRECTIVE ACTION

I made an oral complaint to ABM and a good faith effort to prevent the harassment that was occurring at work from October 6 to November 2, 2014, I promptly reported it to my immediate supervisor of the occurrence ("Exhibit A"), I was never contacted by Human Resources during that time, I was told it was going to be investigated but it was not.

On October 6, 2014, I initially first complained to my immediate supervisor, then on October the 10, 2014, I contacted the District Manager via email ("Exhibit A"), and I was led to believe by my immediate supervisor that my complaint would be investigated or

Privileged Communication & Confidential Information © 2014 Edward Dumas All rights reserved. No part of this publication may be reproduced or transmitted in any form or by any means, electronic or mechanical, including photocopy, recording or any other information storage and retrieval system without prior permission in writing from Edward Dumas.

SEX DISCRIMINATION

RE:

corrected. Instead I was removed by the District Manager, whom is in charge of the entire region for the department I worked under. ABM termed "transfer", put me on termination notice via disciplinary action, and I was demoted from shift supervisor to lobby ambassador without being informed until I arrived at the new worksite. For a detailed account of harassment please refer to the Statement of Facts on page 8 of this appeal for benefits.

I believe I was discriminated because of my sex and/or gender and unlawfully sexually harassed at work; and ABM failed to take any "immediate and corrective action" against sexual harassment as is required by California law. This is contrary to what the California law and public policy mandates to employers and to what the contract terms are for employment between ABM and the Union. This adverse action was designed by ABM management to constructively terminate my employment with them for reporting sexual harassment.

The United States Equal Employment Opportunity Commission (EEOC) publishes guidelines stating that harassment based upon sex is a form of "discrimination". The EEOC Guidelines also give some examples of conduct which, in the agency's view, would give rise to liability for harassment. The Guideless are updated and revised periodically to reflect new developments in the law. The State of California has even stricter guidelines that are statutory law. Copy of EEOC guidelines can be obtained at http://www.eeoc.gov/policy/docs/harassment.html.

"Discrimination" refers to bias in the exercise of personnel management authority on behalf of the ABM, in which has taken some adverse action against me such as adverse job assignment, disciplinary action, promotion and/or demotion. In Roby, "Harassment" refers to the bias that is expressed or communicated through interpersonal relations in the workplace". Roby v. McKesson Corp. (2009) 47 Cal.4th 686, 706 [101 Cal.Rptr.3d 773, 787-788].

The Department must take notice that The California Fair Employment and Housing Act (FEHA) requires and mandates that ABM must take "all reasonable steps necessary to prevent discrimination and harassment from occurring", see California Government Code§ 12940(k). It is ABM's legal duty to perform reasonable steps as the means to explore reasonable solutions in order to prevent and correct harassment in the workplace.

The FEHA specifically prohibits "harassment" as well as "discrimination" at ABM under California Government Code § 12940(a)(h)(j); Discrimination and harassment based on sex, gender, and/or sexual orientation; and sexually harassing conduct under the FEHA

RE:

The FEHA extends protection to independent contractors or persons providing services pursuant to a contract" as well as employees and job applicants.

The FEHA ban on harassment extends to all employers, even ABM, regardless of the number of employees working for the employer. The Department must consider and cannot ignore that California Government Code Section §12940 (a) prohibits "discrimination" in the terms, conditions, or privileges of employment on the basis of "sex", "gender", "gender identity", "gender expression" or "sexual orientation". California Government Code §12940(j)(1) prohibit "harassment" on the basis of "sex", "gender", gender identity," "gender expression" or "sexual orientation".

EXPLORING LEGAL SOLUTIONS AND ABM POLICY

Employer's Duty to Prevent Harassment means that ABM must take all reasonable steps to prevent harassment against me. An employer, like ABM is liable for failing "to take all necessary steps necessary to prevent discrimination and harassment from occurring." California Government Code §12940 (k); Weeks v. Baker & McKenzie (1998) 63 Cal.4th 1128, 1157; Doe v. Capital Cities (1996) 50 Cal.4th 1038, 1053; BAJI No. 2527(4th ed. 2000).

If the harassment has already occurred the duty to maintain a harassment free work environment requires the employer, such as ABM, to take remedial action not only change the harasser's behavior, but to deter potential harassers from unlawful conduct, see Intlekofer v. Turnage (9th Cir. 1992) 973 F2d 773, 778. ABM never took remedial action to change the harasser's unlawful conduct toward me. I followed ABM policy and was deprived equal opportunities in employment for complaining about sexual harassment.

ABM FAILS TO INSITUTE ITS OWN EQUAL EMPLOYMENT POLICY

ABM claims to have an "open door" policy when it comes to equal employment opportunities and/or sexual harassment ("Exhibit B"). According to ABM policy an employee must first discuss the situation with their immediate supervisor within a week of the occurrence who in turn will work with Human Resources to provide a solution or explanation. I did my duty in informing my immediate supervisor and did speak up within a week with my immediate supervisor at ABM. For a detailed account please refer to the "Statement of Facts".

As the harassment worsened and the problem persisted I contacted the District Manager which is also known as the Department or Branch Manager, who was supposed to investigate and provide me with a solution or explanation as claimed in ABM company

Sex Discrimination

RE:

policy. The ABM District Manager who is the acting Department or Branch Manager; did not conduct an investigation, I was never contacted, nor provided with a solution and explanation. I was led to believe there was going to be an investigation, solution and/or explanation. Instead I was treated unfairly and was issued a termination notice (first and final warning) and ABM demoted me for complaining about the sexual harassment.

Whether an employer like ABM has exercised reasonable care to prevent and correct the harassing conduct is determine by "whether the employee's actions as a whole established a reasonable mechanism for prevention and correct" Holly D. v. California Inst. of Technol. (9th Cir 2003) 339 F3d 1158, 1177. ABM never took reasonable care to prevent and correct the harassing behavior against me, in light of me providing notice of the harassment.

My actions to report and declare I was sexually harassed was a reasonable mechanism for prevention and correction. The Ninth Circuit has found that a common way of showing that an employer has established a "reasonable mechanism for prevention" is if the employer has promulgated an appropriate anti-harassment policy that includes a complaint procedure, *although proof of such a policy is not dispositive*. Burlington Indus. Inc. v. Ellerth (1998) 524 US 742, 765, 118 S. Ct. 2257; see, e.g., EEOC v. Hacienda Hotel (9th Cir. 1989) 881 F.2d. 1504, 1516.

I followed ABM's complaint procedure but they failed in instituting their own anti-harassment policy. An employer like ABM, as in Yates v. Avco Corp. (6th Cir 1987) F.2d 630, 635, an employer, who urged confidentiality, did not tell the complainant of his or her rights against harassment, and/or the steps the employer would take to protect their employee can subject the employer to increased liability. After I complained, ABM never consulted me about my rights nor how they would take steps to protect me, and any alleged protection was false and not executed.

The State of California Government Code Section 12940 et al clarifies that ABM should not have stigmatized or penalized me; ABM must have interviewed me and the alleged harasser; any necessary witnesses to the alleged occurences; ABM never communicated to me the progress and conclusion of "the investigation"; ABM has failed to make me whole; ABM has not taken steps to prevent future harassment and discrimination; ABM has not ensured me that there is no retaliation against the me. See Tayborn v. City & County of San Francisco (9th Cir. 2003) 341 F.3d 957, 960. ABM, as in Sarro v. City of Sacramento (1999) 78 F. Supp. 2d 1057, 1064, is now focusing much of their time on the most personal and private aspects of my life, rather than on the alleged harasser and harassment, ABM is not

Privileged Communication & Confidential Information © 2014 Edward Dumas All rights reserved. No part of this publication may be reproduced or transmitted in any form or by any means, electronic or mechanical, including photocopy, recording or any other information storage and retrieval system without prior permission in writing from Edward Dumas.

 RE:

acting appropriately. ABM took no serious steps to show honor and respect for California Laws and the rights of its citizens.

GOOD CAUSE EXISTS FOR LEAVING ABM PURSUANT TO CALIFORNIA PUBLIC POLICY

With respect to ABM's failure to prevent and correct sexual harassment in the workplace, ABM cannot allow me to be sexually harassed in the workplace, that is against California law and public policy. This statute carries a 1 year statute of limitation and requires a government complaint before filing a lawsuit in Court. The Department should not take the side of ABM and presume false facts nor ignore the California Legislative Mandate against discrimination and harassment in the workplace. The Department should not assume that ABM under took an investigation into my complaint of sexual harassment; and the Department cannot ignore that there is ample evidence that I reported the sexual harassment.

ABM never did any investigation into my allegations of sexual harassment at work. ABM is playing both sides of the fence on this legal matter in the hope to absolve the corporation from any legal duty or obligation it had under law. I have since rescinded my signature on the erroneous written warning notice for 'conflict of interest' ("Exhibit D'). ABM has not honored my right to rescission and their breach and/or mistake of contract.

Pursuant to California Unemployment Insurance Code Section §1256.2 (a) states "Except as otherwise provided by subdivision (b), an individual who terminate his or her employment shall not be deemed to have left his or her most recent work without good cause if his or her employer deprived the individual of equal employment opportunities on any basis listed in subdivision (a) 12940 of the Government Code, as those basis are defined in Sections 12926 and 12926.1 of the Government Code."

Subdivision (b) (2) states "An individual who fails to make reasonable efforts to provide the employer with an opportunity to remove any unintentional deprivation of the individuals' equal employment opportunities." This subdivision will exempt subdivision (a); however the Department is acting as the alter ego of ABM in asserting that I failed to "explore all reasonable solutions..." ("Exhibit F"); the Department has falsely assumed that I did not make reasonable efforts to provide the employer with an opportunity to remove "any unintentional deprivation of the individual's equal employment opportunities."

ABM has intentionally deprived me of my equal opportunities and has failed to remedy, restore, and make me whole for the economic injury I have incurred. ABM has operated in bad faith and unlawfully; ABM is not being held accountable for violating California laws but should be held accordingly to due process for their noncompliance.

Privileged Communication & Confidential Information © 2014 Edward Dumas All rights reserved. No part of this publication may be reproduced or transmitted in any form or by any means, electronic or mechanical, including photocopy, recording or any other information storage and retrieval system without prior permission in writing from Edward Dumas.

SEX DISCRIMINATION

RE:

In Thomas v. California Employment Stabilization Commission (1952) 39 Cal.2d 501 [247 P2.d 561] references that the unemployment insurance appeals board is a statutory agency with statewide jurisdiction but without constitutional authority to make final determinations of fact and the benefits provide for by the UI Act are 'property rights' and therefore anyone deprived of a property right by such administrative body is entitled to a limited trial de novo in the Superior Court.

In Pratt v. Local 683, Film Technicians of The Motion Picture and Television Industries (1968) 260 Cal.App.2d 545[67 Cal.Rptr. 483] the Court held that state CUIAB exercises discretionary administrative functions and does not exercise judicial powers in the sense that its decision on the question of whether any employee was or was not discharged for misconduct. The employee's right to receive unemployment insurance benefits should be determinative of her or his right to sue his employer in a court of law for breach of contract of employment. See also Chrysler Corp. v. California Employment Stabilization Commission (1953) 116 Cal.App.2d 8 [253 P.2d 68].

In Pratt the claimant was denied all his legal remedies, even at the trial court level; the Court of Appeals held the trial court reversed in part that decision. The Court also found all throughout the Unemployment Appeals process, the employer made false statements and misrepresentations to the government. ABM has followed the same pattern and the Department should not presume false facts nor assumptions, or become a proxy advocate for their defense to unlawful conduct against me.

Pursuant to Unemployment Insurance Code § 1256 states "An individual is presumed to have been discharged for reasons other than misconduct in connection with his or her work and not to have voluntarily quit without good cause unless his or her employer has given written notice to the contrary to the department as provided in Section 1327, setting forth facts sufficient to overcome the presumption. The presumption provided by this section is rebuttable."

California statutes presumes that an individual has not voluntarily left his work without good cause is established to implement public policy upon payment of benefits to unemployed so as to reduce suffering caused thereby, presumption affects burden of proof in that it imposes upon parties against whom it operates, the employer and the department of human resources, burden of proving non existence of presumed fact, which means that to overcome presumption employee or department must prove by a preponderance of evidence that claimant quit without probable cause or was discharge for misconduct in connection with his work. Perales v. Dept. of Human Resources Development (1973) 32 Cal.App.3d 332 [108 Cal.Rptr. 167].

Privileged Communication & Confidential Information © 2014 Edward Dumas All rights reserved. No part of this publication may be reproduced or transmitted in any form or by any means, electronic or mechanical, including photocopy, recording or any other information storage and retrieval system without prior permission in writing from Edward Dumas.

RE:

In Prescod v. California Unemployment Ins. Appeals Bd. (1976) 57 Cal.App.3d 29[127 Cal.Rptr. 540], where's ones work is made intolerable over period of time by discriminatory acts of employer, such as refusal to reinstate, demotion, or loss of promotional opportunity, there is "good cause'" for leaving employment. It is settled law in California that leaving one's employment because they oppose discrimination or harassment is good and just cause.

While harassing conduct need not occur in workplace in order to render employer liable under Fair Employment and Housing Act, it most occur in work related context. See Capitol City Foods, Inc. v. Superior Court (1992) 5 Cal.App.4th 1042 [7 Cal.Rptr.2d 418]. An employee is not required to use legal terms or buzzwords when opposing discrimination or harassment, see Yanowitz v. L'Oreal USA, Inc. (2005) 103 Cal.App.4th 1021[32 CalRptr.3d 436].

In Greene v. Pomona Unified School Dist. (1995) 32 Cal.App.4th 1216 [38 Cal.Rptr. 2d 770], the court held that there is no need to require unions to become involved with employees' claims of discrimination against their employer based on protected characteristics because employees have remedies available to them through Department of Fair Employment and Housing (DFEH) and the EEOC, as well as civil actions under the FEHA and under Title VII.

It is the legislative intent of the State of California and declared by Governor Arnold Schwarzenegger that "Equal employment opportunity for all individual is the policy of the State of California in all its activities. All state officials, managers, and supervisor shall vigorously enforce this policy."

ABM DID NOT PERFORM THE MANDATORY TRAINING OR EDUCATION IN HARASSMENT AS REQUIRED BY CALIFORNIA LAW

To the best of my knowledge and belief, ABM did not fully comply with California Government Code §12950.1 (a) and never provided me with at least two hours of classroom or other effective interactive training and education regarding sexual harassment to all supervisory employees in California, as the law requires. It is the employers duty to train and educate on how to prevent and correct sexual harassment in the workplace. It is the employees duty to report it promptly, in which I did. The sexual harassment never ceased and they failed to investigate the harassment that was occurring against me. ABM never provided the proper legal training as required, nor took immediate and corrective legal action. The disciplinary action is pretextual, invalid, and unexecutable pursuant to the union contract and California's Public Policy against Discrimination and Harassment.

Privileged Communication & Confidential Information © 2014 Edward Dumas All rights reserved. No part of this publication may be reproduced or transmitted in any form or by any means, electronic or mechanical, including photocopy, recording or any other information storage and retrieval system without prior permission in writing from Edward Dumas.

SEX DISCRIMINATION

 RE:

California Government Code §12950.1 (a) further requires for ABM to train all new supervisory employees within six months of their assumption of a supervisory position. The training and education required by this section shall include information and practical guidance regarding the federal and state statutory provisions concerning the prohibition against and the prevention and correction of sexual harassment and the remedies available to victims of sexual harassment in employment.

The State of California mandates that ABM must provide training and education that shall also include practical examples aimed at instructing supervisors in the prevention of harassment, discrimination and retaliation, and shall be presented by trainers or educators with knowledge and expertise in the prevention of harassment, discrimination, and retaliation. I believe ABM failed to provide this training to me as a shift supervisor; I do not recall receiving any anti-harassment training at ABM as required by the State of California.

California Government Code §12950.1 (d) states that even if the training and education required by this part of California law did not reach me it shall not result in and of itself in liability to ABM; and even if ABM complied with this section, it does not necessarily insulate ABM from liability for sexual harassment of any current or former employee.

California Government Code §12950.1 (f) states that the training and education required by this section is intend to establish and minimum threshold and should not discourage nor relieve any employer from providing for longer more frequent, or more elaborate training and education regarding workplace harassment or other forms of unlawful discrimination in order to meet its obligations to take all reasonable steps necessary to prevent and correct harassment and discrimination in the workplace.

RESERVATION OF RIGHTS AND RIGHT TO PRIVACY

I reserves the right, upon completion of a lawful investigation and discovery, to tender and to file supplemental and amended allegations as may be appropriate under the applicable law. I further reserve the right to privacy as provided under California Article 1, Section 1, privacy. Shaffer v. Superior Court (1995) 33 Cal.App.4th 993 [39 Cal.Rptr.2d 506]. In Tylo v. Superior Court (1997) 55 Cal.App.4th 1379 [64 Cal.Rptr.2d 731]; Barrenda L. v. Superior Court (1998) 65 Cal.App.4th 794[76 Cal.Rptr.2d 727]. In addition to the rights vested to me under The United States Constitution and Bill of Rights.

Pursuant to the California Civil of Civil Procedure § 2017.220 (a) states "In any civil action alleging conduct that constitutes sexual harassment...any party seeking discovery concerning the plaintiff's sexual conduct with individuals other than the alleged perpetrator shall establish specific facts showing that there is good cause for that discovery

RE:

concerning the plaintiff's sexual conduct with individuals other than the alleged perpetrator shall establish specific facts showing that there is good cause for that discovery and that the matter sought to be discovered is relevant to the subject matter of the action and reasonably calculated to lead to the discovery of admissible evidence. This showing shall be made by noticed motion, accompanied by a meeting and confer declaring under Section 2016.040, and shall not be made or considered by the court at an ex parte hearing."

ABM has demonstrated an intent to side-step this Civil Procedure and has miscontrued, misrepresented, and/or omitted the facts to The California Employment Development Department. ABM has acted as if it is above the rule of law and does not honor nor respect California Laws and Public Policy. ABM has treated me unfairly by law and by contract and is opposed to preventing harassment and discrimination in their workplace.

STATEMENT OF FACTS

Sexual Harassment Incidents at 800 S. Hope Street

January 27, 2014: After I was scheduled for a series of job interviews for a Security Officer position with ABM Scheduler ▇▇▇, ABM Manager ▇▇▇, and ABM District Manager ▇▇▇. I was hired to start as a Security Shift Supervisor and started working for ABM at the location known as 800 S. Hope Street, Los Angeles, California, for $13.40 per hour, *and under a written contract with ABM management and SEIU Labor Organization*. The location is under business contract for security services between CALSTRS (CBRE acting agent) and ABM.

January 27, 2014 to October 5, 2014: I worked as a Shift Supervisor and Security Officer for *ABM at* 800 S. Hope Street; I worked in the security division at this building with no disciplinary issues and was given customer compliments from time to time.

Sunday, October 5, 2014: I was harassed by a non-employee, named ▇▇▇, in ▇▇▇ she would get me fired from my job. I did not accept her offer and told ▇▇▇ to leave me alone. (Exhibit A "Declaration of ▇▇▇").

Monday, October 6, 2014: *I had a complaint about someone harassing me in the building and I promptly notified my immediate supervisor*, ABM Manager ▇▇▇. ▇▇▇ did not leave me alone and became harassing toward me at work. 'Crank calls' at the security desk station *began to come through at various times*, ▇▇▇ spoke curse words at me *when she walked by, even whispering profanity to me* while I was working at the security desk.

Privileged Communication & Confidential Information © 2014 Edward Dumas All rights reserved. No part of this publication may be reproduced or transmitted in any form or by any means, electronic or mechanical, including photocopy, recording or any other information storage and retrieval system without prior permission in writing from Edward Dumas.

SEX DISCRIMINATION

Tuesday, October 7, 2014: I continued receiving crank calls at *the* security desk. **I notified Manager** ▮▮▮ regarding the crank calls, curse words, and harassing behavior toward me by ▮▮▮. **I was told to just document it by ABM Manager** ▮▮▮ and I became increasingly more afraid of her.

Wednesday, October 8, 2014: I started regular work shift at 11:00PM, for a graveyard shift, and I was receiving multiple crank calls throughout the night. My co-worker, Security Officer ▮▮▮, noticed the strange behavior ▮▮▮ was exhibiting towards me throughout the workweek and on the graveyard shift. ▮▮▮'s harassing behavior was negatively affecting me at the workplace.

Thursday, October 9, 2014: **I**, *again*, **informed ABM Manager** ▮▮▮ that building employee ▮▮▮ behavior toward me was just getting worse; as the crank calling persisted at the desk all throughout my shift, when she would appear at the security desk she would continue to use curse words at me, act strangely by saying that she's "cracking", "dying", "can't live", passing me notes in sexual nature, and looking at me in a strange manners. **I asked ABM Manager** ▮▮▮ **to report the unlawful harassment to ABM Corporate**. I explained to ABM Manager ▮▮▮ that if these incidents continue to go unreported then there can be major liabilities; I specifically stated to ABM Manager ▮▮▮ that "...[W]e need to protect the client, ABM, and our jobs". I was feeling like the harasser's behavior was so intentional as to sabotage my job and work performance, I needed ABM to get more involved. ABM Manager ▮▮▮ stated to me that he called ABM District Manager ▮▮▮, and/or ABM Security Director ▮▮▮, his immediate supervisor, and informed me that the *ABM District Manager wants me to write a statement*.

Friday, October 10, 2014: **I wrote a statement about the incident** on October 5, 2014, I made a Declaration under penalty of perjury; I arrived at the worksite, **I emailed** the Declaration along with a note, attached as evidence, written to me by ▮▮▮, **and awaited a response from ABM. I never received a response nor call from ABM Human Resources or ABM Management;** *I was led to believe* **that there was going to be an investigation.** ABM Manager ▮▮▮ stated, "...the wheels are rolling...its starting...",thus leading me to believe that there was going to be *a prompt and fair investigation; to investigate my harassment complaint*.

October 11 to 16, 2014:

I kept reporting the harassing behavior by ▮▮▮ **to my immediate supervisor and no one still spoke with me about my complaint**. I was receiving multiple crank calls

RE: ███

at the security desk where I was stationed; also, how building employee ███ would speak curse words at me such as "███ you" or would walk by the security desk and whisper to me '███'; even as far as making suicidal insinuations at times when she would approach me by myself at the security desk. I felt awkward and simply stayed alert in case her behavior became physical. I attempted to give ABM Manager ███ the two notes she gave me but he <u>ignored</u> reading the note(s).

When ███ was present at the building, at the time I was working at the security desk, she had often and continued to speak curse words at me such as "███ you", "you mother ███" "son of a ███", and "you're so full of ███". ███ would pass me explicit sexual notes but I disregarded them because her behavior was unwelcomed.

<u>Friday, October 17, 2014:</u> I worked for the ABM Security Director ███ worksite, with ABM District Manager ███ and ABM Scheduler ███. I spoke with ███ as to if she had knowledge of my complaint about possible sexual harassment at work; she stated that she was unaware of the situation. None of the above named Managers ever discussed nor investigated my concern or complaint regarding building employee ███'s behavior.

<u>Saturday, October 18, 2014 to Sunday, October 19, 2014:</u> I continued to receive crank calls and when building employee ███ walked by, she would speak curse words at me. **No one from ABM Human Resources or ABM Management ever discussed or investigated the harassment that was occurring.**

<u>Monday, October 20, 2014:</u> I attended a building training meeting and ABM District Manager ███ was present but did not speak with me in regards to my sexual harassment complaints against building employee ███. **No one from ABM ever discussed nor investigated my complaint about what has become a hostile work environment.**

<u>Tuesday, October 21, 2014; Wednesday, October 22, 2014; Thursday, October 23, 2014:</u> I continued to receive crank calls and when building employee ███ was present she would speak curse words at me; I asked my co-workers if anyone from the company has talked to them about my harassment concerns regarding ███'s behavior and verified that **no one from ABM has talked to them to investigate the basis of my claim of sex harassment.** Building employee ███ began bothering other Security Officers on another shift, as I was informed.

Friday, October 24, 2014: Off

Privileged Communication & Confidential Information © 2014 Edward Dumas All rights reserved. No part of this publication may be reproduced or transmitted in any form or by any means, electronic or mechanical, including photocopy, recording or any other information storage and retrieval system without prior permission in writing from Edward Dumas.

SEX DISCRIMINATION

RE: ███████

Saturday, October 25, 2014//Sunday, October 26, 2014: No one from ABM Human Resources or ABM Management ever called me nor discussed my complaint and concerns about building employee ███████ harassing me at work. I attempted to forward the letter(s) she was giving me but the ABM Manager ███████ did not want to read them.

Monday, October 27 -28, 2014: (Company held a Meeting for a Fire Drill; Building was evacuated for a Fire Drill)

Wednesday October 29, 2014: I was receiving crank calls at work (Graveyard).

Thursday, October 30, 2014: After working from 11:00PM to 7:00AM, I received a phone call at home about 9:00AM from ABM Scheduler ███████, wanting to me to go an ABM corporate office for a meeting with ABM District Manager ███████. I inquired what kind of meeting would this be, if it is about the incidents, and if I would need my Union Representative, ███████ stated to me that "███████ thinks highly of you" and "your going to have to talk to him about that".

Friday, October 31, 2014: OFF

Saturday, November 1, 2014: I was receiving crank calls at the security desk.

Sunday, November 2, 2014: ███████ argued with me regarding keeping a Tenant's glass door closed and secure; co-worker ███████ was present.

Monday, November 3, 2014: I meet with ███████ whom presented me with a first and final written warning for violating ABM's conflict of interest policy, told me that "the Union would not disagree with [us], it is better to have a job than no job...", and I was to be removed to another worksite or would not have employment with the company.

Tuesday, November 4, 2014: I experienced a loss of wages, as I would have worked my regularly scheduled shift. *I utilized the complaint procedure ABM had in place on October 6, 2014, which was to report it to my immediate supervisor, then to later write a statement, and wait for something to happen such as a transfer and/or training.* No one from ABM still has not talked to me about the harassment incidents that had occurred at ABM.

Wednesday, November 5, 2014: I arrived at the new worksite in where I was brought into Robert Ramirez's office and he informed that I was demoted and that any mistake I make, "even a wrong ███████ and I would be terminated. Mr. ███████ stated to the effect that I would start receiving lesser pay, I pressed this issue of a pay cut with him, and he stated that "he really does not know anything". I informed him at approximately

Privileged Communication & Confidential Information © 2014 Edward Dumas All rights reserved. No part of this publication may be reproduced or transmitted in any form or by any means, electronic or mechanical, including photocopy, recording or any other information storage and retrieval system without prior permission in writing from Edward Dumas.

RE:

11:47AM that I am quitting ABM by "throwing in the towel" and will seek legal remedies and action.

Thursday, November 6, 2014: I filed for unemployment benefits pursuant to having to quit for good cause in lieu of being sexually harassed for four weeks, I promptly reported it when it first started, and no one from ABM ever investigated, corrected, nor prevented the harassment; I was never informed I was to be demoted, changed in job position, given less privileges, and would get a pay reduction at the "meeting" held by ABM District Manager on 11/3/14; I was never compensated for the meeting.

November 10, 2014: I filed an intake with the EEOC.

November 26, 2014: I received a letter from the EEOC, per ███, regarding my intake and a one page informational sheet ("Exhibit C").

November 27, 2014 to December 11, 2014: I am currently processing the EEOC complaint so I can move forward with securing my rights by Court in order to file a lawsuit, as needed. ("Exhibit G").

December 12-21, 2014: Interviewed by California EDD, the representative stated and questioned to me in that employers do not have a duty to protect their employees from harassment and falsely presumed that ABM did an investigation and took "immediate and corrective action" as is required by California Law. Benefits denied by EDD; EDD states "[I] did not explore all reasonable solutions before I quit" ("Exhibit F").

December 27, 2014: I am currently filing an appeal with the CUIAB.

Sex Discrimination

FOR EDD LEGAL REVIEW

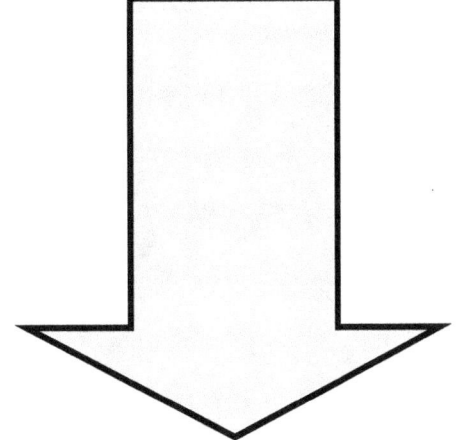

Privileged Communication & Confidential Information © 2014 Edward Dumas All rights reserved. No part of this publication may be reproduced or transmitted in any form or by any means, electronic or mechanical, including photocopy, recording or any other information storage and retrieval system without prior permission in writing from Edward Dumas.

The EDD, EEOC, & Superior Court Legal Forms

'rint

Subject: Fwd: ███ Declaration RE Quid Pro Quo Incident
From: 800 Hope Security
To:
Date: Monday, October 13, 2014 3:33 PM

---------- Forwarded message ----------
From: **800 Hope Security**
Date: Fri, Oct 10, 2014 at 10:21 AM
Subject: ███ Declaration RE Quid Pro Quo Incident
To: ███   ███   ███
              800 Hope Security

Please find my attached Declaration regarding the incident of quid pro quo sex harassment I reported and Exhibit A for supporting evidence of such.

I apologize for any inconvenience I may have caused you.

Feel free to contact me for further investigation.

Truthfully,

███

SEX DISCRIMINATION

Pre-Initial Complaint/ In Pro Per

SUPERIOR COURT OF THE STATE OF CALIFORNIA

COUNTY OF LOS ANGELES - CENTRAL DISTRICT

STANLEY MOSK COURTHOUSE

███████,
    Complainant,

v.

███████,
    Respondent.

Case No.:

DECLARATION OF ███████

RE: QUID PRO QUO SEXUAL HARRASMENT

Date: Friday, October 10, 2014

I, ███████ SAY AND DECLARE AS FOLLOWS:

1. I am a Complainant in this legal issue, and if called as a witness, I could and would testify competently to these facts. I hereby reserve my rights of privacy under the California Constitution, Article 1, Section 1, privacy.

2. I disclose the facts set forth regarding this initial complaint against a female employee of a subtenant at the location inwhere I am contracted to work to perform professional services and labor. I have never made nor advanced any offers for sex in exchange for work at work.

DECLARATION RE QUID PRO QUO SEXUAL HARRASMENT

1   3. The female employee is known as ▓▓▓▓ herein referred to as the "Respondent".
2 The business the Respondent is employed at is known as "▓▓▓▓▓▓▓▓▓LLC"
3 (herein "▓▓▓▓"). ▓▓▓▓ operates and subcontracts its lease from the location inwhere I am
4 contracted to perform professional services and labor.
5   4. On October 5, 2014, at approximately 6:00PM (PST) I discussed ▓▓▓▓ with the
6 Respondent ▓▓▓▓▓▓▓▓▓▓▓▓▓▓▓▓▓▓▓▓▓▓▓ The Respondent demanded
7 terms and conditions to be set forth regarding ▓▓▓▓▓▓▓▓▓▓▓▓▓▓▓
8 I did not agree with the Respondent's terms and conditions, so I explained to the Respondent that
9 I could not ▓▓▓▓▓▓▓s for the terms and conditions she demanded from me.
10   5. The Respondent was angry and screaming at me so I started to walk away▓▓▓▓
11 ▓▓▓▓ the Respondent she screamed and demanded that if ▓▓▓▓▓▓▓
12 ▓▓▓▓, she will make sure that I am fired from my job at the location inwhere I provide
13 my professional services and labor. I did not accept the Respondent's offer and told her that I did
14 not want to ▓▓▓▓▓▓▓ The Respondent starting to ▓▓▓▓▓▓
15 ▓▓▓▓▓▓.
16   6. On October 6, 2014, at 3:00PM I arrived to my job and informed my immediate supervisor
17 of the incident that occurred outside of the workplace. At 4:26PM the Respondent provided me
18 with a typed letter, herein "Exhibit A".▓▓▓▓▓▓▓▓▓▓▓▓▓▓▓▓
19 ▓▓▓▓▓▓▓▓▓▓▓▓▓▓▓▓▓▓.
20   I hereby declare under the penalty of perjury under laws of the State of California that the
21 foregoing is true and correct, Executed in Los Angeles, California on October 10, 2014.

                                              , declarant

DECLARATION RE QUID PRO QUO SEXUAL HARRASMENT

PAGE 132 IS REDACTED*

Sex Discrimination

"EXHIBIT B"

FOR EDD LEGAL REVIEW

Privileged Communication & Confidential Information © 2014 Edward Dumas All rights reserved. No part of this publication may be reproduced or transmitted in any form or by any means, electronic or mechanical, including photocopy, recording or any other information storage and retrieval system without prior permission in writing from Edward Dumas.

Employee Policy Handbook

of underrepresented groups, to develop an Affirmative Action Program, and take extra steps for implementing those reasonable goals through outreach, recruitment, training, and other special activities and commitments.

Any goals that are established are not intended as rigid, inflexible quotas that must be met, but rather as targets reasonably attainable by applying every good faith effort in implementing these plans. The use of goals in the Company's plans is not intended to discriminate against any individual or group of individuals with respect to any employment opportunity for which they are qualified on the grounds that they are not the beneficiaries of Affirmative Action themselves. Nothing in the Company's Affirmative Action Plans is intended to sanction the discriminatory treatment of any person. Thus, the Company's plans have been developed in strict reliance upon the guidelines on Affirmative Action issued by the U.S. Dept. of Labor.

Equal Employment Opportunity: Open Door

Suggestions for improving ABM are always welcome. At some time, employees may have a complaint, suggestion, or question about their job, working conditions or treatment they are receiving. Employee good-faith complaints, questions, and suggestions also are of concern to the Company. The Company has established an "open door" practice to promote effective communication between employees and management in resolving personnel problems.

An employee who encounters problems concerning any aspect of employment by the Company is encouraged to:

1. First discuss the situation with their immediate supervisor within a week of the occurrence who will in turn work with Human Resources to provide a solution or explanation.

2. If the employee is not satisfied with the proposed solution, cannot discuss it with the immediate supervisor, or the problem persists, the employee should contact the Department or Branch Manager or the division's head of Human Resources, who will investigate and provide a solution or explanation.

3. If the problem persists, the employee may contact the ABM Industries' Human Resource Department or the Compliance Hotline at 1-877-253-7804 (abmhotline.ethicspoint.com).

The company encourages employees to bring the matter to Human Resources as soon as possible if they believe that their immediate supervisor has failed to resolve it.

This procedure, which the Company believes is important for both the employee and the Company, cannot guarantee that every problem will be resolved to the employee's satisfaction. However, ABM values employee observations and employees should feel free to raise issues of concern, in good faith, without fear of retaliation.

Equal Employment Opportunity ("EEO"): Policy Against Harassment in the Workplace

Purpose of this Policy

Professional behavior is expected and required of all ABM employees. The Company's intent is to provide all employees with a workplace environment consistent with ABM's core values of Respect, Fairness and Dignity. Employees who are respected and valued and who are not distracted by discrimination, harassment or other forms of unprofessional or unacceptable conduct can fully contribute their skills and talents to enhance ABM's performance. Accordingly, ABM does not tolerate workplace discrimination or harassment based on race, religion, gender, national origin, age, disability, sexual orientation, veteran or any other status protected by law.

This policy is designed to promote a culture of Respect, Fairness and Dignity. To achieve this goal, this policy prohibits both illegal conduct and unprofessional, offensive conduct that is disruptive to teamwork and productivity. This policy applies equally to interactions between ABM employees as well as interactions between ABM employees, customers, vendors, tenants and other third-parties.

Prohibited Conduct

Prohibited conduct includes offensive or derogatory verbal comments or jokes based on any personal characteristic unrelated to job performance. Obscene gestures, display of offensive or sexual visual material, unwanted sexual advances and physical touching or blocking of movement are also prohibited. Submission to sexual advances in order to get, keep or advance in a job, is a serious form of sexual harassment. If you are not sure if your conduct is appropriate for the workplace ask: "Would I want to see my behavior portrayed on the front page or the evening news?" If the answer is "no," then stop what you are doing. If you are unsure about the answer, you should contact Human Resources.

Employee Responsibilities

Speak Up: If you are offended by conduct in the workplace, we encourage you to respond immediately by objecting directly to the offender, which is often very effective. If you are uncomfortable objecting to the offender, or if the conduct continues, report the conduct using the Company's reporting procedures described below. Keep in mind that if you fail to respond to harassment by objecting or reporting it, ABM cannot help resolve the situation or address any misconduct. If you witness offensive conduct, report it using the reporting procedures below. Preferences based on familial or romantic relationships are not appropriate in ABM's workplace. If you see favoritism occurring, report it using the procedures below.

ABM takes seriously all concerns about employee treatment and maintaining a professional workplace environment and prohibits retaliation against individuals who report violations of this policy in good faith. If you observe or experience retaliation, please report it using the reporting procedures below. Retaliation is defined as any conduct or harm that would have the effect of discouraging an employee to make a complaint.

Sex Discrimination

"EXHIBIT C"

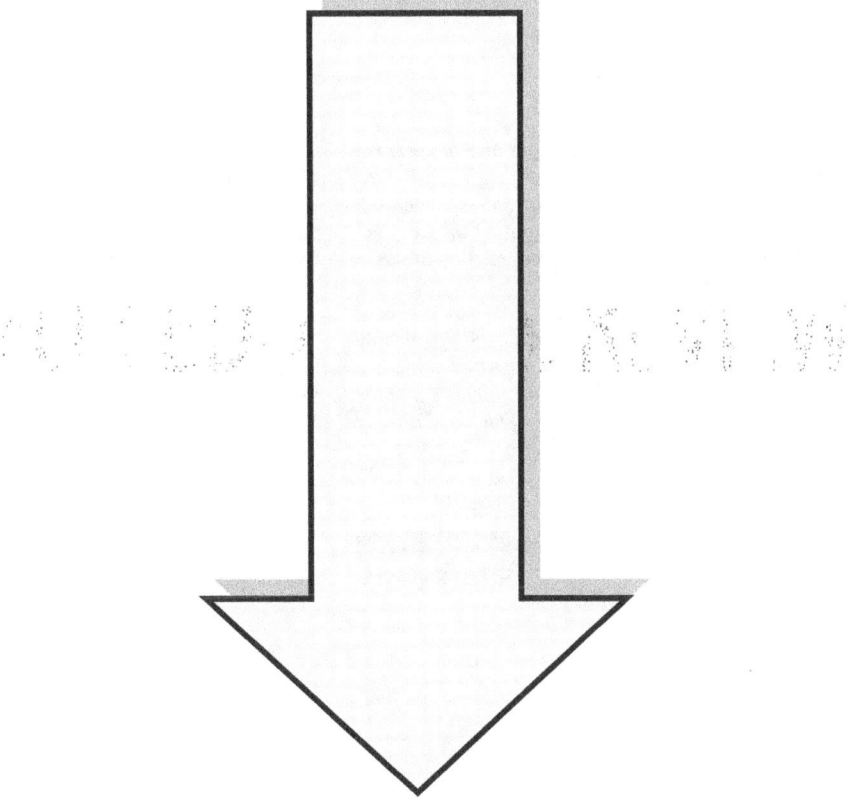

U.S. EQUAL EMPLOYMENT OPPORTUNITY COMMISSION
Los Angeles District Office

255 E. Temple Street, 4th Floor
Los Angeles, CA 90012
Intake Information Group: (800) 669-4000
Intake Information Group TTY: (800) 669-6820
Los Angeles Status Line: (866) 408-8075
Los Angeles Direct Dial: (213) 894-1096
TTY (213) 894-1121
FAX (213) 894-1118

Date: November 20, 2014

Respondent: ABM
EEOC Charge Number: ▓▓▓▓▓▓

Dear Mr. ▓▓▓▓▓:

Your correspondence (*letter, intake questionnaire other communication*) concerning allegations of employment discrimination by the Respondent named above has been received by our office and is in the process of being reviewed. The correspondence has been assigned the above-referenced charge number. We have also notified the Respondent that you are filing a charge, which the EEOC is required to do. Upon completion of the review you will be contacted regarding further processing.

Be advised, the EEOC is located in a U.S. Courthouse and anyone attempting to enter must present valid United States state or federal identification (state driver's license, state I.D. card, U.S. passport, or a similar document) to gain entrance into the building. If you do not have United States identification, please contact EEOC at (213) 894-1000 for additional information.

Sincerely,

▓▓▓▓▓▓
CRTIU Supervisor

Office Hours: Monday – Friday, 8:00 a.m. – 4:30 p.m.
Website: www.eeoc.gov
Enclosure: Information Sheet for Charging Parties

Sex Discrimination

"EXHIBIT D"

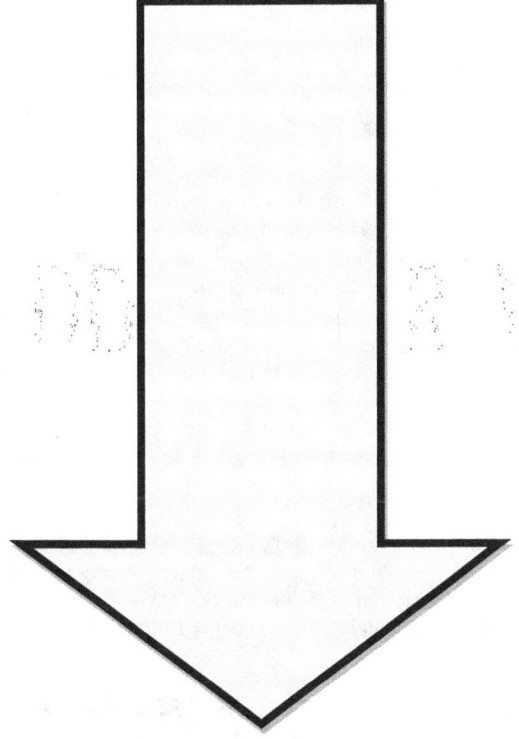

Privileged Communication & Confidential Information © 2014 Edward Dumas All rights reserved. No part of this publication may be reproduced or transmitted in any form or by any means, electronic or mechanical, including photocopy, recording or any other information storage and retrieval system without prior permission in writing from Edward Dumas.

The EDD, EEOC, & Superior Court Legal Forms

Subject: Recissition and Breach of Contract
From: ███
To: ███
Date: Monday, December 1, 2014 2:09 PM

I hereby rescind my signature on the Warning Notice that was issued to me on or around November 3, 2014, at approximately 2:00PM (PST), pursuant to the Los Angeles Master Collective Bargaining Agreement (Contract), Article 4, Discipline and Discharge, Section 4.2 herein states:

"Warning notices shall be issued within ten days after the Employer knew or should have known of the offense. A copy of the warning shall be sent to the Union. Each warning notice shall contain a place for the employee to sign to acknowledge receipt without admitting guilt."

Pursuant to Contract, the Warning Notice regarding the alleged "Conflict of Interest" was in fact a breach of contract because you failed, within ten days, as prescribed by Contract. Nevertheless, you knew I became friends with someone in the building; therefore the warning notice **is not valid and is hereby declared null and void.**

I further declare I was constructively terminated due to quid pro quo sexual harassment in the workplace and the failure to take corrective action to prevent such further harassment from occurring.
I experienced loss of wages, privileges and benefits, and was unjustly demoted for complaining about an employee from another company in the building sexually harassing me.

Please note that I complained to you about Ms. ███ LLC, sexually harassing me on October 6, 2014, I wrote a *Declaration, under penalty of perjury*, on October 10, 2014, and emailed it to you. I saw you in at least in two separate and distinct meetings throughout the month and you never discussed the sexual harassment complaint with me at all.

It was not until October 30, 2014, that I was notified by ███ of a meeting desired by you in regards to "the incident", I inquired if this is a disciplinary meeting, if I would need my Union Representative at this meeting, and if this meeting would be compensated. ███ was silent and simply responded, "███ thinks highly of you, you're going to have to talk to him when he is here."

I meet with you on November 3, 2014, with ███ present but silent, at the scheduled meeting at 2:00PM in where you had me waiting for thirty to forty-five minutes in the lobby with no information, parking accommodation, or union representation. You stated a take or leave it demand, inwhere I would be transferred to a different location, inwhere I would be training and working with the 'Director of Security' OR I would not be employed.

SEX DISCRIMINATION

I found the adverse action, new terms and conditions set forth unacceptable after learning that I was demoted, along with a potential pay-cut, and it has not been tolerable working for an employer who does not compensate correctly on a consistent basis. Therefore, please forward me a copy of timesheets from January 27, 2014 to November 5, 2014, for all the times I had worked, "clocked in", or "wrote in", whether it was by myself or someone else, for everyday I had worked.

Please attach this letter and my Declaration RE Quid Pro Quo Sexual Harassment to the Warning Notice, along with any other additional information you receive from the EEOC, as should be sent to the Union along with the original warning notice.

Feel free to contact me if you have any comments or questions at 213 ▓▓▓▓▓▓▓

"EXHIBIT E"

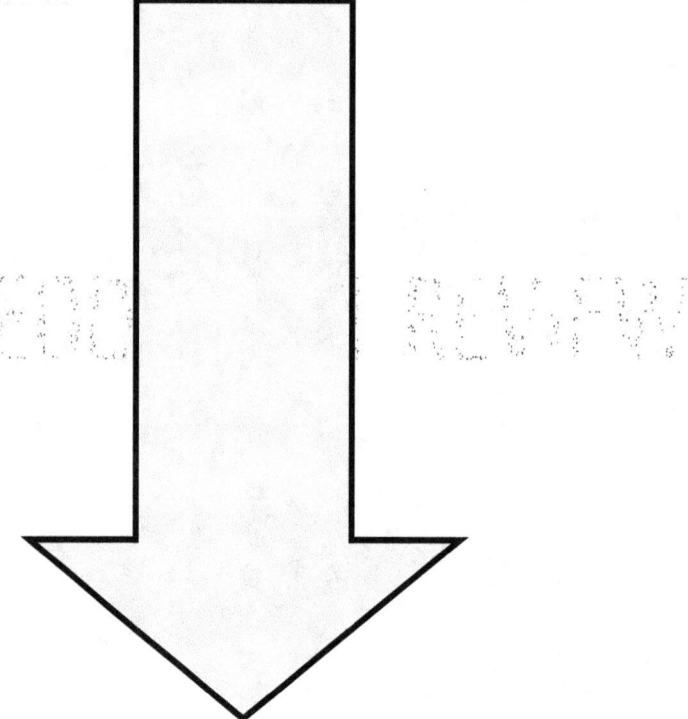

Sex Discrimination

deductions were made, together with a monthly list of the employees for whom it has deducted dues and on whose behalf it is remitting dues. The list shall include the first and last name of each employee, the total amount of dues which were deducted, and the Social Security number or other unique nine (9) digit employee identifier number associated with the individual employee.

All deduction authorization forms must be submitted to the Employer within six (6) months from the date the employee completed the form. The Employer will not process deduction authorization forms submitted in excess of six (6) months after their completion.

2.4 The Union will furnish the forms to be used for authorization. The Employer will furnish the Union with a duplicate copy of all signed authorizations, unless another procedure has been adopted.

2.5 The Union will completely defend and indemnify and hold the Employer free and harmless against any and all claims, damages, suits or other forms of liability whatsoever that shall arise out of or by reason of action taken by the Employer at the Union's request for the purpose of complying with any of the provisions of Article 2, including the Employer's termination of any employee for the failure to pay dues or an agency fee, including court costs and reasonable attorney fees. The Union shall have the right to select counsel to represent the Employer to contest, litigate, administer and/or settle any legal action with the Employer's consent, which shall not be unreasonably withheld.

ARTICLE 3
NO DISCRIMINATION

The Union and the Employer agree they shall not discriminate in violation of federal or state law against any applicant or employee in hiring, promotions, assignments, suspensions, discharge, terms and conditions of employment, wages, training, recall or lay-off status, because of race, color, ancestry, religion, creed, national origin, age, sex, maternity status, sexual orientation, gender expression, veteran status, or against a qualified individual with a disability (defined by the Americans with Disabilities Act). No employee or applicant for employment covered by this Agreement shall be discriminated against because of membership in the Union or activities on behalf of the Union.

ARTICLE 4
DISCIPLINE AND DISCHARGE

4.1 The Employer shall be free to discharge employees for refusal to obey lawful orders, incompetency, misrepresentation, intoxication, or any just cause. An employee who has not completed his or her probationary period may be disciplined or discharged without just cause and without recourse to the Grievance and Arbitration procedure set forth in Article 25.

4.2 The Employer shall be free to discipline any employee who commits an infraction, which, while not being sufficient to constitute just cause for discharge, is sufficient to warrant some lesser disciplinary action. However, no employee who has completed the probationary period will be discharged for offenses, which do not in and of themselves constitute just cause to discharge unless the employee has progressed through the discipline process and been given the opportunity to correct his/her behavior.

Warning notices shall be issued within ten (10) days after the Employer knew or should have known of the offense. A copy of the warning shall be sent to the Union. Each warning notice shall contain a place for the employee to sign to acknowledge receipt without admitting guilt.

Warning or disciplinary notices may not be considered as a part of the Employer's discipline process after twelve (12) months and shall be no longer valid for the purpose of discipline.

4.3 In addition to those circumstances mentioned elsewhere in this Agreement, just cause circumstances for discharge shall include, but not be limited to, unlawful use or unlawful possession of controlled substances, intoxication, insubordination, theft, excessive absenteeism, gross negligence, failure to comply with reasonable rules, policies or directives promulgated by the Employer and clearly communicated to the employee (where such failure to comply constitutes serious misconduct or creates a safety concern), use of unnecessary force or disrespectful treatment of a tenant, visitor or employee and mobility or unwillingness to be trained to fulfill existing or modified security needs of the Employer, the building owner or its tenants. The Union further understands and agrees that the Employer provides an important service to its tenants of a personalized nature to fulfill their security needs, as those needs are perceived by the Employer, the building owner and the tenants. Accordingly, the provisions of this Section shall be implemented and interpreted by the parties and by an arbitrator in arbitration proceedings so as to give significant consideration to such needs.

4.4 The Employer will discharge any employee who is denied registration or whose registration is canceled by the Department of Consumer Affairs of the State of California or any other governmental agency.

Employees who have renewed their registration and document this with a receipt or similar proof by the end of the BSIS grace period, but have not yet received their new registration cards, shall not be denied work, subject to BSIS regulations.

Any employee, who by reason of the requirements of his job assignment must pass a test prescribed by any governmental agency or obtain a permit from any governmental agency and is not able to pass the test to obtain such a permit, shall be removed from the job. The employee will then be offered the first available job for which the employee is qualified that becomes available within the same dispatch area. If the employee refuses the first available job for which the employee is qualified and which is located in his/her geographic area, he/she may be permanently removed from the payroll. Discharge under this Article for failure to possess a license, except as limited above in this Section, shall be without recourse to the Grievance Procedure of Article 25.

"EXHIBIT F"

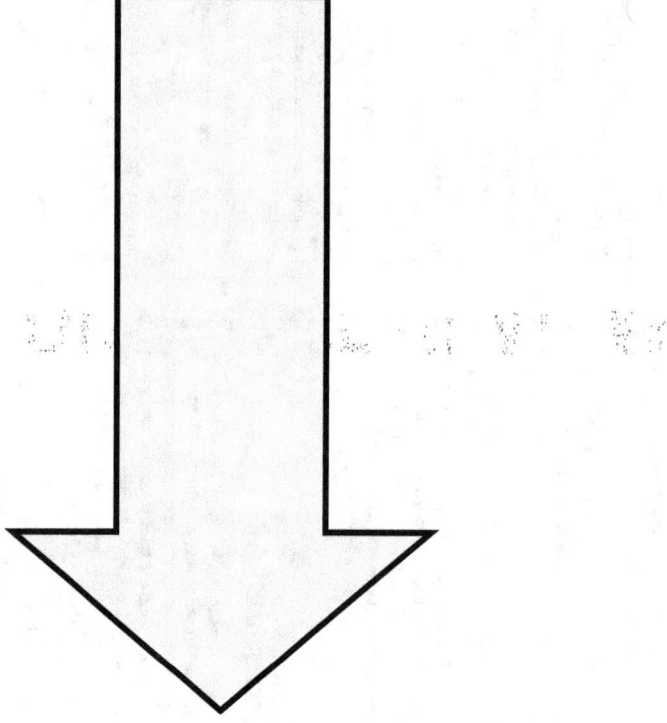

Sex Discrimination

EMPLOYMENT DEVELOPMENT DEPT
SAN BERNARDINO PAC
PO BOX 641
SAN BERNARDINO CA 92402-0641

NOTICE OF DETERMINATION

DATE MAILED   12/11/14
BENEFIT YEAR BEGAN   03/30/14

EDD TELEPHONE NUMBERS:
ENGLISH   1-800-300-5616
SPANISH   1-800-326-8937
CANTONESE   1-800-547-3506
MANDARIN   1-866-303-0706
VIETNAMESE   1-800-547-2058
TTY   1-800-815-9387

SSA NUMBER

YOU ARE NOT ELIGIBLE TO RECEIVE BENEFITS UNDER CALIFORNIA UNEMPLOYMENT INSURANCE CODE SECTION 1256 BEGINNING 11/02/14 AND CONTINUING UNTIL YOU RETURN TO WORK AFTER THE DISQUALIFYING ACT AND EARN $2250.00 OR MORE IN BONA FIDE EMPLOYMENT, AND YOU CONTACT THE ABOVE OFFICE TO REOPEN YOUR CLAIM.

YOU QUIT YOUR LAST JOB WITH ABM ONSITE SERVICES BECAUSE YOU FELT THE WORKING CONDITIONS WERE INTOLERABLE. YOU DID NOT EXPLORE ALL REASONABLE SOLUTIONS BEFORE YOU QUIT. AFTER CONSIDERING AVAILABLE INFORMATION, THE DEPARTMENT FINDS THAT YOU DO NOT MEET THE LEGAL REQUIREMENTS FOR PAYMENT OF BENEFITS. SECTION 1256 PROVIDES - AN INDIVIDUAL IS DISQUALIFIED IF THE DEPARTMENT FINDS HE VOLUNTARILY QUIT HIS MOST RECENT WORK WITHOUT GOOD CAUSE OR WAS DISCHARGED FOR MISCONDUCT FROM HIS MOST RECENT WORK. SECTION 1260A PROVIDES - AN INDIVIDUAL DISQUALIFIED UNDER SECTION 1256 IS DISQUALIFIED UNTIL HE/SHE, SUBSEQUENT TO THE DISQUALIFYING ACT, PERFORMS SERVICES IN BONA FIDE EMPLOYMENT FOR WHICH HE/SHE RECEIVES REMUNERATION EQUAL TO OR IN EXCESS OF FIVE TIMES HIS OR HER WEEKLY BENEFIT AMOUNT.

APPEAL:

YOU HAVE THE RIGHT TO FILE AN APPEAL IF YOU DO NOT AGREE WITH ALL OR PART OF THIS DECISION.

TO APPEAL, YOU MUST DO ALL OF THE FOLLOWING:

A. COMPLETE THE ENCLOSED APPEAL FORM (DE1000M) OR WRITE A LETTER STATING THAT YOU WANT TO APPEAL THIS DECISION. IF YOU WRITE A LETTER TO APPEAL, EXPLAIN THE REASON WHY YOU DO NOT AGREE WITH THE DEPARTMENT'S DECISION. WRITE YOUR SOCIAL SECURITY NUMBER ON EACH DOCUMENT YOU SUBMIT TO THE DEPARTMENT. (TITLE 22, CALIFORNIA CODE OF REGULATIONS (CCR), SECTION 5008).

B. MAIL THE DE1000M OR YOUR LETTER TO THE ADDRESS OF THE OFFICE LISTED ON THE FIRST PAGE OF THIS DECISION.

C. FILE YOUR APPEAL WITHIN TWENTY (20) DAYS OF THE MAIL DATE OF THIS NOTICE OR NO LATER THAN 12/31/14.

YOUR HANDBOOK, "A GUIDE TO BENEFITS AND EMPLOYMENT SERVICES", GIVES MORE INFORMATION ABOUT APPEALS. IF YOU DO NOT HAVE A HANDBOOK, CONTACT THE OFFICE LISTED ON THE FIRST PAGE OF THIS NOTICE.

APPEAL INFORMATION:

WHEN YOUR APPEAL IS RECEIVED, YOUR CASE WILL BE REVIEWED. IF THE DECISION REMAINS THE SAME, WE WILL SEND YOUR APPEAL TO THE OFFICE OF APPEALS. IF YOU APPEAL AFTER THE 20 DAYS, YOU MUST INCLUDE THE REASON FOR THE DELAY. THE ADMINISTRATIVE LAW JUDGE WILL DETERMINE WHETHER YOU HAD GOOD CAUSE FOR THE DELAY. IF THE ADMINISTRATIVE LAW JUDGE DETERMINES YOU DID NOT HAVE GOOD CAUSE FOR SUBMITTING YOUR APPEAL LATE, YOUR APPEAL WILL BE DISMISSED.

THE OFFICE OF APPEALS WILL SEND YOU A LETTER WITH THE DATE, PLACE, AND TIME OF YOUR HEARING AND A PAMPHLET EXPLAINING APPEAL HEARING PROCEDURES. AT THE HEARING, THE ADMINISTRATIVE LAW JUDGE WILL LISTEN TO YOU, EXAMINE THE FACTS, AND MAKE A DECISION. YOU MAY HAVE A REPRESENTATIVE OR SOMEONE ELSE HELP YOU.

IF YOU ARE CLAIMING CONTINUING BENEFITS:

WHILE YOU WAIT FOR THE ADMINISTRATIVE LAW JUDGE'S DECISION, YOU MUST CONTINUE TO MAIL YOUR CLAIM FORMS TO THE EDD. IF YOU DO NOT RECEIVE CLAIM FORMS OR A FORM FROM THE OFFICE OF APPEALS, CONTACT THE OFFICE LISTED ON THE FIRST PAGE OF THIS NOTICE. IF THE ADMINISTRATIVE LAW JUDGE DECIDES YOU ARE ELIGIBLE FOR BENEFITS; WE CAN ONLY PAY BENEFITS IF CLAIM FORMS WERE RECEIVED FOR THAT WEEK.

OTHER SERVICES: CONTACT EDD FOR INFORMATION ABOUT (1) JOB REFERRALS, (2) DISABILITY INSURANCE, (3) OTHER EDD SERVICES (4) SERVICES OFFERED BY OTHER AGENCIES.

DE1080 CZ   REV. 1 (06-05)   (CLU)

Sex Discrimination

"EXHIBIT G"

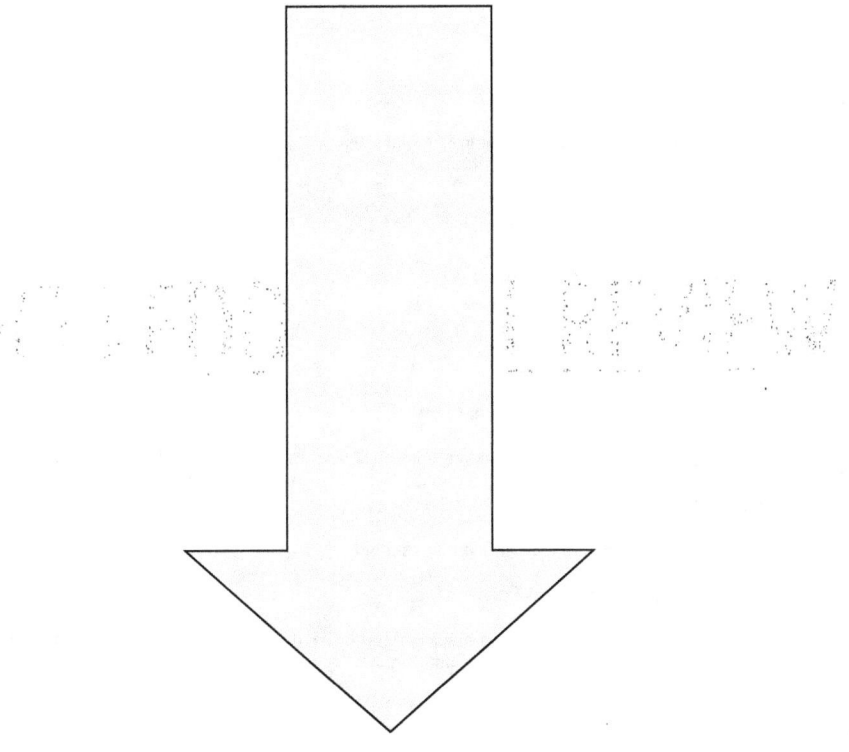

The EDD, EEOC, & Superior Court Legal Forms

U.S. Equal Employment Opportunity Commission
Los Angeles District Office

255 E. Temple St. 4th
Los Angeles, CA 90012

(213) 894-1096
TTY (213) 894-1121
Fax: (213) 894-1118

Respondent: ABM
EEOC Charge No.: 480-2015 ▮▮▮
FEPA Charge No.:

December 16, 2014

Dear ▮▮▮

This is with reference to your recent written correspondence or intake questionnaire in which you alleged employment discrimination by the above-named respondent. The information provided indicates that the matter complained of is subject to the statute(s) checked off below:

[X] Title VII of the Civil Rights Act of 1964 (Title VII)

[ ] The Age Discrimination in Employment Act (ADEA)

[ ] The Americans with Disabilities Act (ADA)

[ ] The Equal Pay Act (EPA)

[ ] The Genetic Information Nondiscrimination Act (GINA)

The attached EEOC Form 5, Charge of Discrimination, is a summary of your claims based on the information you provided. Because the document that you submitted to us constitutes a charge of employment discrimination, we have complied with the law and notified the employer that you filed a charge.

To enable proper handling of this action by the Commission you should:

(1) Review the enclosed charge form and make corrections.

(2) Sign and date the charge in the bottom left hand block where I have made an "X". For purposes of meeting the deadline for filing a charge, the date of your original signed document will be retained as the original filing date.

(3) Return the signed charge to this office.

Please sign and return the charge within thirty (30) days from the date of this letter. Under EEOC procedures, if we do not hear from you within 30 days or receive your signed charge within 30 days, we are authorized to dismiss your charge and issue you a right to sue letter allowing you to pursue the matter in federal court. Please be aware that after we receive your signed Form 5, the EEOC will send a copy of the charge to California Department Of Fair Employment & Housing 2218 Kausen Drive Suite 100 Elk Grove, CA 95758 as required by our procedures. If that agency processes the charge, it may require the charge to be signed before a notary public or an agency official.

SEX DISCRIMINATION

Please use the "EEOC Charge No." listed at the top of this letter whenever you call us about this charge. Please also notify this office of any change in address or of any prolonged absence from home. Failure to cooperate in this matter may lead to dismissal of the charge.

Please also read the enclosed brochure, "What You Should Know Before You File A Charge With EEOC," for answers to frequently asked questions about employee rights and the EEOC process. If you have any questions, please call me at the number listed below. If you have to call long distance, please call collect.

Sincerely,

Ivan Aguilar
Investigator

Office Hours: Monday – Friday, 8:00 a.m. - 4:30 p.m.
www.eeoc.gov

Enclosure(s)
    Copy of EEOC Form 5, Charge of Discrimination
    Copy of EEOC Uniform Brochure, "What You Should Know Before You File A Charge With EEOC."

"EXHIBIT H"

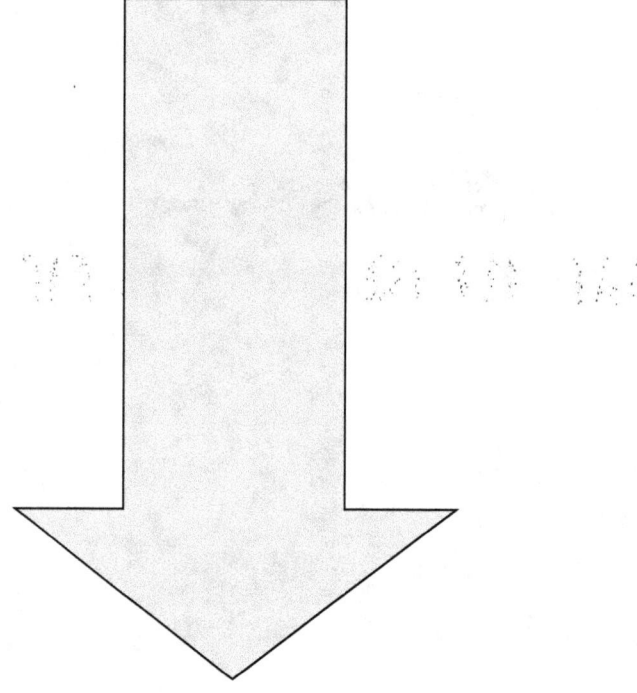

SEX DISCRIMINATION

LABOR COMMISSIONER, STATE OF CALIFORNIA

BUREAU OF FIELD ENFORCEMENT
STATE OF CALIFORNIA-DEPARTMENT OF INDUSTRIAL RELATIONS
DIVISION OF LABOR STANDARDS ENFORCEMENT

OFFICE USE ONLY
TAKEN BY: _____ DATE FILED: _____ INDUSTRY: _____

Please print legibly or type. Fill out this form if you would like to report a widespread violation of workplace laws (e.g., wage and hour, child labor, workers' compensation, or recordkeeping laws) by an employer that affects all or a group of employees working for the employer. If you are claiming only unpaid wages on behalf of yourself and do not wish to report a widespread violation of the law by your employer that also affects other workers, then fill out the DLSE Form 1 (Initial Report or Claim) to file an individual wage claim, instead of this form.

REPORT OF LABOR LAW VIOLATION

SECTION 1. REPORTING PARTY (INDIVIDUAL OR REPRESENTATIVE)

NAME OF REPORTING PARTY: Edward _____ IF INTERPRETER IS NEEDED, INDICATE LANGUAGE: _____
ADDRESS: _____ CITY: _____ STATE: CA ZIP: _____
HOME PHONE: (___) _____ CELL/OTHER PHONE: (___) _____ E-MAIL (if available): _____

If you are represented by a lawyer or other advocate, enter your ADVOCATE and ORGANIZATION information:
NAME: N/A ORGANIZATION NAME: _____
ADDRESS: _____ CITY: _____ STATE: _____ ZIP: _____
HOME PHONE: (___) _____ CELL/OTHER PHONE: (___) _____ E-MAIL (if available): _____

SECTION 2. EMPLOYER REPORTED

EMPLOYER BUSINESS NAME: ABM
ADDRESS: _____ CITY: Los Angeles STATE: CA ZIP: 90015
PHONE: (___) TYPE OF BUSINESS: Security Services, Facility Services TOTAL EMPLOYEES: 107,000
ENTITY TYPE: ✓ CORPORATION INDIVIDUAL PARTNERSHIP LLC LLP OTHER (explain): _____
OWNER'S NAME: N/A NAME AND JOB TITLE OF PERSON IN CHARGE: Gilbert Naranjo, District Manager

	ADDRESS CITY, STATE, ZIP	EMPLOYER STILL OPERATING THERE?	BUSINESS HOURS	TOTAL EMPLOYEES
EMPLOYER'S MAIN WORK LOCATION	LA, CA, 90015	✓ YES NO UNKNOWN	9-5p	
OTHER WORK LOCATION (if any, whether or not you worked there)	LA, CA, 90010	✓ YES NO UNKNOWN	8-5p	
OTHER WORK LOCATION (if any, whether or not you worked there)	LA, CA, 90067	✓ YES NO UNKNOWN		

IS THE EMPLOYER COVERED BY WORKERS' COMPENSATION INSURANCE? ✓ YES NO UNKNOWN
IS THERE A UNION CONTRACT? ✓ YES NO DID YOUR JOB INVOLVE PUBLIC WORKS? YES ✓ NO
EMPLOYER'S VEHICLE LICENSE PLATE NUMBER: _____

SECTION 3. WORK HOURS AND WAGES

DO YOU OR DID YOU WORK FOR THE EMPLOYER? ✓ YES NO IF "YES":
DATE OF HIRE: 01 / 27 / 14 LAST DAY OF WORK (if applicable): 11 / 05 / 15 ✓ QUIT FIRED STILL EMPLOYED
DID THE EMPLOYER DESIGNATE WHAT TIME THE WORKDAY BEGAN FOR EMPLOYEES? ✓ YES NO DON'T KNOW IF "YES":
WHAT TIME DID THE EMPLOYER DESIGNATE? SUN/12 ✓ AM PM
DID THE EMPLOYER DESIGNATE WHICH DAY OF THE WEEK THE WORKWEEK BEGAN? ✓ YES NO DON'T KNOW IF "YES":
WHAT DAY DID THE EMPLOYER DESIGNATE? ✓ SUNDAY MONDAY TUESDAY WEDNESDAY THURSDAY FRIDAY SATURDAY

WHAT IS THE NORMAL OR STANDARD WORK SCHEDULE FOR EMPLOYEES DURING THE WEEK? PROVIDE YOUR BEST ESTIMATE OF THE START AND END TIMES AND NUMBER OF HOURS WORKED FOR EACH WORK DAY. (If employees did not work standard schedules, skip to the next question.)

Day	Start Time	AM/PM	End Time	AM/PM	Hours Worked	
SUNDAY	START TIME: ___	AM PM	END TIME: ___	AM PM	HOURS WORKED: ___	
MONDAY	START TIME: ___	AM PM	END TIME: ___	AM PM	HOURS WORKED: ___	
TUESDAY	START TIME: ___	AM PM	END TIME: ___	AM PM	HOURS WORKED: ___	TOTAL HOURS
WEDNESDAY	START TIME: ___	AM PM	END TIME: ___	AM PM	HOURS WORKED: ___	WORKED PER
THURSDAY	START TIME: ___	AM PM	END TIME: ___	AM PM	HOURS WORKED: ___	WEEK:
FRIDAY	START TIME: ___	AM PM	END TIME: ___	AM PM	HOURS WORKED: ___	
SATURDAY	START TIME: ___	AM PM	END TIME: ___	AM PM	HOURS WORKED: ___	

BOFE 1 (Rev. 11/2012)

SECTION 3. WORK HOURS AND WAGES (continued)

DO EMPLOYEES WORK DIFFERENT SCHEDULES OR IRREGULAR HOURS SO YOU CANNOT PROVIDE A STANDARD WORK SCHEDULE? ✓ YES   NO

IF "YES," BRIEFLY DESCRIBE THE DIFFERENT SCHEDULES OR IRREGULAR WORK HOURS AS BEST AS YOU CAN: _____

WHEN IS THE NORMAL OR STANDARD SCHEDULED MEAL PERIOD FOR EMPLOYEES?
 START TIME: _____ AM PM   END TIME: _____ AM PM   ✓ THERE IS NO STANDARD SCHEDULED MEAL PERIOD

WHAT IS THE AVERAGE LENGTH OF TIME FOR AN EMPLOYEE'S MEAL PERIOD? 30   MINUTES   HOURS

WHO SET THE WORK SCHEDULE? (FULL NAME AND JOB TITLE/POSITION): MARILYN GARCIA, SCHEDULER

WHAT DAY IS PAY DAY?   DAILY
 WEEKLY ON _____   ✓ BI-WEEKLY ON (Once every two weeks) FRIDAY _____
 MONTHLY ON _____   SEMI-MONTHLY ON (Twice a month) _____

WHO PAYS EMPLOYEES? (FULL NAME AND JOB TITLE/POSITION): UNKNOWN

ARE EMPLOYEES PAID BY THE HOUR? ✓ YES   NO   IF "YES," HOW MUCH? $_____ PER HOUR
 VARIES (EXPLAIN): Pay structures vary throughout the corporation.

ARE EMPLOYEES PAID A FIXED AMOUNT OF WAGES (OR SALARY), REGARDLESS OF THE NUMBER OF HOURS WORKED? ✓ YES   NO
 IF "YES," HOW MUCH? $_____   PER DAY   PER WEEK   EVERY 2 WEEKS   SEMI-MONTHLY   MONTHLY
 VARIES (EXPLAIN): Varies on position and location of the employee per se.

ARE EMPLOYEES PAID BY PIECE RATE? YES   NO   IF "YES," HOW MUCH? $_____ PER (Describe Unit) _____
 PIECE RATES VARY (EXPLAIN): DON'T KNOW

HOW ARE EMPLOYEES PAID? ✓ CHECK   CASH
 BOTH CHECK & CASH   OTHER METHOD (EXPLAIN): _____
 ✓ METHOD OF PAYMENT VARIES PER EMPLOYEE OR JOB POSITION (EXPLAIN): GIFTS AND BONUSES ARE PROVIDED.

IF EMPLOYEES ARE PAID IN CASH, DOES THE EMPLOYER KEEP CASH PAYMENT RECORDS OR LOGS?   YES   NO   ✓ DON'T KNOW

DOES THE EMPLOYER KEEP TIME RECORDS OF HOURS WORKED BY EMPLOYEES?   YES   NO   ✓ DON'T KNOW

WHAT LANGUAGES ARE SPOKEN BY EMPLOYEES? ✓ ENGLISH   ✓ SPANISH   MIXTEC   TRIQUE   CANTONESE   MANDARIN   KOREAN
 VIETNAMESE   TAGALOG   CAMBODIAN   HMONG   THAI   PUNJABI   HINDI   RUSSIAN   OTHER: _____

SECTION 4. SUSPECTED VIOLATIONS OF EMPLOYER

The boxes below describe conduct by an employer that violates the law. Please put a check mark in the box(es) if the employer engages in, or any employee or employees have experienced, any of the following violations:

☐ **NO WORKERS' COMPENSATION INSURANCE**

☐ **CHILD LABOR VIOLATIONS:**
 ☐ No valid work permit(s)
 ☐ No valid entertainment work permit(s)
 ☐ Minor(s) work excessive or prohibited hours
 ☐ Minor(s) work in hazardous conditions
 Estimated number of minors affected: _____

☑ **MINIMUM WAGE VIOLATIONS:**
 ☐ Paid below minimum wage
 ☐ Not paid at all for overtime hours worked
 ☑ Not paid for all hours worked, including unpaid travel time and try-out time
 ☐ Paycheck issued with insufficient funds
 ☐ Asked employee to pay back wages paid
 ☑ No split shift premium pay
 Estimated number of employees affected: _____

☑ **OVERTIME VIOLATIONS:**
 ☐ Not paid daily overtime for hours worked over 8 hours per day (or 10 hours per day for farmworkers)
 ☑ Not paid weekly overtime for hours worked over 40 hours per week
 ☑ Not paid double time for hours worked over 12 hours per day
 ☐ Not paid overtime for working on the 7th consecutive workday in a workweek
 Estimated number of employees affected: _____

BOFE 1 (Rev. 11/2012)

Sex Discrimination

SECTION 4 - SUSPECTED VIOLATIONS OF EMPLOYER (continued)

[✓] OTHER UNPAID WAGES:
- [ ] Wages are not paid at the contracted rate
- [✓] No reporting time premium pay
- [✓] No premium pay for missing meal or rest periods

Estimated number of employees affected: _____

[ ] PAY STUB VIOLATIONS:
- [ ] Paid by check or cash without an itemized wage deduction statement
- [ ] Itemized wage deduction statement provided but not accurate and/or incomplete
- [ ] Itemized wage deduction statement not provided at least semi-monthly

Estimated number of employees affected: _____

[ ] MEAL PERIOD VIOLATIONS:
- [ ] 30-minute off-duty meal period not provided by the end of the 5th hour of work
- [ ] Second 30-minute off-duty meal period not provided when working more than 10 hours
- [ ] Meal period provided but less than 30 minutes

Estimated number of employees affected: _____

[ ] REST BREAK VIOLATIONS:
- [ ] For work days between 3.5 hours and up to 6 hours per day, not allowed to take a 10-minute rest break
- [ ] For work days of more than 6 hours and up to 10 hours per day, not allowed to take two 10-minute rest breaks
- [ ] For work days of more than 10 hours and up to 14 hours per day, not allowed to take three 10-minute rest breaks

Estimated number of employees affected: _____

[✓] PAY DATE VIOLATIONS:
- [ ] No fixed pay date
- [✓] Late payment of wages

Estimated number of employees affected: _____

[✓] RECORD KEEPING VIOLATIONS:
- [✓] Daily time records are not kept or inaccurate
- [✓] Payroll records are not kept or inaccurate
- [✓] No notice to new hires (under Labor Code Section 2810.5)

[✓] BUSINESS EXPENSE VIOLATIONS:
- [✓] Uniforms not reimbursed or illegally charged to employees
- [ ] Tools, supplies or equipment not reimbursed or illegally charged to employees
- [ ] Illegal charges for cash shortages, breakage, or loss of equipment

Estimated number of employees affected: _____

[✓] FAILURE TO POST:
- [✓] Applicable Industrial Welfare Commission Order not posted
- [ ] Minimum Wage Order 2001 not posted
- [✓] Pay day notice not posted
- [ ] Workers' compensation insurance notice not posted
- [ ] Rate of compensation not posted (for farmworkers only)

[ ] MISCLASSIFICATION:
- [ ] Employees misclassified as independent contractors
- [ ] Salaried employees misclassified as exempt employees

Estimated number of employees affected: _____

[ ] LICENSING/REGISTRATION VIOLATIONS:
- [ ] Unlicensed construction contractor
- [ ] Contracted with unlicensed construction contractor
- [ ] Unlicensed farm labor contractor
- [ ] Unregistered garment contractor or manufacturer
- [ ] Unregistered car wash

[ ] FAILURE TO PROVIDE LACTATION ACCOMMODATIONS

Estimated number of employees affected: _____

[✓] OTHER VIOLATIONS (briefly explain):
Failure to provide suitable Seats, pursuant to IWC 4-2001, § 14.Seats

Estimated number of employees affected: _____

Please provide any other information about your complaint that you believe is important for the Labor Commissioner to know:
Time records are often altered and changed. Other employees have experienced late payment of wages and not paid for all hours worked; it is unknown to me how many are affected; I was told by my immediate Supervisor that "...there is no overtime to be paid, even if you have to stay overtime" when my relief was late.

Please provide the following information for any minors under the age of 18 who work for the employer:

FULL NAME (first and last name, and any "nick" names)	AGE	JOB POSITION/ TYPE OF WORK PERFORMED	NORMAL WORK SCHEDULE	HOW WAS THE MINOR PAID (by check, in cash, both cash and check, or other method)?

MAY YOUR NAME BE USED IN AN INVESTIGATION? [ ] YES [✓] NO
DO YOU WANT DLSE TO KEEP YOUR NAME AND CONTACT INFORMATION CONFIDENTIAL? * [✓] YES [ ] NO

I HEREBY CERTIFY THAT THE INFORMATION ABOVE IS A TRUE STATEMENT TO THE BEST OF MY KNOWLEDGE.
SIGNED: ███████████ DATE: 11/20/2014
PRINT NAME: ███████████

* DLSE will maintain confidentiality as appropriate in each case and to the extent provided for under the law. Information may need to be released in some cases.

"EXHIBIT I"

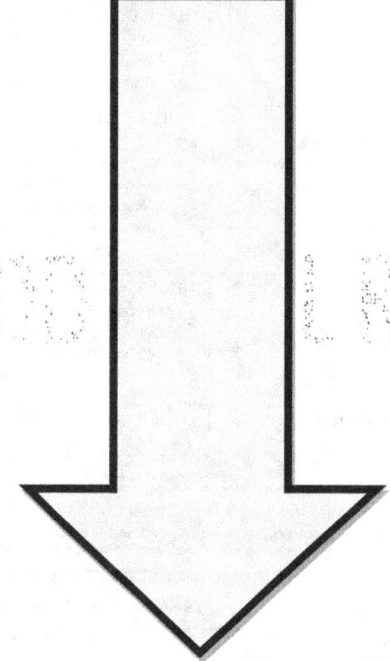

SEX DISCRIMINATION

DECEMBER 17, 2014

(Additional, Other, and Confidential Information)

I am writing in response to my interview with the *California Employment Development Department* on December 12, 2014. I hold that pursuant to California law, ABM should not be allowed take the position that a Corporation can let an employee be sexually harassed at work and not take any reasonable steps to prevent it.

In my interview on 12/10/14 at approximately 9:30AM, the interviewer assumed that my former employer, ABM, conducted an investigation into my sexual harassment allegations at work, with no factual basis to form that assumption. I explained that there was no investigation; I was removed or constructively transferred to another location four weeks after I had complained about someone constantly sexually harassing me at work; ABM failed to take "*immediate* and appropriate corrective action" according to what the law states and mandates to covered employers (see **Government Code § 12940(j)(1)**). Please note "immediate" is a legal requirement for employers to instantly take any reasonable steps to stop harassment.

ABM's District Manager's decision to remove me was executed four weeks later after I initially complained about sexual harassment to him and I consistently inquired if anyone was going to investigate the unlawful harassment or the harasser. ABM did nothing and took no steps to prevent the unlawful harassment from occurring during my work shifts. ABM took me off work or constructively suspended me for one day on 11/4/14 before removing me to another location and demoting me to another position four weeks after I complained about sexual harassment at work, in addition to a final notice, seasoned for wrongful termination.

Employers operating in California are obligated to take immediate action against harassment in the workplace and, moreover, are to provide anti-harassment training to new supervisors within the first six months of new hire. I was never provided that particular training as a newly hired supervisor which is required and mandated by law. (see **California Government Code §12950.1**)

It is settled law in California that if any covered employer fails in their duty to prevent or correct unlawful harassment, then they are liable for harassment that has occurred at the workplace. Pursuant to California law, specifically see **Government Code § 12940(j)(1)**, which makes it unlawful for employers to allow:

"... harassment of an employee, an applicant, or a person providing services pursuant to a contract by an employee, other than an agent or supervisor, shall be unlawful if the entity, or its agents or supervisors, knows or should have known of this conduct and fails to take immediate and appropriate corrective action. An employer may also be responsible for the acts of nonemployees, with respect to sexual harassment of employees, applicants, or persons providing services pursuant to a contract in the workplace, where the employer, or its agents or supervisors, knows or should have known of the conduct and fails to take immediate and appropriate corrective action. In reviewing cases involving the acts of nonemployees, the extent of the employer's control and any other legal responsibility that the employer may have with respect to the conduct of those non employees shall be considered. An entity shall take all reasonable steps to prevent harassment from occurring. Loss of tangible job benefits shall not be necessary in order to establish harassment."

Furthermore, pursuant to the California Attorney General's Office, Civil Rights Handbook, Third Edition, 2001, states on page 30: "...under Unemployment Insurance Code section 1256.7, you also have good cause to quit your job if you are sexually harassed by your employer [footnote]. Accordingly, if you are discriminated against on any of the basis set forth in section 125.2 or are sexually harassed, you may not be disqualified from receiving unemployment insurance benefits if you quit your job."

The Attorney General goes on to state how one must meet all other requirements to be eligible for unemployment and for more information regarding my rights to contact your Department for assistance. This is problematic because in my interview the Department took the position that some type of sexual harassment is legal and the employer did a good job in removing me after being sexually harassed at work for four weeks.

I am very concerned because accordingly the California Attorney General goes on to state further on page 30:

"It is very important to note that if you do quit your job because you have been discriminated against by your employer and file a claim for unemployment insurance benefits, your employer may appeal any EDD determination that you should receive benefits. If this occurs, you may wish to seek the advice of an attorney. Under California law, if you should subsequently lose your unemployment insurance case, your employer may then be able to use that decision against you in any subsequent discrimination case which you might file with some other governmental agency or in court. In other words, a loss in the unemployment insurance case may prevent you from prevailing in another forum under a different set of laws."

In addition, ABM does not fully comply with California Labor Code provisions; please find a confidential copy of the Labor Violation Report as supporting evidence for good cause; please find a copy of the EEOC correspondence as supporting evidence for my initial government complaint for good cause.

Feel free to contact me if you have any comments or questions at   or Email me at

Truthfully,

Sex Discrimination

SEX DISCRIMINATION

DECISION BY THE ADMINISTRATIVE LAW JUDGE MICHAEL KURZ (DISCRIMINATORY)

CALIFORNIA UNEMPLOYMENT INSURANCE APPEALS BOARD

INGLEWOOD OFFICE OF APPEALS
9800 South La Cienega Blvd - Ste 901
INGLEWOOD CA 90301

(310) 337-4302

Claimant-Appellant

Case No.
Issue(s): 1256
Date Appeal Filed: 12/29/2014

EDD: 0410   BYB: 03/30/2014

Date and Place of Hearings(s):
(1) 01/20/2015   Long Beach

Parties Appearing:
*Claimant

* Indicates Party Appeared by Written Statement

DECISION

The decision in the above-captioned case appears on the following page(s).

The decision is final unless appealed within 20 calendar days from the date of mailing shown below. See the attached "Notice to Parties" for further information on how to file an appeal. If you are entitled to benefits and have a question regarding the payment of benefits, call EDD at 1-800-300-5616.

Michael Kurz, Administrative Law Judge

FILE COPY

Date Mailed: JAN 28 2015

Case No.: ▮▮▮▮
CLT/PET: ▮▮▮▮
Parties Appearing: Claimant
Parties Appearing by Written Statement: Claimant

Inglewood Office of Appeals
ALJ: Michael Kurz

ISSUE STATEMENT

The claimant appealed from a determination disqualifying the claimant for unemployment benefits under Unemployment Insurance Code section 1256. The issue in this case is whether the claimant left the most recent employment voluntarily without good cause.

FINDINGS OF FACT

The claimant worked for ten months as a security officer. His last day of work was November 4, 2014 and his final rate of pay was $13.40 an hour.

The claimant voluntarily quit because he was being transferred as a result of his complaints about a tenant in the building that he was a security officer for.

The claimant did not like being transferred and therefore quit his job. The claimant alleged that he was being harassed by a tenant in the building. The claimant brought this to the employer's attention, and while the employer was investigating they decided to transfer the claimant. Instead of going with the transfer, allowing the investigation to play out, the claimant instead became upset, angry, and voluntarily quit.

At the time the claimant quit he did not have another job lined up.

REASONS FOR DECISION

An individual is disqualified for benefits if he or she left his or her most recent work voluntarily without good cause. (Unemployment Insurance Code, section 1256.)

There is good cause for voluntarily leaving work where the facts disclose a real, substantial, and compelling reason of such nature as would cause a reasonable person genuinely desirous of retaining employment to take similar action. (Precedent Decision P-B-27.)

Good cause for leaving work must be determined in light of the actual or real cause of the separation in issue. (Precedent Decision P-B-8.)

▮▮▮-150128

SEX DISCRIMINATION

Employment security statutes are designed to avoid the menace of economic insecurity, and not to make work pleasant. Petty irritations are a part of everyday living, and no work is conducted in an atmosphere of complete sweetness and light. If irritations are not material and substantial they must be borne, and do not constitute good cause for leaving work. (*Department of Industrial Relations v. Mann* (1950) 35 Ala.App. 505, 50 So.2d 780.)

"'An employee may not be unreasonably sensitive to his [or her] working environment. .... Every job has its frustrations, challenges, and disappointments; these are inherent in the nature of work. An employee is protected from ... unreasonably harsh conditions, in excess of those faced by his [or her] co-workers. He [or she] is not, however, guaranteed a working environment free of stress.'" (*Turner v. Anheuser-Busch, Inc.* (1994) 7 Cal.4th 1238; citing with approval *Goldsmith v. Mayor and City of Baltimore* (4th Cir. 1993) 987 F.2d 1064.)

Section 1256.5 (formerly section 1256.7) of the Unemployment Insurance Code provides that sexual harassment is good cause for leaving employment if a reasonable effort is made to preserve the employment relationship in cases in which such effort would not be futile. "Sexual harassment" includes unwelcome sexual advances, requests for sexual favors, and any other verbal, visual or physical conduct of a sexual nature when any of the following occur:

(1) Submission to the conduct is either explicitly or implicitly made a condition of the employment.

(2) Submission to or rejection of the conduct is used as the basis for employment decisions affecting the individual.

(3) The conduct has the purpose or effect of interfering unreasonably with the individual's job performance or creating an intimidating, hostile or offensive working environment.

In Precedent Decision P-B-475 the claimant's co-worker engaged in conduct ranging from comments about the claimant's body and undergarments to pestering the claimant to accompany him on social outings. The co-worker finally grabbed the claimant's buttocks. The Appeals Board held that a reasonable woman would feel the co-worker's acts had created an intimidating, hostile and offensive environment.

In Precedent Decision P-B-8 the claimant quit because of dissatisfaction with a rotating shift, but without any complaint to management or any request to be assigned to a different shift or location. The appeals board held that an individual genuinely desirous of retaining employment would have complained, thus affording management an opportunity to make an adjustment. The claimant's failure to do so negated any good cause which might otherwise have existed for quitting.

In this instance, the claimant voluntarily quit his most recent employment without good cause. The claimant's complaints involved the fact that he had dated a woman that worked in the building who was not a co-employee. The claimant alleged that that woman then began to harass him and wanted him to be in a relationship. As soon as he expressed this to the employer the employer began an investigation, and as a result, the claimant was transferred. The claimant took this to mean that he was being retaliated against rather than the fact that the employer was attempting to resolve the situation and was separating the parties.

At the time the claimant quit he did not have another job lined up. Further, the claimant did not give the employer an opportunity to attempt to resolve the matters, or, the claimant simply disagreed with the fact that the employer was removing him from the situation because he was the one complaining about the situation. In any event, whatever good cause the claimant had, was negated by the fact that the claimant did not provide the employer reasonable opportunity to resolve the matter. Further, it appears that the employer was attempting to resolve the matter by transferring the claimant to another station given the fact the employer had no control over the person the claimant was alleging was harassing him. The employer's actions were not unreasonable given the claimant's persistent complaints. Under these circumstances the claimant voluntarily quit without good cause and accordingly is disqualified for benefits under section 1256 of the code.

DECISION

The determination of the department is affirmed. The claimant is disqualified for benefits under 1256 of the code. Benefits are denied.

SD:cb/em 2/1

4

SEX DISCRIMINATION

Case No. ▓▓▓▓▓

INGLEWOOD OFFICE OF APPEALS
9800 South La Cienega Blvd - Ste 901
INGLEWOOD CA 90301
Telephone: (310) 337-4302
Fax: (310) 337-4392

DECISIONS SENT TO

▓▓▓▓▓▓▓▓▓▓

NOTICE OF DEFAMATION OF CHARACTER AND DEMAND FOR RETRACTION TO THE EDD

Office of Appeals Case File Number ▇▇▇▇

FROM: ▇▇▇▇▇▇▇▇▇)

JANUARY 26, 2015

IMMEDIATE ATTENTION TO THE FOLLOWING PERSONS:

TO: The Employment Development Department; The San Bernardino PAC"; "L. Robinson"; and "Representative CRL" (herein referred as the "RECIEPIENTS");

SUBJECT: NOTICE of Defamation of Character, Untrue/Unfair Reporting, & Altering Evidence: Demand for Redaction, Retraction, and/or Deletion

NOTICE: My written and oral statements are true, in furtherance of direct and physical evidence that I was discriminated against and allowed to be harassed at ABM. The above named "RECIEPIENTS" must cease, retract and/or, as applicable, redact the defamatory statements made against me.

This governmental agency and its agents have made alterations and severely prejudiced my claim as if they were the Judge and Jury in all legal matters. My statement that I "reported someone sexually harassing me at the location known as "▇▇▇ ▇ ▇▇▇▇" is true and cannot be disputed by ANY of YOU as a matter of FACT. Nevertheless, as it is has come to my immediate attention, as to the specific details, on January 15, 2015, upon review of my case file number ▇▇▇▇▇▇ at the Inglewood Office of Appeals, CIUAB.

Herein, the named above "RECIEPIENTS" did indeed alter physical and direct evidence; subjected me to unfair and untrue governmental reporting for defamatory and discriminatory purposes in violation of my personal and civil rights. The named government insurance agency and persons, whether by initial and/or initial and name, plus department, are herein referred to as the "RECIEPIENTS".

The RECIEPIENTS have shown hatred, prejudice, and with a negligent-reckless disregard for the truth in their report of me with malice. The RECIEPIENTS have constructed

© 2015 L. Edward Dumas. All rights reserved. No part of this publication may be reproduced or transmitted in any form or by any means, electronic or mechanical, including photocopy, recording or any other information storage and retrieval system without prior permission in writing from L. Edward Dumas.

Sex Discrimination

Office of Appeals Case File Number

information in a document known as "Report of Claim Status VQ" and misrepresented the truth as the erroneous basis to defame and discriminate against me in this prejudiced report. The RECIPIENTS have acted unlawfully in the furtherance of altering valid evidence in support of my litigation against a company (ABM) that currently discriminates against their own workers for reporting harassment in their workplace. A fact well known by another governmental agency is known as the EEOC.

Please look up the EEOC, its authority, guidance, rules, regulations, and current cases it has been involved in such as ABM. It is the EEOC's glorious task as to help eliminate and eradicate discrimination in America; and denial of equal opportunities in the American workplace. It has been the RECIEPIENTS shameful task as to help aggravate and exacerbate discrimination and denial of true and fair reporting from claims discrimination stemming from the workplace in the State of California. This behavior displayed by the RECIEPIENTS can be viewed as truly Anti-American by way of contempt of my civil rights vested in the US and California Constitutions, in addition to Statutory and Declaratory laws.

The RECIEPIENTS, as it must be noted, should have been educated in the EEOC and equal opportunity in the workplace in general. The RECIEPIENTS' insensitivity and alterations of evidence demonstrate a suppression of my civil rights and their tendency to encourage American Companies to lie about its unlawful employment practices. Direct and physical evidence has now been altered and attempted to have been destroyed by the RECIPIENTS, not just defamatory and discriminatory on its face, but a suppression of civil rights on its face.

The Recipients have not honored my personal and civil rights and have merely attempted to suppress them in accordance with ABM, who has intentionally deprived me of equal opportunities by law and now here comes the RECIEPIENTS to their rescue. Only simply to aid and abet the discrimination and unfair business practices by ABM.

The RECIPIENTS have prejudicially misconstrued and falsely constructed parts of their report, altering previous evidence, in order to act in bad faith, discriminate, and treat me

© 2015 L. Edward Dumas. All rights reserved. No part of this publication may be reproduced or transmitted in any form or by any means, electronic or mechanical, including photocopy, recording or any other information storage and retrieval system without prior permission in writing from L. Edward Dumas.

Office of Appeals Case File Number

unfairly. The statement and fact that "I was demoted and given less terms" is a fact and cannot be disputed but only has been to date by the RECIEPIENTS. The government and its own agents have reported with falsity, assumed falsely with a reckless disregard for the truth and law, and in turn discriminated against me because of my protected characteristics.

The RECIPIENTS are working as a proxy agent and advocate for a company (ABM) that allows its workers to be discriminated against freely, with prejudice, and harassed at work with no attempts to stop the unlawful conduct, whether it be a female and even a male.

The California Government, along with Federal Mandated-Funds, are being manipulated by paying these RECIEPIENTS, inadvertently, to assist ABM, in suppressing my civil rights, free of charge. At the same time, all the while making me suffer for it, but not limited to defending myself where there is no res judicata. It is as if the RECIEPIENTS were being paid by ABM in order to collaterally estop my employment discrimination case from going forward. How convenient for ABM.

The statement, entered as data on the Report Claim of Status, states that I "cannot describe a valid compelling reason for the quit." Is not a fact of the "FINAL INCIDENT". This is a alteration and discriminatory conclusion of the facts, not the facts itself. As the RECIEPIENTS would not find a "valid" reason; because the interviewer on about 12/10/14 acted unprofessionally, reversely discriminated, and displayed hatred and disbelief towards me.

I have told the truth in this matter, I told the truth that I was demoted and indeed threatened with a pay cut. I have no motive to lie and be subject to humiliation by ABM and now I have to be subject to humiliation by YOU.

One of the RECIPIENTS stated to me in the interview, that they did not think that the "employer" could or had the duty to stop harassment against their workers in the workplace. This statement was never documented nor referenced in the "Record of Claim Status Interview VQ". This statement was not documented by the RECIEPIENTS because it would have showed their discriminatory state of mind and intent to have altered evidence

© 2015 L. Edward Dumas. All rights reserved. No part of this publication may be reproduced or transmitted in any form or by any means, electronic or mechanical, including photocopy, recording or any other information storage and retrieval system without prior permission in writing from L. Edward Dumas.

SEX DISCRIMINATION

Office of Appeals Case File Number

in order to suppress my civil rights under California law, in addition to Federal prohibitions. The RECIEPIENTS are truly misplaced and prejudicially apply a double standard in this and other fashions.

The RECIEPIENTS had intentionally acted with false predicates and assumptions in order to frustrate, confuse, and obscure my telephone interview. The RECIEPIENTS made insensitive and irrelevant statements, particularly with regards to my experience. I had gone through a lot for 32 days at ABM with regards to harassment and discrimination and should not have been subject to disbelief and humiliation.

The "Report of Claim Status VQ" is not a truthful and fair report of my written statements. This document has been produced for the sole purpose altering evidence in the anticipation of further litigation in order to justify harassment, discrimination, and thus render me ineligible for benefits. This shows not only an intent to unethically and collaterally estop my good faith litigation but operates with the intent to alter evidence in support of discrimination and harassment in the State of California.

The RECIEPIENTS have unjustly denied me benefits and have altered physical evidence as described in the California Evidence Code 250 and the California Code of Civil Procedure 2031.010.

The unfair and falsely fabricated information produced and published for the benefit of an Employer that allows harassment and discrimination in their workplace was made with malice, and a negligent reckless disregard for the truth is unconscionable.

The RECIEPIENTS have acted with the intent to alter physical and direct evidence in my case. The above named RECIEPIENTS of this correspondence has slandered me in a false and unprivileged publication. They may have orally uttered and also communicated by mechanical and other means in writing, such as the "Report of Claim Status VQ".

In this so-called "Report" they have directly injured me in the respect that my character, pending litigation in other jurisdictions, professional license, and trade that has imputed to me general disqualification. The RECIPIENTS have also injured me by imputing in those

© 2015 L. Edward Dumas. All rights reserved. No part of this publication may be reproduced or transmitted in any form or by any means, electronic or mechanical, including photocopy, recording or any other information storage and retrieval system without prior permission in writing from L. Edward Dumas.

Office of Appeals Case File Number ▉▉▉▉

respects to which the other litigation and my occupation peculiarly requires such as being truthful and making factual reports. The RECIPIENTS have also imputed something with reference to my profession and trade that has natural tendency to lessen it "profits" or in my case, like "profits" such as business opportunities, my value added labor, and professional marketability. The RECIPIENTS have imputed to me an impotence or a want of chastity; or which, by natural conquest, has caused me damage.

Each RECIPIENTS' acts of libel is defamatory of me without the necessity of explanatory matter, such as an inducement, innuendo or other extrinsic fact, which is said to be a libel "on its face". I can and intend to prove that the RECIPIENTS' statements are libelous on its face and are actionable, I can further prove I have suffered special damage as a proximate result thereof. The RECIPIENTS have violated my personal rights and put forth in writing, printing, as a fixed representation to the eye, which exposes me to hatred, contempt ridicule, or obloquy, or which has caused and may cause me to be shunned or avoided now, and now has a tendency to injure me in my occupation.

The RECIPIENTS have shown hatred and contempt of ridicule of me because of my protected characteristics. The RECIPIENTS have exposed and shown hatred of me because I was a male complaining about a female sexually harassing me at work. The RECIPIENTS have acted not only with reverse discriminatory conduct; but have further acted with malice and negligence, with a complete reckless disregard for the truth in order to paint a picture of me as a liar and thus damaging my reputation and rights to litigation. The RECIEPIENTS have shown hatred and ill will toward me because I am a whistleblower and have complained about discrimination before.

SPECIAL NOTICE: I further assert that I have a constitutional right to privacy and privilege that I have not waived and previously asserted; and right to unprejudiced information in this report and other related litigation. Statements and references documenting sex outside the workplace are private per se and should be redacted in this

© 2015 L. Edward Dumas. All rights reserved. No part of this publication may be reproduced or transmitted in any form or by any means, electronic or mechanical, including photocopy, recording or any other information storage and retrieval system without prior permission in writing from L. Edward Dumas.

Sex Discrimination

Office of Appeals Case File Number ▇▇▇▇

report. This report should not make reference to sex and dating outside the workplace because the context misplaces the information in a fashion that prejudices me to a third party reader. It also prejudices me in pending litigation that would only be allowed by a noticed motion and hearing in an actual court of law.

IMPORTANT NOTICE: Retraction, redaction, and or deletion must be immediate and without delay, the above named recipients must notify the CUIAB-Inglewood Office of Appeals with the utmost sense of urgency. A copy of the retraction, redaction, and or deletion must be forwarded to me as quickly as possible without expense to me. The retraction, redaction, and or deletion along with this notice attached to it should be copied into the case file ▇▇▇▇. The previous "Report of Claim Status VQ" should be removed from the case file no ▇▇▇▇.

This provides evidence that I attempted to informally resolve this matter within 20 days for retraction, deletion, and/or redaction; I have demanded for retraction, deletion, and/or redaction of an unfair and untrue report of my claim before filing a lawsuit. Also within the six month period of complaining about a governmental agency to itself.

I have also incurred damages that I reserve the right to file a claim for reimbursement of those damages, is herein not waived.

Truthfully,

© 2015 L. Edward Dumas. All rights reserved. No part of this publication may be reproduced or transmitted in any form or by any means, electronic or mechanical, including photocopy, recording or any other information storage and retrieval system without prior permission in writing from L. Edward Dumas.

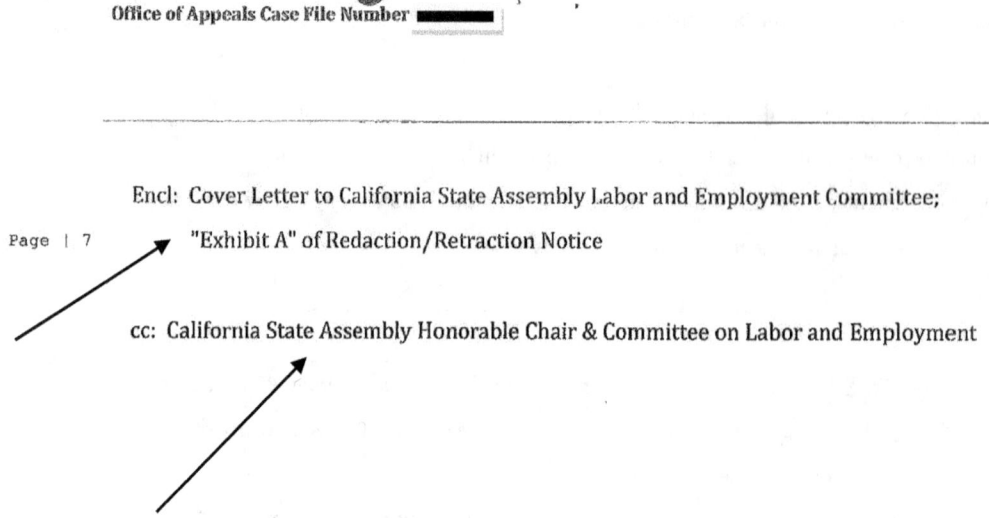

Encl: Cover Letter to California State Assembly Labor and Employment Committee; "Exhibit A" of Redaction/Retraction Notice

cc: California State Assembly Honorable Chair & Committee on Labor and Employment

© 2015 L. Edward Dumas. All rights reserved. No part of this publication may be reproduced or transmitted in any form or by any means, electronic or mechanical, including photocopy, recording or any other information storage and retrieval system without prior permission in writing from L. Edward Dumas.

SEX DISCRIMINATION

Office of Appeals Case File Number ▇▇▇▇

"EXHIBIT A"
of
Retraction/Redact Notice

These Statements, but not limited to the following, that have altered the evidence with falsity, negligence, and a reckless disregard for the facts of this case and show Prejudice in the "Summary of Material Facts and Reason For Decision" must be immediately retracted, redacted, and/or deleted without delay are:

"CLMT ADMITS HE WASN'T TOLD IF IT WAS A PAY CUT"

Comment [x1]: This statement is prejudicial, false, and misleading; thus alters physical and direct evidence.

HE ADMITS THAT HE DIDNT TALK TO UPPER MGMT UNTIL HE QUIT."

Comment [x2]: This sentence is an intentional misconstruction of the facts thus altering direct and physical evidence to be false and misleading. Statement designed to alter evidence.

"CLMT DID NOT HAVE COMPELLING REASON FOR THE QUIT"

Comment [x3]: False and misleading conclusion based on reverse discrimination by agents of EDD; acted with malice and disregard for the truth.

"CLMT STS THAT HE...REC'D A PAY CUT"

Comment [x4]: Statement is in direct contradiction of "Comment [x2]" and is an alteration of physical and direct evidence of my witness statement. Stated in contradiction as a reckless disregard for the truth.

"CLMT NEVER HAD FACTS SHOWING THAT HE WAS DEMOTED".

Comment [x5]: Reckless and disregard for the truth and libelous on its face; my witness statement and declaration shows that I was demoted. No person who had wrote this as a "fact" witnessed my demotion but falsely assume that I was not demoted, when I was in fact demoted.

DID NOT EXPLORE ALL REASONABLE ALTERNATIVES PRIOR TO QUITTING"

Comment [x6]: Not a fact and intentionally stated in order to discriminate against me in order to deny me eligibility for benefits. Stated with malice and negligence.

"CMT CANNOT DESCRIBE A VALID COMPELLING REASON FOR THE QUIT. ASKED HIM MULTIPLE TIMES".

Comment [x7]: Not a fact but disregard for the truth of this legal matter and intentionally put forth in a negative fashion in order to discriminate against me further to deny me benefits for being deprived of equal opportunities under the law. Stated with malice and an intent to further discriminate.

JANUARY 26, 2015 [re: ▇▇▇ v. ABM]

The EDD, EEOC, & Superior Court Legal Forms

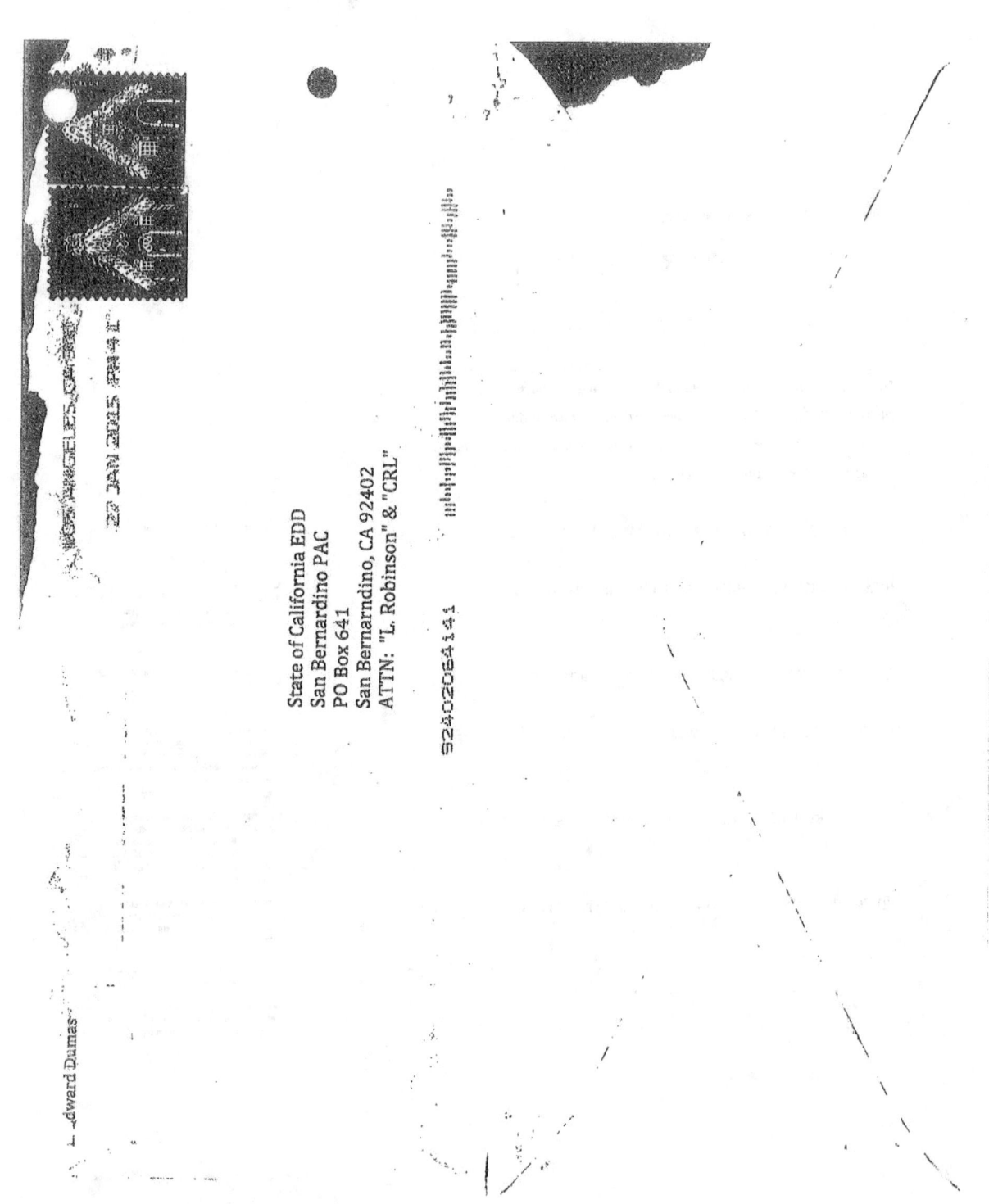

LOS ANGELES, CA
27 JAN 2015 PM 4 L

Edward Dumas

State of California EDD
San Bernardino PAC
PO Box 641
San Bernarndino, CA 92402
ATTN: "L. Robinson" & "CRL"

92402064141

SEX DISCRIMINATION

SENATOR RICARDO LARA
CONSTITUENT SERVICES
AUTHORIZATION FORM

I have sought the assistance of Senator Ricardo Lara on a matter which may require the release of information contained in records maintained by your agency and which may be prohibited from dissemination under the Privacy Act of 1974.

I hereby authorize you to release all relevant portions of my records and to discuss problems involved in this case with Senator Ricardo Lara and with any authorized member of his staff until the matter is resolved.

Printed Name

Address

Describe your situation in detail:

The EDD has denied me rights under California law and has made unfair and untrue reporting of me by altering direct evidence, in order to unjustly deny me benefits and aid a Corporation that discriminates and allows harassment in its workplace.

I worked for a company known as "ABM" in Los Angeles from 1/26/14 to 10/6/14 with no disciplinary issues; then I was harassed at work for about a month from 10/6/14 to 11/2/14, I kept reporting the harassment to company management and ended up being discriminated for reporting it by the Corporate Office -team of ABM.

So I "quit" or was "constructively terminated" for having been discriminated by receiving a demotion and punished for reporting the harassment. I filed for unemployment and informed the EDD as to why I had to leave for good cause.

The agent of the EDD met me with unprofessionalism, extreme skepticism, and disbelief from the very beginning of the "telephone interview".

I was told by the EDD agent to the effect, that the employer does not have to do anything to stop harassment in the workplace, they asserted to me that there is nothing an employer can really do. I believe that this is completely false, untruthful, and contrary to California law. I believe this was said in order to make me stop interviewing and because I was disbelieved by the agent because I am a male complaining about sex harassment.

As I was already frustrated because of the EDD agents unprofessionalism, I became upset and confused at the insensitive comment. The EDD agent continued to twist up my words and tried to contradict the facts I was stating in the phone interview. So the phone interview went "sour" and I was told by the agent that they would contact the employer to see if they had investigated the harassment. The company never investigated the harassment while it was occurring at the location in where I was working at.

Ultimately, I was denied by the EDD twice, before issuing a letter around 12/18/14, and then after issuing a written statement and exhibits on 12/30/14. On 12/30/14 the EDD constructed their "Report of Claim Status VQ" And the EDD agent(s) wrote up a prejudicial, untrue, and unfair "Report of Claim Status" on specific parts of this report in order to discredit my claim and pending litigation against ABM. Specific sentences inserted in their report are simply untrue, such as their claim that I never had "facts showing I was demoted".

There untrue and unfair report of me is altering evidence in this and pending litigation in another jurisdiction. The EDD is altering evidence and giving an unfair advantage to a multi-billion dollar Corporation that discriminates against some of their workers. The unfair and untrue report made against me violates Civil Code 47 and Code of Civil Procedure 2031.010.

On 1/15/15, I requested to an Administrative Law Judge in the Inglewood Office of Appeals (CIUAB) to order a subpoena of documents and video footage in ABM's possession in support of my case. The ALJ unjustly denied my lawful request and further prejudiced me in support of ABM and EDD, by stating that he did not think the video could be played and this is not a place for "free discovery". The same ALJ stated that the employer is not a party to the action. The ALJ stated that I should not make the subpoena request because it would notify the employer that I am appealing for benefits when it is the EDD disputing my unemployment benefits.

The ALJ denied me rights to discovery allowed under the law and there is no recourse in the CIUAB that I know of to appeal or file a writ for the denial of the subpoena, regardless of whether ABM was "a party" or not.

A hearing date was set in Long Beach Office of Appeals at 2:30PM on 1/20/15; I was the only person that was scheduled to appear in this case. So I appeared by written declaration, under penalty of perjury, in addition to other legal documents in support of my eligibility.

SEX DISCRIMINATION

I informed the desk clerk at the Long Beach Office of Appeals that the EDD is the only one disputing my claim, my rights are not being respected, and the desk clerk stated that it "does not matter to me".

I informed the desk clerk how I felt about my rights being suppressed by the Government and the disparate treatment by the EDD. I submitted my legal documents in support of my eligibility claim to the desk clerk. I have not received any correspondence as to the ALJ's decision of my case. My rights and case seems to not matter to anyone at the EDD or CIUAB.

I had made a separate complaint to the EDD about the disparaging remarks made by the EDD agent. I received a letter, dated 1/21/15, from an EDD 'EEO Compliance Manager' who stated to the effect that they will not investigate their agent for the disparate treatment and disparaging remarks made against me. The EDD claims that I have not provided "enough" information to investigate itself.

On 1/26/15 I faxed a seven page letter to the State Assembly Labor and Employment Committee providing information as to the unfair and untrue aspects in the "Report of Claim Status VQ". I have attached the letter in this email that I had faxed to the Assembly Committee.

The committee representative informed me to contact my local State official for help with constituent services. I believe that some of the statements made by the EDD are unfair and untrue, and violate my personal and civil rights.

The EDD has published this "Report" in support of a Corporation that allows its employees to be harassed and discriminated against. ABM just had a Federal Court Consent Decree lifted regarding harassment in their workplace. I believe ABM punished me because I was another employee reporting harassment in their workplace and may cause them more Government regulation such as Court Ordered EEO Monitoring of their business practices; which was mandated for 3 years. And now ABM is free discriminate against their employees with no government regulation at all; the EDD seems to be supporting this unlawful behavior.

The EDD agents' "Report of Claim Status VQ" must be fair and accurate but it not. The parts that the EDD has asserted as a material fact is not evidence but subjective conclusions of an agent or department that knows nothing about the facts of my case. My intent is to resolve this within the Government and not have to feel that I have to file a lawsuit against my Government.

I would like for your Office to look into this matter and if possible encourage some oversight with an agency that does not honor California laws and public policy. Thank you.

Signature_____   Date 1/27/2015

Office of Appeals Case File Number ▮▮▮▮▮

FROM: ▮▮▮▮▮▮▮▮▮▮)

JANUARY 26, 2015

IMMEDIATE ATTENTION TO THE FOLLOWING PERSONS:

TO: The Employment Development Department; The San Bernardino PAC"; "L. Robinson"; and "Representative CRL" (herein referred as the "RECIEPIENTS");

SUBJECT: NOTICE of Defamation of Character, Untrue/Unfair Reporting, & Altering Evidence: Demand for Redaction, Retraction, and/or Deletion

NOTICE: My written and oral statements are true, in furtherance of direct and physical evidence that I was discriminated against and allowed to be harassed at ABM. The above named "RECIEPIENTS" must cease, retract and/or, as applicable, redact the defamatory statements made against me.

This governmental agency and its agents have made alterations and severely prejudiced my claim as if they were the Judge and Jury in all legal matters. My statement that I "reported someone sexually harassing me at the location known as ' ▮▮▮▮▮ is true and cannot be disputed by ANY of YOU as a matter of FACT. Nevertheless, as it is has come to my immediate attention, as to the specific details, on January 15, 2015, upon review of my case file number 5393929 at the Inglewood Office of Appeals, CIUAB.

Herein, the named above "RECIEPIENTS" did indeed alter physical and direct evidence; subjected me to unfair and untrue governmental reporting for defamatory and discriminatory purposes in violation of my personal and civil rights. The named government insurance agency and persons, whether by initial and/or initial and name, plus department, are herein referred to as the "RECIEPIENTS".

The RECIEPIENTS have shown hatred, prejudice, and with a negligent-reckless disregard for the truth in their report of me with malice. The RECIEPIENTS have constructed

© 2015 L. Edward Dumas. All rights reserved. No part of this publication may be reproduced or transmitted in any form or by any means, electronic or mechanical, including photocopy, recording or any other information storage and retrieval system without prior permission in writing from L. Edward Dumas.

Sex Discrimination

Office of Appeals Case File Number ▮▮▮▮▮

information in a document known as "Report of Claim Status VQ" and misrepresented the truth as the erroneous basis to defame and discriminate against me in this prejudiced report. The RECIPIENTS have acted unlawfully in the furtherance of altering valid evidence in support of my litigation against a company (ABM) that currently discriminates against their own workers for reporting harassment in their workplace. A fact well known by another governmental agency is known as the EEOC.

Please look up the EEOC, its authority, guidance, rules, regulations, and current cases it has been involved in such as ABM. It is the EEOC's glorious task as to help eliminate and eradicate discrimination in America; and denial of equal opportunities in the American workplace. It has been the RECIEPIENTS shameful task as to help aggravate and exacerbate discrimination and denial of true and fair reporting from claims discrimination stemming from the workplace in the State of California. This behavior displayed by the RECIEPIENTS can be viewed as truly Anti-American by way of contempt of my civil rights vested in the US and California Constitutions, in addition to Statutory and Declaratory laws.

The RECIEPIENTS, as it must be noted, should have been educated in the EEOC and equal opportunity in the workplace in general. The RECIEPIENTS' insensitivity and alterations of evidence demonstrate a suppression of my civil rights and their tendency to encourage American Companies to lie about its unlawful employment practices. Direct and physical evidence has now been altered and attempted to have been destroyed by the RECIPIENTS, not just defamatory and discriminatory on its face, but a suppression of civil rights on its face.

The Recipients have not honored my personal and civil rights and have merely attempted to suppress them in accordance with ABM, who has intentionally deprived me of equal opportunities by law and now here comes the RECIEPIENTS to their rescue. Only simply to aid and abet the discrimination and unfair business practices by ABM.

The RECIPIENTS have prejudicially misconstrued and falsely constructed parts of their report, altering previous evidence, in order to act in bad faith, discriminate, and treat me

© 2015 L. Edward Dumas. All rights reserved. No part of this publication may be reproduced or transmitted in any form or by any means, electronic or mechanical, including photocopy, recording or any other information storage and retrieval system without prior permission in writing from L. Edward Dumas.

Office of Appeals Case File Number ▇▇▇▇▇

unfairly. The statement and fact that "I was demoted and given less terms" is a fact and cannot be disputed but only has been to date by the RECIEPIENTS. The government and its own agents have reported with falsity, assumed falsely with a reckless disregard for the truth and law, and in turn discriminated against me because of my protected characteristics.

The RECIPIENTS are working as a proxy agent and advocate for a company (ABM) that allows its workers to be discriminated against freely, with prejudice, and harassed at work with no attempts to stop the unlawful conduct, whether it be a female and even a male.

The California Government, along with Federal Mandated-Funds, are being manipulated by paying these RECIEPIENTS, inadvertently, to assist ABM, in suppressing my civil rights, free of charge. At the same time, all the while making me suffer for it, but not limited to defending myself where there is no res judicata. It is as if the RECIEPIENTS were being paid by ABM in order to collaterally estop my employment discrimination case from going forward. How convenient for ABM.

The statement, entered as data on the Report Claim of Status, states that I "cannot describe a valid compelling reason for the quit." Is not a fact of the "FINAL INCIDENT". This is a alteration and discriminatory conclusion of the facts, not the facts itself. As the RECIEPIENTS would not find a "valid" reason; because the interviewer on about 12/10/14 acted unprofessionally, reversely discriminated, and displayed hatred and disbelief towards me.

I have told the truth in this matter, I told the truth that I was demoted and indeed threatened with a pay cut. I have no motive to lie and be subject to humiliation by ABM and now I have to be subject to humiliation by YOU.

One of the RECIPIENTS stated to me in the interview, that they did not think that the "employer" could or had the duty to stop harassment against their workers in the workplace. This statement was never documented nor referenced in the "Record of Claim Status Interview VQ". This statement was not documented by the RECIEPIENTS because it would have showed their discriminatory state of mind and intent to have altered evidence

© 2015 L. Edward Dumas. All rights reserved. No part of this publication may be reproduced or transmitted in any form or by any means, electronic or mechanical, including photocopy, recording or any other information storage and retrieval system without prior permission in writing from L. Edward Dumas.

SEX DISCRIMINATION

Office of Appeals Case File Number ▓▓▓▓

in order to suppress my civil rights under California law, in addition to Federal prohibitions. The RECIEPIENTS are truly misplaced and prejudicially apply a double standard in this and other fashions.

The RECIEPIENTS had intentionally acted with false predicates and assumptions in order to frustrate, confuse, and obscure my telephone interview. The RECIEPIENTS made insensitive and irrelevant statements, particularly with regards to my experience. I had gone through a lot for 32 days at ABM with regards to harassment and discrimination and should not have been subject to disbelief and humiliation.

The "Report of Claim Status VQ" is not a truthful and fair report of my written statements. This document has been produced for the sole purpose altering evidence in the anticipation of further litigation in order to justify harassment, discrimination, and thus render me ineligible for benefits. This shows not only an intent to unethically and collaterally estop my good faith litigation but operates with the intent to alter evidence in support of discrimination and harassment in the State of California.

The RECIEPIENTS have unjustly denied me benefits and have altered physical evidence as described in the California Evidence Code 250 and the California Code of Civil Procedure 2031.010.

The unfair and falsely fabricated information produced and published for the benefit of an Employer that allows harassment and discrimination in their workplace was made with malice, and a negligent reckless disregard for the truth is unconscionable.

The RECIEPIENTS have acted with the intent to alter physical and direct evidence in my case. The above named RECIEPIENTS of this correspondence has slandered me in a false and unprivileged publication. They may have orally uttered and also communicated by mechanical and other means in writing, such as the "Report of Claim Status VQ".

In this so-called "Report" they have directly injured me in the respect that my character, pending litigation in other jurisdictions, professional license, and trade that has imputed to me general disqualification. The RECIPIENTS have also injured me by imputing in those

© 2015 L. Edward Dumas. All rights reserved. No part of this publication may be reproduced or transmitted in any form or by any means, electronic or mechanical, including photocopy, recording or any other information storage and retrieval system without prior permission in writing from L. Edward Dumas.

Office of Appeals Case File Number ▮▮▮▮▮▮

respects to which the other litigation and my occupation peculiarly requires such as being truthful and making factual reports. The RECIPIENTS have also imputed something with reference to my profession and trade that has natural tendency to lessen it "profits" or in my case, like "profits" such as business opportunities, my value added labor, and professional marketability. The RECIPIENTS have imputed to me an impotence or a want of chastity; or which, by natural conquest, has caused me damage.

Each RECIPIENTS' acts of libel is defamatory of me without the necessity of explanatory matter, such as an inducement, innuendo or other extrinsic fact, which is said to be a libel "on its face". I can and intend to prove that the RECIPIENTS' statements are libelous on its face and are actionable, I can further prove I have suffered special damage as a proximate result thereof. The RECIPIENTS have violated my personal rights and put forth in writing, printing, as a fixed representation to the eye, which exposes me to hatred, contempt ridicule, or obloquy, or which has caused and may cause me to be shunned or avoided now, and now has a tendency to injure me in my occupation.

The RECIPIENTS have shown hatred and contempt of ridicule of me because of my protected characteristics. The RECIPIENTS have exposed and shown hatred of me because I was a male complaining about a female sexually harassing me at work. The RECIPIENTS have acted not only with reverse discriminatory conduct; but have further acted with malice and negligence, with a complete reckless disregard for the truth in order to paint a picture of me as a liar and thus damaging my reputation and rights to litigation. The RECIEPIENTS have shown hatred and ill will toward me because I am a whistleblower and have complained about discrimination before.

SPECIAL NOTICE: I further assert that I have a constitutional right to privacy and privilege that I have not waived and previously asserted; and right to unprejudiced information in this report and other related litigation. Statements and references documenting sex outside the workplace are private per se and should be redacted in this

© 2015 L. Edward Dumas. All rights reserved. No part of this publication may be reproduced or transmitted in any form or by any means, electronic or mechanical, including photocopy, recording or any other information storage and retrieval system without prior permission in writing from L. Edward Dumas.

Sex Discrimination

Office of Appeals Case File Number ▮▮▮▮

report. This report should not make reference to sex and dating outside the workplace because the context misplaces the information in a fashion that prejudices me to a third party reader. It also prejudices me in pending litigation that would only be allowed by a noticed motion and hearing in an actual court of law.

IMPORTANT NOTICE: Retraction, redaction, and or deletion must be immediate and without delay, the above named recipients must notify the CUIAB-Inglewood Office of Appeals with the utmost sense of urgency. A copy of the retraction, redaction, and or deletion must be forwarded to me as quickly as possible without expense to me. The retraction, redaction, and or deletion along with this notice attached to it should be copied into the case file ▮▮▮▮. The previous "Report of Claim Status VQ" should be removed from the case file no. ▮▮▮▮.

This provides evidence that I attempted to informally resolve this matter within 20 days for retraction, deletion, and/or redaction; I have demanded for retraction, deletion, and/or redaction of an unfair and untrue report of my claim before filing a lawsuit. Also within the six month period of complaining about a governmental agency to itself.

I have also incurred damages that I reserve the right to file a claim for reimbursement of those damages, is herein not waived.

Truthfully,

▮▮▮▮

© 2015 L. Edward Dumas. All rights reserved. No part of this publication may be reproduced or transmitted in any form or by any means, electronic or mechanical, including photocopy, recording or any other information storage and retrieval system without prior permission in writing from L. Edward.Dumas.

Office of Appeals Case File Number ▇▇▇▇

Encl: Cover Letter to California State Assembly Labor and Employment Committee;
"Exhibit A" of Redaction/Retraction Notice

cc: California State Assembly Honorable Chair & Committee on Labor and Employment

© 2015 L. Edward Dumas. All rights reserved. No part of this publication may be reproduced or transmitted in any form or by any means, electronic or mechanical, including photocopy, recording or any other information storage and retrieval system without prior permission in writing from L. Edward Dumas.

SEX DISCRIMINATION

Office of Appeals Case File Number ▇▇▇

"EXHIBIT A"
of
Retraction/Redact Notice

These Statements, but not limited to the following, that have altered the evidence with falsity, negligence, and a reckless disregard for the facts of this case and show Prejudice in the "Summary of Material Facts and Reason For Decision" must be immediately retracted, redacted, and/or deleted without delay are:

"CLMT ADMITS HE WASN'T TOLD IF IT WAS A PAY CUT"

HE ADMITS THAT HE DIDNT TALK TO UPPER MGMT UNTIL HE QUIT."

"CLMT DID NOT HAVE COMPELLING REASON FOR THE QUIT"

"CLMT STS THAT HE...REC'D A PAY CUT"

"CLMT NEVER HAD FACTS SHOWING THAT HE WAS DEMOTED".

DID NOT EXPLORE ALL REASONABLE ALTERNATIVES PRIOR TO QUITTING"

"CMT CANNOT DESCRIBE A VALID COMPELLING REASON FOR THE QUIT. ASKED HIM MULTIPLE TIMES".

JANUARY 26, 2015 [re: ▇▇▇ v. ABM]

The EDD, EEOC, & Superior Court Legal Forms

Case No.: ▉▉▉▉▉▉
CLT/PET: ▉▉▉▉▉▉
Parties Appearing: Claimant
Parties Appearing by Written Statement: Claimant

Inglewood Office of Appeals
ALJ: Michael Kurz

ISSUE STATEMENT

The claimant appealed from a determination disqualifying the claimant for unemployment benefits under Unemployment Insurance Code section 1256. The issue in this case is whether the claimant left the most recent employment voluntarily without good cause.

FINDINGS OF FACT

The claimant worked for ten months as a security officer. His last day of work was November 4, 2014 and his final rate of pay was $13.40 an hour.

The claimant voluntarily quit because he was being transferred as a result of his complaints about a tenant in the building that he was a security officer for.

The claimant did not like being transferred and therefore quit his job. The claimant alleged that he was being harassed by a tenant in the building. The claimant brought this to the employer's attention, and while the employer was investigating they decided to transfer the claimant. Instead of going with the transfer, allowing the investigation to play out, the claimant instead became upset, angry, and voluntarily quit.

At the time the claimant quit he did not have another job lined up.

REASONS FOR DECISION

An individual is disqualified for benefits if he or she left his or her most recent work voluntarily without good cause. (Unemployment Insurance Code, section 1256.)

There is good cause for voluntarily leaving work where the facts disclose a real, substantial, and compelling reason of such nature as would cause a reasonable person genuinely desirous of retaining employment to take similar action. (Precedent Decision P-B-27.)

Good cause for leaving work must be determined in light of the actual or real cause of the separation in issue. (Precedent Decision P-B-8.)

SEX DISCRIMINATION

Employment security statutes are designed to avoid the menace of economic insecurity, and not to make work pleasant. Petty irritations are a part of everyday living, and no work is conducted in an atmosphere of complete sweetness and light. If irritations are not material and substantial they must be borne, and do not constitute good cause for leaving work. (*Department of Industrial Relations v. Mann* (1950) 35 Ala.App. 505, 50 So.2d 780.)

"'An employee may not be unreasonably sensitive to his [or her] working environment. ... Every job has its frustrations, challenges, and disappointments; these are inherent in the nature of work. An employee is protected from ... unreasonably harsh conditions, in excess of those faced by his [or her] co-workers. He [or she] is not, however, guaranteed a working environment free of stress.'" (*Turner v. Anheuser-Busch, Inc.* (1994) 7 Cal.4th 1238; citing with approval *Goldsmith v. Mayor and City of Baltimore* (4th Cir. 1993) 987 F.2d 1064.)

Section 1256.5 (formerly section 1256.7) of the Unemployment Insurance Code provides that sexual harassment is good cause for leaving employment if a reasonable effort is made to preserve the employment relationship in cases in which such effort would not be futile. "Sexual harassment" includes unwelcome sexual advances, requests for sexual favors, and any other verbal, visual or physical conduct of a sexual nature when any of the following occur:

(1) Submission to the conduct is either explicitly or implicitly made a condition of the employment.

(2) Submission to or rejection of the conduct is used as the basis for employment decisions affecting the individual.

(3) The conduct has the purpose or effect of interfering unreasonably with the individual's job performance or creating an intimidating, hostile or offensive working environment.

In Precedent Decision P-B-475 the claimant's co-worker engaged in conduct ranging from comments about the claimant's body and undergarments to pestering the claimant to accompany him on social outings. The co-worker finally grabbed the claimant's buttocks. The Appeals Board held that a reasonable woman would feel the co-worker's acts had created an intimidating, hostile and offensive environment.

In Precedent Decision P-B-8 the claimant quit because of dissatisfaction with a rotating shift, but without any complaint to management or any request to be assigned to a different shift or location. The appeals board held that an individual genuinely desirous of retaining employment would have complained, thus

affording management an opportunity to make an adjustment. The claimant's failure to do so negated any good cause which might otherwise have existed for quitting.

In this instance, the claimant voluntarily quit his most recent employment without good cause. The claimant's complaints ▬▬▬▬▬▬▬▬▬▬▬▬▬▬▬▬▬▬▬▬▬▬▬▬▬▬▬ who was not a co-employee. The claimant alleged that that woman then began to harass him and wanted him to be in a relationship. As soon as he expressed this to the employer the employer began an investigation, and as a result, the claimant was transferred. The claimant took this to mean that he was being retaliated against rather than the fact that the employer was attempting to resolve the situation and was separating the parties.

At the time the claimant quit he did not have another job lined up. Further, the claimant did not give the employer an opportunity to attempt to resolve the matters, or, the claimant simply disagreed with the fact that the employer was removing him from the situation because he was the one complaining about the situation. In any event, whatever good cause the claimant had, was negated by the fact that the claimant did not provide the employer reasonable opportunity to resolve the matter. Further, it appears that the employer was attempting to resolve the matter by transferring the claimant to another station given the fact the employer had no control over the person the claimant was alleging was harassing him. The employer's actions were not unreasonable given the claimant's persistent complaints. Under these circumstances the claimant voluntarily quit without good cause and accordingly is disqualified for benefits under section 1256 of the code.

DECISION

The determination of the department is affirmed. The claimant is disqualified for benefits under 1256 of the code. Benefits are denied.

SD:cb/em 2/1

SEX DISCRIMINATION

ACKNOWLEDGEMENT LETTER

CALIFORNIA UNEMPLOYMENT INSURANCE APPEALS BOARD

In the Matter of

AB Case No.: AO

ALJ Decision No.:

Appellant: CLAIMANT
CHO-BYB: 0

Date Mailed: February 13, 2015

ACKNOWLEDGEMENT LETTER

The California Unemployment Insurance Appeals Board has received an appeal from the Board Appellant listed above requesting a review of the Administrative Law Judge's decision in the case shown above. If there is another party in the case listed above, the Appeals Board is sending a copy of the appeal to that party for its records.

It is not necessary for you to do anything further for the Appeals Board to review the case and issue a decision. Another hearing will not be held. A decision will be based on the audio recording and exhibits admitted at the hearing. If the board appeal was not filed on time, the Appeals Board will inform you in its decision on whether good cause is found for the delay.

The party that did not file the board appeal cannot respond to the board appeal and cannot submit new or additional evidence unless the Appeals Board grants permission. The Appeals Board will notify that party if permission is granted.

Let us know if you change your mailing address. If you submit documents, write the AO Case Number listed above on all the documents. If there is another party listed above, send a copy of all the documents to that party and fill out the Proof of Service form. Mail, fax or deliver all the documents and the completed Proof of Service form to:

CUIAB   PHONE: (916) 263-6803
P O Box 944275   FAX: (916) 263-6837
SACRAMENTO CA 94244-2750

FILE COPY   Claimant

4012NRR-No Rec Req-02/18/2010   MMC

The EDD, EEOC, & Superior Court Legal Forms

CALIFORNIA UNEMPLOYMENT INSURANCE APPEALS BOARD

In the Matter of

AB Case No.: AO-

ALJ Decision No.:

Appellant: CLAIMANT
CHO-BYB:

Date Mailed: February 13, 2015

ACKNOWLEDGEMENT LETTER

The California Unemployment Insurance Appeals Board has received an appeal from the Board Appellant listed above requesting a review of the Administrative Law Judge's decision in the case shown above. If there is another party in the case listed above, the Appeals Board is sending a copy of the appeal to that party for its records.

It is not necessary for you to do anything further for the Appeals Board to review the case and issue a decision. Another hearing will not be held. A decision will be based on the audio recording and exhibits admitted at the hearing. If the board appeal was not filed on time, the Appeals Board will inform you in its decision on whether good cause is found for the delay.

The party that did not file the board appeal cannot respond to the board appeal and cannot submit new or additional evidence unless the Appeals Board grants permission. The Appeals Board will notify that party if permission is granted.

Let us know if you change your mailing address. If you submit documents, write the AO Case Number listed above on all the documents. If there is another party listed above, send a copy of all the documents to that party and fill out the Proof of Service form. Mail, fax or deliver all the documents and the completed Proof of Service form to:

CUIAB
P O Box 944275
SACRAMENTO CA 94244-2750

PHONE: (916) 263-6803
FAX: (916) 263-6837

EDD:0410

Claimant

4012NRR-No Rec Req-02/18/2010

MMC

SEX DISCRIMINATION

CALIFORNIA UNEMPLOYMENT INSURANCE APPEALS BOARD

In the Matter of

AB Case No.: AO ▮

ALJ Decision No.: ▮

Appellant: CLAIMANT
CHO-BYB: 04 ▮

Date Mailed: February 13, 2015

ACKNOWLEDGEMENT LETTER

The California Unemployment Insurance Appeals Board has received an appeal from the Board Appellant listed above requesting a review of the Administrative Law Judge's decision in the case shown above. If there is another party in the case listed above, the Appeals Board is sending a copy of the appeal to that party for its records.

It is not necessary for you to do anything further for the Appeals Board to review the case and issue a decision. Another hearing will not be held. A decision will be based on the audio recording and exhibits admitted at the hearing. If the board appeal was not filed on time, the Appeals Board will inform you in its decision on whether good cause is found for the delay.

The party that did not file the board appeal cannot respond to the board appeal and cannot submit new or additional evidence unless the Appeals Board grants permission. The Appeals Board will notify that party if permission is granted.

Let us know if you change your mailing address. If you submit documents, write the AO Case Number listed above on all the documents. If there is another party listed above, send a copy of all the documents to that party and fill out the Proof of Service form. Mail, fax or deliver all the documents and the completed Proof of Service form to:

CUIAB
P O Box 944275
SACRAMENTO CA 94244-2750

PHONE: (916) 263-6803
FAX: (916) 263-6837

4012NRR-No Rec Req-02/18/2010

MMC

CUIAB DECISION BY CALIFORNIA UNEMPLOYMENT INSURANCE APPEALS BOARD MEMBERS ELLEN CORBETT AND MICHAEL ALLEN (UNLAWFUL)

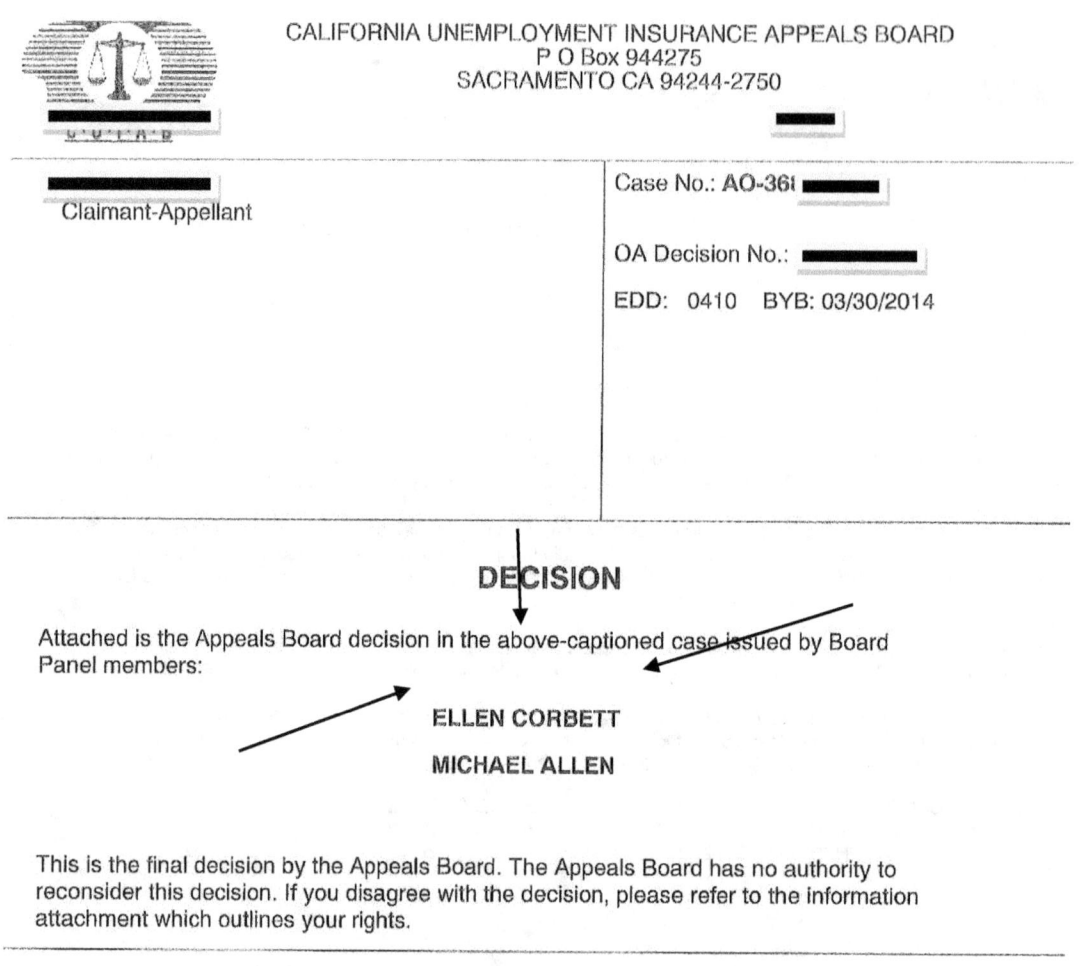

SEX DISCRIMINATION

Case No.: AO- ▮▮▮
Claimant: ▮▮▮▮▮▮

The claimant appealed from the decision of the administrative law judge that held the claimant disqualified for unemployment insurance benefits under section 1256 of the Unemployment Insurance Code.

We have carefully and independently reviewed the record in this case, and have considered the contentions raised on appeal. We find no material errors in the issue statement or in the findings of fact as modified below. The expanded reasons for decision properly apply the law to the facts. Therefore, we adopt the issue statement, the modified findings of fact, and the expanded reasons for decision as our own.

We modify the findings of fact as follows.

In the second sentence of the first paragraph we delete the date of "November 4, 2014," and replace it with the date of "November 5, 2014."

After the first sentence of the third paragraph we add the following. The claimant felt the new position was a "demotion" and thought there may be a pay cut associated with the new assignment.

At the end of the last sentence of the third paragraph we add the words "during his first day working in the new assignment."

We expand the reasons for decision by adding the following after the second sentence of the last paragraph.

At the time of the claimant's separation he had already been transferred to a new work assignment and was therefore no longer being subjected to any sexual harassment. As such, any prior sexual harassment would not have provided good cause for his resignation. Although the claimant alleged that the new assignment constituted a "demotion," he failed to provide any facts upon which to make such a finding and admitted he had been given no specific information concerning any actual reduction in pay resulting from the transfer.

On appeal to this Board, the claimant appears to contend that a representative of the Employment Development Department intentionally reported false information in a "Report of Claim Status VQ," and that any information provided in that report should therefore not be considered. It is unclear from the claimant's

written argument what specific information he is alleging is false. Clearly some of the information contained in that report reflects the conclusions of the interviewer. The purpose of that report is for the interviewer to record information as well as the basis for a determination, which would be a conclusion. However, we do not find that the decision issued by the administrative law judge relied on anything other than the facts contained in the record.

In reviewing appeals from decisions of administrative law judges, this Board follows the principle that the findings of the trier of fact will not be disturbed unless they are against the weight of the evidence. Since we find no material error in this case, we will not substitute our judgment for that of the administrative law judge. (Precedent Decision P-B-10.)

The decision of the administrative law judge is affirmed. The claimant is disqualified under code section 1256. Benefits are denied as provided in the appealed decision.

Sex Discrimination

Case No. AO- █████

P O Box 944275
SACRAMENTO, CA 94244-2750
Telephone: (916) 263-6619
Fax: (916) 263-6836

DECISIONS SENT TO

█████

The EDD, EEOC, & Superior Court Legal Forms

NOTICE OF RELATED CASES

CM-015

ATTORNEY OR PARTY WITHOUT ATTORNEY (Name, State Bar number, and address):

Long Beach, CA 90806

TELEPHONE NO.:   FAX NO. (Optional):
E-MAIL ADDRESS (Optional):
ATTORNEY FOR (Name): in pro per

SUPERIOR COURT OF CALIFORNIA, COUNTY OF LOS ANGELES - CENTRAL
STREET ADDRESS: 111 N. Hill Street
MAILING ADDRESS: 111 N. Hill Street
CITY AND ZIP CODE: Los Angeles 90012
BRANCH NAME: Stanley Mosk Courthouse

PLAINTIFF/PETITIONER:

DEFENDANT/RESPONDENT: ABM Onsite Services - West, Inc.

CASE NUMBER:

JUDICIAL OFFICER:
Hon. Judge James C. Chalfant

DEPT.:

NOTICE OF RELATED CASE

Identify, in chronological order according to date of filing, all cases related to the case referenced above.

1. a. Title: _____ v. ABM Onsite Services West Inc. et al.
   b. Case number:
   c. Court: [✓] same as above
      [ ] other state or federal court (name and address):
   d. Department: 31
   e. Case type: [ ] limited civil [✓] unlimited civil [ ] probate [ ] family law [ ] other (specify):
   f. Filing date: 6/6/2016
   g. Has this case been designated or determined as "complex?" [ ] Yes [✓] No
   h. Relationship of this case to the case referenced above (check all that apply):
      [✓] involves the same parties and is based on the same or similar claims.
      [✓] arises from the same or substantially identical transactions, incidents, or events requiring the determination of the same or substantially identical questions of law or fact.
      [✓] involves claims against, title to, possession of, or damages to the same property.
      [✓] is likely for other reasons to require substantial duplication of judicial resources if heard by different judges.
         [ ] Additional explanation is attached in attachment 1h
   i. Status of case:
      [✓] pending
      [ ] dismissed [ ] with [ ] without prejudice
      [ ] disposed of by judgment

2. a. Title: _____ v. California Unemployment Ins. Appeals Board (ABM Onsite Services West Inc.)
   b. Case number:
   c. Court: [✓] same as above
      [ ] other state or federal court (name and address):
   d. Department: 85

Form Approved for Optional Use
Judicial Council of California
CM-015 [Rev. July 1, 2007]

NOTICE OF RELATED CASE

Cal. Rules of Court, rule 3.300
www.courtinfo.ca.gov

SEX DISCRIMINATION

CM-015

PLAINTIFF/PETITIONER:	CASE NUMBER:
DEFENDANT/RESPONDENT: ABM Onsite Services - West, Inc.	

2. *(continued)*
    e. Case type: ☐ limited civil ☐ unlimited civil ☐ probate ☐ family law ☒ other *(specify)*: Mandamus
    f. Filing date: 9-22-2015
    g. Has this case been designated or determined as "complex?" ☐ Yes ☒ No
    h. Relationship of this case to the case referenced above *(check all that apply)*:
        ☒ involves the same parties and is based on the same or similar claims.
        ☒ arises from the same or substantially identical transactions, incidents, or events requiring the determination of the same or substantially identical questions of law or fact.
        ☒ involves claims against, title to, possession of, or damages to the same property.
        ☒ is likely for other reasons to require substantial duplication of judicial resources if heard by different judges.
            ☐ Additional explanation is attached in attachment 2h
    i. Status of case:
        ☐ pending
        ☐ dismissed ☐ with ☐ without prejudice
        ☒ disposed of by judgment

3. a. Title: _____ v. ABM Onsite Services West Inc.
    b. Case number: _____
    c. Court: ☒ same as above
            ☐ other state or federal court *(name and address)*:
    d. Department: 90
    e. Case type: ☐ limited civil ☐ unlimited civil ☐ probate ☐ family law ☒ other *(specify)*: SmallClaim
    f. Filing date: 5-21-2015
    g. Has this case been designated or determined as "complex?" ☐ Yes ☒ No
    h. Relationship of this case to the case referenced above *(check all that apply)*:
        ☒ involves the same parties and is based on the same or similar claims.
        ☒ arises from the same or substantially identical transactions, incidents, or events requiring the determination of the same or substantially identical questions of law or fact.
        ☒ involves claims against, title to, possession of, or damages to the same property.
        ☒ is likely for other reasons to require substantial duplication of judicial resources if heard by different judges.
            ☐ Additional explanation is attached in attachment 3h
    i. Status of case:
        ☐ pending
        ☐ dismissed ☐ with ☐ without prejudice
        ☒ disposed of by judgment

4. ☐ Additional related cases are described in Attachment 4. Number of pages attached: ____

Date: _____

_____   ▶ _____
(TYPE OR PRINT NAME OF PARTY OR ATTORNEY)   (SIGNATURE OF PARTY OR ATTORNEY)

NOTICE OF RELATED CASE

	CM-015
PLAINTIFF/PETITIONER: ▓▓▓▓▓	CASE NUMBER:
DEFENDANT/RESPONDENT: ABM Onsite Services - West, Inc.	▓▓▓▓▓

PROOF OF SERVICE BY FIRST-CLASS MAIL
NOTICE OF RELATED CASE

(NOTE: You cannot serve the Notice of Related Case if you are a party in the action. The person who served the notice must complete this proof of service. The notice must be served on all known parties in each related action or proceeding.)

1. I am at least 18 years old and not a party to this action. I am a resident of or employed in the county where the mailing took place, and my residence or business address is (specify):

   ▓▓▓▓▓

2. I served a copy of the *Notice of Related Case* by enclosing it in a sealed envelope with first-class postage fully prepaid and (check one):
   a. ☐ deposited the sealed envelope with the United States Postal Service.
   b. ☑ placed the sealed envelope for collection and processing for mailing, following this business's usual practices, with which I am readily familiar. On the same day correspondence is placed for collection and mailing, it is deposited in the ordinary course of business with the United States Postal Service.

3. The *Notice of Related Case* was mailed:
   a. on (date): 6/24/2016
   b. from (city and state): Los Angeles, California

4. The envelope was addressed and mailed as follows:

   a. Name of person served:
   California Unempl. Ins. Appeals Board
   Street address: 2400 Venture Oaks Way #100
   City: Sacramento
   State and zip code: CA 95833

   c. Name of person served:
   Honorable Judge Samantha Jessner
   Street address: 111 N. Hill Street
   City: Los Angeles
   State and zip code: CA 90012

   b. Name of person served:
   ABM Onsite Services - West, Inc.
   Street address: 818 W. 7th Street, #930
   City: Los Angeles
   State and zip code: CA 90017

   d. Name of person served:
   Honorable Judge James C. Chalfant
   Street address: 111 N. Hill Street
   City: Los Angeles
   State and zip code: CA 90012

☐ Names and addresses of additional persons served are attached. (You may use form POS-030(P).)

I declare under penalty of perjury under the laws of the State of California that the foregoing is true and correct.

Date: 6/24/2016

_____   ▶   _____
(TYPE OR PRINT NAME OF DECLARANT)   (SIGNATURE OF DECLARANT)

SEX DISCRIMINATION

CUIAB COVER LETTER AND BLANK DISCRIMINATION FORM IN RESPONSE TO LEGISLATIVE COMPLAINTS

State of California - Edmund G. Brown, Jr., Governor
California Labor & Workforce Development Agency

California Unemployment Insurance Appeals Board
2400 Venture Oaks Way, Suite 300
Sacramento, CA 95833

April 25, 2017

Mr. ████████
████████████████
████████████████

Dear Mr. ████:

Recently, the Office of California Assembly Speaker Anthony Rendon shared your correspondence regarding a board appeal decision from the California Unemployment Insurance Appeals Board (CUIAB). Your letter alleges discrimination in the board appeal decision process.

Please find attached a CUIAB Discrimination Complaint Form. If you would like to file an official complaint, please complete the form and return to CUIAB's Equal Employment Opportunity Officer at 3517 Camino Del Rio South, Suite 310, San Diego, CA 92108.

Once we receive your completed form, the CUIAB will be able to conduct an investigation into your complaint.

Sincerely,

LORI KUROSAKA
Assistant Director

cc: Elena Gonzales, Executive Director

STATE OF CALIFORNIA
California Unemployment Insurance Appeals Board

DISCRIMINIATION COMPLAINT FORM
CONFIDENTIAL

Instructions: This form may be used when filing a complaint of discrimination, harassment, or retaliation. All complaints may be filed with the California Unemployment Insurance Appeals Board's (CUIAB) EEO Office, Martha Silva, located at 3517 Camino del Rio South, Suite 310, San Diego, CA 92108. Telephone number is (619) 521-3346.

Please try to answer all questions that may apply to your situation. You may use additional paper if additional space is needed. If you have any documents that support your complaint, please attach them to this Discrimination Complaint Form. For example, if you are complaining about disability discrimination and have completed a Request for Reasonable Accommodation form, attach it to this complaint form.

1. **COMPLAINANT INFORMATION:**

Name: _____ Classification: _____

Home Address: _____ Home Telephone Number: _____

Division/ Unit: _____ Work Telephone Number: _____

2. **BASIS OF COMPLAINT:**
Select a protected group category that best identifies the alleged discrimination, harassment, or retaliation. Checking boxes that do not apply may delay your complaint:

- [ ] AGE (over 40 years old)
- [ ] ANCESTRY (national or cultural origin)
- [ ] COLOR (skin color)
- [ ] DISABILITY
    - [ ] Physical
    - [ ] Mental
    - [ ] Medical Condition
- [ ] GENDER IDENTITY
- [ ] GENETIC CHARACTERISTICS
- [ ] MARITAL STATUS (divorced, married, never married, separated, widowed, etc.)
- [ ] NATIONAL ORIGIN (birth site, language, accent)
- [ ] POLITICAL AFFILIATION (membership or association with a political party or special interest group)
- [ ] PREGNANCY (childbirth or related medical condition)
- [ ] RACE (belonging to one of the anthropological racial/ethnic groups: American Indian, Asian, Black, Filipino, Hispanic, Pacific Islander or White)
- [ ] RELIGION (spiritual beliefs)
- [ ] SEX (gender – female or male)
- [ ] SEXUAL HARASSMENT (unwelcome attention of a sexual nature)
- [ ] SEXUAL ORIENTATION (bisexual, heterosexual, or homosexual)
- [ ] RETALIATION (retaliation for filing an EEO discrimination complaint, involved in an EEO complaint, or for opposing illegal discriminatory employment practices)
- [ ] VETERAN'S STATUS

3. **PERSON AND/OR ENTITY YOU ARE COMPLAINING ABOUT:**

Name: _____ Classification: _____

Division/Unit: _____ Immediate Supervisor: _____

Sex Discrimination

STATE OF CALIFORNIA
California Unemployment Insurance Appeals Board

4. **What** happened to you? How do you believe you were discriminated, harassed or retaliated against?

5. **Why** do you believe you are being discriminated, harassed, or retaliated against?

6. **Where** did the alleged act of discrimination, harassment, or retaliation occur?

7. **When** did the last alleged act of discrimination, harassment, or retaliation occur? Please be as specific as possible on this date, and indicate whether the discrimination, harassment, or retaliation was continuous or is still ongoing?

8. **Who** witnessed or has knowledge of the alleged act of discrimination, harassment, or retaliation? Please list the names of any and all witnesses.

9. **How** were you affected by the alleged acts of discrimination, harassment, or retaliation?

10. **Were** other individuals subjected to the same alleged discriminatory, harassment, or retaliation conduct? If so, please provide names and telephone numbers if possible.

11. **What** would you like CUIAB to do as a result of your complaint? In other words, what remedy would you like?

	Yes	No
Have you discussed your complaint with your Supervisor?	☐	☐
Have you filed your complaint with any other state or federal agency?	☐	☐

CUIAB makes every effort to protect confidentiality in any investigation, but cannot guarantee absolute confidentiality. An employee's right to due process and equitable treatment requires CUIAB to interview many individuals during the course of an investigation. Confidentiality will be protected and honored to as great a degree as is legally possible. However, anonymity and complete confidentiality cannot be guaranteed once a complaint is made known to CUIAB alleging behavior that may involve CUIAB policies. You can assist in protecting confidentiality by keeping the proceedings of any interview with you strictly confidential.

ASSURANCE AND SIGNATURE

I affirm that the above information is true to the best of my knowledge, information, and belief.

Complainant Signature: _____   Date: _____

www.ingramcontent.com/pod-product-compliance
Lightning Source LLC
Chambersburg PA
CBHW060412220526
45465CB00008B/2854